The Global Organ Shortage

The Global Organ Shortage

Economic Causes, Human Consequences, Policy Responses

T. Randolph Beard, David L. Kaserman, and Rigmar Osterkamp

With a Foreword by Friedrich Breyer

STANFORD ECONOMICS AND FINANCE
An Imprint of Stanford University Press
Stanford, California

Stanford University Press
Stanford, California

Special discounts for bulk quantities of Stanford Economics and Finance are available to corporations, professional associations, and other organizations. For details and discount information, contact the special sales department of Stanford University Press. Tel: (650) 736-1782, Fax: (650) 736-1784

Printed in the United States of America on acid-free, archival-quality paper

Library of Congress Cataloging-in-Publication Data

Beard, T. Randolph (Thomas Randolph), author.
    The global organ shortage : economic causes, human consequences, policy responses / T. Randolph Beard, David Kaserman, and Rigmar Osterkamp ; with a foreword by Friedrich Breyer.
        pages cm
    Includes bibliographical references and index.
    ISBN 978-0-8047-8409-2 (cloth : alk. paper)
    1. Procurement of organs, tissues, etc.—Government policy.   2. Procurement of organs, tissues, etc.—Economic aspects.   3. Donation of organs, tissues, etc.—Government policy.   4. Donation of organs, tissues, etc.—Economic aspects.   I. Kaserman, David L., author.   II. Osterkamp, Rigmar, author.   III. Title.
    RD129.5.B43 2012
    362.17'83—dc23

Typeset by Newgen in 10.5/14 Bembo

In memory of David L. Kaserman (1947–2008)

Contents

Illustrations

Figures

Tables

Foreword

Every day, 30 U.S. citizens die from the failure of a vital organ while still waiting for a suitable transplant, and similar figures—relative to population size—are reported from all of the other developed countries. It is one of the few problems of modern health care that cannot be solved by pouring more money into the existing system. The reason is that the rate of organ donations is simply not sufficient. Another tragic fact is that hundreds of thousands of people with end-stage renal disease (ESRD) can be kept alive only by renal dialysis. They have to be treated three times a week, at high costs and greatly reduced quality of life, while most of them would be much better off after receiving a transplant. At the same time, hundreds of millions of people have two healthy kidneys, and many of them would be willing to part with one of them if only they were adequately compensated for the (small) risk attached to the surgery and any possible pain and discomfort. That society in principle accepts this additional risk for living donors is obvious because living kidney donation is a very common procedure among relatives.

These facts describe a severe shortage of human transplants. Economics tells us that shortages can be alleviated by acting either on the demand or on the supply side. In the particular case of human organs, the demand is more or less fixed by medical need (e.g., reducing the rate of kidney failure by persuading people to eat less and exercise more is an extremely slow process). The supply, however, can be and is in fact influenced by policy measures and regulations. The most important feature in this respect is the universally established rule that all organ donations must be altruistic and no compensation may be paid to the donor. And it is this very rule that the authors of this book—three economists who have studied the problem for decades—hold accountable for the lack of adequate supply and thus for the enormous pain and suffering caused by the shortage of organ transplants.

This book is "provocative" in the best sense of the word: its purpose is to provoke a new discussion not only on how to increase the procurement of organ transplants, but on the very nature of health care policy in the United States, in Europe, and in many other developed countries. Is it better to prevent unnecessary pain, suffering, and early death, or is it more important to comply with certain widely held normative convictions such as "no commodification of the human body"?

The authors must be congratulated for providing a comprehensive overview of the severity of the problem, the reasons for the failure of existing institutions, and the potential of alternative proposals to solve the problem. Of course, at the heart of this book is their own proposal to create a system of donor compensation that meets ethical criteria. The authors argue their case very carefully and forcefully, but they may not be able to convince all those readers who are skeptical of using monetary incentives in matters of life and death. (On the other hand, why does no one object to paying doctors and nurses for their services?) At the very least, however, the book should spur a discussion of what we all can do to solve one of the most pressing health care problems of our time.

Friedrich Breyer

Preface

The extent of the global organ shortage is horrifying. Tens of thousands of patients die every year around the world due to the shortage of organs. Even the "lucky ones" may languish on waiting lists for years until an organ is made available to them. Moreover, due to the shortage, a global black market for organs—mainly kidneys—has developed, and it has been rightly criticized for unfairness and even exploitation. In the course of our work, we have arrived at the conviction that the dire situation that patients in need of an organ are facing is—not exclusively but overwhelmingly—the consequence of the primary element of organ procurement systems implemented practically all over the world: exclusive reliance on uncompensated donation. Our main motivation in writing this book is to contribute to a change in the current organ procurement policy.

We have, however, a private motive, and, to us, it is ultimately the most compelling. David Kaserman, one of the authors, responded to the profound challenge that his congenital kidney disease presented in a manner that many would be unable to imitate: he applied his training as an economist to his predicament as an organ transplant patient, and he concluded that the medical misery in which he found himself had an *economic* cause. David Kaserman made several significant contributions to economics, especially in the areas of vertical integration, competitive market analysis, and regulation, but he felt more engaged by his work on the organ shortage than on any other topic. As his health deteriorated (partially as a consequence of the long-term use of drugs designed to block rejection of his transplant), his focus on the organ shortage became stronger, and he was actively engaged in work on this book at the time of his death. Our decision to complete this project is our way of honoring his memory.

T. Randolph Beard
Rigmar Osterkamp

Acknowledgments

This book is the outcome of a four-year intense collaboration among three economists, two Americans and a German. It was one of the American authors, David Kaserman of Auburn University, who encouraged the other to take the global organ shortage problem more seriously. He was the guiding light for this book. We say "was" because David died in January 2008 in the renal intensive care unit of the University of Alabama at Birmingham Hospital. He designed the outline of the whole book and wrote drafts or outlines for most of the chapters. David deserves the most credit for the success of this book.

We were fortunate to be able to present seminars in Munich and elsewhere, where we received many valuable criticisms. We are very much indebted to the contributions made by Professor Friedrich Breyer, University of Konstanz; Dr. Detlef Bösebeck, regional chair of the German organ procurement network DSO; Michael Horvath of the Technical University of Munich; Professor Clifton Perry Esq., Auburn University Department of Political Science; Professor Thomas Gutmann of the University of Münster Faculty of Law; Dr. Charles Diskin; John Covell of MIT; theologian Andreas Peltzer of Windhoek, Namibia; and Auburn economists Bob Ekelund, Mike Stern, Richard Saba, Hyeongwoo Kim, Mark Thornton, and John Jackson. All of these individuals provided suggestions, criticisms, and support, although none of them should be blamed, in any way, for any errors, nor for our conclusions. If nothing else, in this process of writing this book, we learned that compensation for organ donors is a topic that generates very strong opinions on all sides.

Finally, we would like to express our gratitude for the patience and support we received and the stimulating discussions we had with our and David's loved ones: Lois Kaserman, Leslie Beard, Erna Sutter, and Judith Osterkamp.

T. Randolph Beard, Auburn
David L. Kaserman (1947–2008)
Rigmar Osterkamp, Munich
January 2012

The Global Organ Shortage

1

Introduction

Do not go gentle into that good night. . . . Rage, rage against the dying of the light.
Dylan Thomas

The organ transplantation policies adopted by the vast majority of the world's nations have failed. Although transplantation provides the best, and often the only, effective therapy for many otherwise fatal conditions, the great benefits transplantation could provide go largely unrealized because of failures in the organ acquisition process. In the United States, for example, more than 10,000 persons die every year either awaiting transplantation or as a result of deteriorating health exacerbated by the shortage of organs. More than 350,000 kidney patients receive dialysis treatment at an average annual cost of over $75,000. Similar statistics can be observed in many other wealthy countries. In poor countries, the problems are often masked by inadequate public health resources: countries in which dialysis is generally unavailable do not exhibit waiting lists because their end-stage renal disease patients die quickly. Patients needing transplants of organs other than kidneys receive less attention due to their smaller numbers, but in such cases no therapeutic alternative to transplantation, such as dialysis, exists. These patients usually die quickly, and thus receive less attention than those on dialysis.

Organ transplantation, especially in the cases of kidneys and livers, has shown itself to be by far the best medical response to a variety of life-threatening conditions. Further, numerous studies have established the large financial savings many transplants provide, even in less-than-ideal patient populations. Patients receiving successful transplants often enjoy substantial improvements in the qualities of their lives, including being able to work, care for family members, and so on. As a result, it is nearly universally agreed that a large expansion in transplantation activity, at least for kidneys and livers, is unambiguously desirable from virtually any point of view. Further, it is nearly universally agreed that, on purely medical grounds, there exist sufficient, or more than sufficient, numbers of suitable organs, currently unutilized, which could in principle be used to support a large increase in transplant operations. Such an expansion would save many tens of thousands of lives annually and would reduce the burden on public health insurance funds by many billions of dollars or euros. Lives saved, pain eliminated, costs reduced—what could be more worthwhile? And yet, despite these essentially undisputed facts, the deaths, suffering, and costs continue, year after year, all over the world. How can this be?

The problems of organ transplantation and the shortages of organs represent perhaps the most complex and morally controversial medical issue aside from abortion and euthanasia. In the "organ problem," one comes face to face with such topics as the meaning of personhood, the proper treatment of the bodies of deceased persons, the ethics of rationing a life-saving yet extremely finite resource, the meaning and definition of death, the problems attendant on the mechanical maintenance of human life beyond its "natural" limits, black markets, and so on. Add to these very difficult questions the often conflicting religious and cultural traditions, and toss in many billions of dollars of public expenditure and powerful special interest groups, and one has a perfect recipe for conflict, controversy, and public policy gridlock.

Yet, it is the contention of this book that the problems of organ transplantation, and the shortages of organs for that purpose, are in no sense unsolvable. Although one may hope, and perhaps reasonably expect, that scientific advances such as cloning will one day allow transplant patients to receive tailor-made organs grown from their own cells, it is both unnecessary and irresponsible to fail to act now just because ultimately the problem may be resolved by technical means. Rather, we have the means now to resolve the shortage over a reasonable period if we choose to do so. The primary problems are not technological but are instead political and moral. Establishing this thesis is a primary purpose of this book.

As economists, we must confess to the typical economist's bias toward cynical, financially based explanations for human behavior. However, any prospect for true reform, which we feel must include meaningful donor compensation, is dependent on taking the opposing arguments seriously and vanquishing them on their own terms. Hence, we cannot avoid entering the moral arena and battling the moral objections using the tools of ethics and philosophy. This book, therefore, is not solely composed of economic analyses and financial calculations.

Our conclusions are relatively simple: any practical solution to the organ shortages under current technological means must involve paying meaningful compensation to donors for their willingness to donate. All available evidence, fairly evaluated, suggests that compensation will be effective in greatly increasing the availability of organs for transplant. Compensation may be paid both to the families of deceased donors and to living donors (in the case of kidneys). We propose the establishment of public monopsony buyers for organs and argue that such a system may be adequately managed to produce greatly improved patient outcomes while saving money and avoiding serious moral failings. The distribution of organs will be handled on purely medical grounds, presumably within the existing national and international organ procurement systems. The probable levels of compensation necessary to secure substantially increased organ supplies are likely to be modest in comparison to the cost savings arising from expansion of transplantation, at least for kidneys and livers. In the case of kidneys, the costs of dialysis, its medical side effects, and the sizes of end-stage renal disease populations suggest that huge savings in both lives and medical expenditures are readily available. It is true that it will be more difficult to make such claims in the case of certain other transplants, such as lungs or hearts, and the resolution of such problems is important. However, the case for greatly expanded renal transplantation therapy is incontrovertible.

The proposal to compensate donors is, of course, an old one. Indeed, it is quite difficult to think of any other system where begging is the sole legal means of obtaining a supply of goods. From the perspective of the economist, price controls are the fundamental cause of the observed shortages, and very little convincing is necessary. For many physicians, medical societies, and sociologists, however, this linkage is not compelling. Many doctors, for example, argue that compensation would result in fewer organs or organs of poorer quality, undermining the entire transplantation system. Others suggest that any increase in the numbers of organs available would result in increased enrollment on transplant waiting lists. Still others suggest that many of those on renal transplant waiting lists are not legitimate candidates for transplants, so the extent of the alleged shortage is overblown. Some medical ethicists, while perhaps accepting the potential of compensation to increase organ supply, reject the entire notion on moral grounds, often predicated on Kantian ideas of the objectification of the human body/human person. Others confuse the notion of compensating donors within a regulated, transparent public system with a Dickensian, free-for-all "organ bazaar," in which poor citizens of Third World nations are duped into selling parts of their bodies for the benefit of the undeserving wealthy. (Somewhat ironically, this is precisely the case today with the black market, a consequence of the current system.) These are deep waters, emotionally speaking—so deep that they have been sufficient to maintain the current procurement system despite its unsatisfactory performance. Our task in this book is to address each of these lines of argument with an effective refutation, and, because these are not entirely economic challenges, we cannot hope to vanquish them solely using economic arguments. But economics will be our primary tool, and for that we cannot apologize.

The format of the book reflects, to some degree, the evolution of the organ shortage problem itself. We begin in Chapter 2 with a history of transplantation medicine, highlighting those developments that made the miracle of human solid organ transplants possible. Our current system of unpaid donation evolved in an environment in which transplants from strangers were technically infeasible. When the family unit was itself the sole "organ procurement organization," the prohibition of compensation had no practical effect. The discovery of cyclosporin and similar drugs, however, pushed the state of the science well beyond the boundaries drawn by public policy. With the widespread public funding of hemodialysis therapy came the kidney transplant waiting list, now a baleful constant of modern life in industrialized countries.

Chapter 3 evaluates the consequences of this "altruistic" donation system. Several hundred thousand people have died awaiting transplants (primarily for kidneys) since 1980. Waiting lists are long in many (though not all) industrialized countries, especially for kidneys and livers. Severe shortages of organs have led to steadily decreasing standards for deceased donors, and despite continuous improvement in antirejection therapy and organ handling protocols, medical outcomes with substandard organs are generally worse. The proliferation of living-donor transplants stands as a testimony to the inability of many national authorities to increase postmortem sources to meet demands. Black or "gray" market transplant activities and so-called "transplant tourism" have become widespread.

Chapter 4 makes the medical and financial case for large increases in transplant activity. We review studies that examine in detail the social costs and benefits of various transplants, and we find, consistent with overwhelming medical opinion, that transplantation is the best and most cost-effective treatment for a number of serious disorders. In the case of kidney transplants and end-stage renal disease, one can justify paying very large compensation to donors (or their families) based solely on savings to public health funds. Many billions of dollars or euros are lost every year through continued reliance on the current system of organ procurement. In contrast, it is more difficult to rationalize large increases in certain other transplant procedures purely based on direct medical cost effects. It is unlikely, given current technological constraints and life expectancies, that large expansions in heart-lung transplants will "pay for themselves" in this sense.

Chapter 5 considers the sources of the current crisis, with special emphasis on the role of the "price control" imposed by bans on donor compensation. We lay the blame for the shortage primarily on this aspect of the current system. However, it is not accurate to say that this prohibition is the only example of defective incentives in the organ procurement effort. The widespread use of monopsony structures in organ procurement, characterized by geographic exclusivity in donor recruitment, may also be problematic, as are other moral hazards endemic to the ways in which transplant centers and others are compensated. Public responses to the organ shortage, manifested in steadily rising rates of living-donor transplants, also present an obstacle, and we document a pattern of intertemporal substitution between deceased and living-donor organs. In particular, increases in deceased-donor organ supplies reduce future living-donor supplies to some degree, potentially undermining efforts to expand transplants through deceased-donor recruitment. A defective incentive to organ donation is also created by the rule that nondonors are treated the same as willing donors if they should ever need an organ. Finally, we examine the political economy of the shortage system and identify potential conflicts of interest among interested parties. Because organs are jointly supplied by deceased donors, increases in the numbers of deceased donors may also increase pressure to perform more transplants of other solid organs, increasing total medical costs. This fact may be relevant in explaining the public positions of some insurance funds in the compensation debate, at least in Europe. This effect should not apply to efforts to increase living-donor kidney supplies through compensation.

The poor performance of the organ procurement mechanism has given rise to many proposals for reform that fall short of donor compensation. Chapter 6 reviews what one might term "piecemeal" reform proposals, both implemented and hypothetical. Many such efforts have not been very useful, but several, such as presumed consent, pairwise exchanges, and best practice efforts (such as the Organ Donor Breakthrough Collaborative, or ODBC, in the United States), have measurable benefits. Some possible innovations, such as donation to a waiting list, have yet to be evaluated in practice.

Chapter 7 addresses the moral and ethical issues surrounding the compensation proposal. As is clear from the preceding discussion, we cannot find these arguments persuasive. Human life is a very great value indeed, and it is surely incumbent on anyone arguing against donor compensation to make an extremely compelling case. As economists, we are admittedly consequentialists in these matters. In fact, we find the arguments presented by opponents of compensation to be very weak. It appears that much of the informed opposition may actually represent a deep and understandable aversion to the prospect of poor donors selling their organs for the benefit of wealthy patients, albeit this aversion is couched in an ethical language.

In Chapter 8 we come to the specifics of our proposal. We describe institutional arrangements for the introduction of compensation. We provide a simple mathematical analysis of the likely appearance of a socially directed monopsony procurement organization and establish several propositions regarding the forms compensation might take. We suggest that, in general, both living and deceased-donor kidneys would be rewarded by such an entity, and at differing levels, at least in the early stages and in countries with severe shortages. We review the limited empirical evidence relevant to the question of organ compensation rates, and we argue that payments are likely to be well below those levels at which cost savings are consumed in acquisition expenses. On the contrary, it is quite likely that organ acquisition will be cheaper under a compensation program. We review the performances of legal markets for other body parts, such as those for blood products and sperm, and find no inherent and obvious difficulty with a regulated compensation scheme. We also address the issue of the effect of offering compensation on altruistic donation levels. Criteria for organ recipients, as well as donor evaluation and enrollment, are also reviewed. We argue that the introduction of compensation for organ donation, for both deceased donors (all organs) and living donors (kidneys), could be implemented quickly in many countries. Trials are an obvious first step.

Chapter 9 summarizes our recommendations. On balance, we think it is fair to say that the existing system is unacceptable. Current procurement efforts do not utilize the strongest and most efficient means of obtaining additional organs for transplantation. Compensation will increase the number of organs available with no reduction in their quality. Huge amounts of money, and many thousands of lives, could be saved by this reform. No person needs to be unfairly exploited to accomplish this. Indeed, it is the current system, with its unnecessary deaths, thriving black markets, and astronomical public costs, which represents exploitation in its most unjust sense. Of course, if everyone agreed with these opinions and with the evidence presented to support them, it would be difficult to see how the current system could have survived to the present day. That it has survived, however, is obvious. Explaining how we got to this point and, more importantly, how we can get away from it is our purpose. If this effort hastens the demise of the present system for obtaining organs for transplantation, then we shall be very glad indeed.

2

The Evolution of Organ Transplantation
and Procurement Policy

Introduction

Before we can successfully diagnose the underlying causes of the organ shortage and prescribe an effective remedy, it is useful to examine the origins of the
current system of organ procurement and transplantation. Accordingly, in this
chapter we describe the historical paths that have led to modern transplantation technology and the organ procurement policy that supports it.

We acquaint the reader with the genesis, advances, and constraints of organ
transplant technology—and we hope to instill some appreciation for this rather
amazing medical achievement. We continue with a description of the important aspects of an organ transplant process. We list the types of transplants and
sources of organs, and we examine the patients' perspective. The focus of a later
section of this chapter is the existing procurement system, established practically worldwide, and its philosophical-ideological base: altruistic donation. The
chapter ends with a summary of these discussions.

In the Beginning:
The Technological Challenges and Advancements
Early History and Advances

The familiarity and almost routine nature of modern organ transplantation mask the incredible achievements that have led to this important tool

of modern medicine. Indeed, the first reported transplant that most people remember was the one performed by the Saints Cosmas and Damian. The miracle reportedly occurred in the late second century CE, and it is still commemorated in the Liturgy of the Mass of the Roman Catholic Church.[1] As portrayed by many pious artists over the centuries, the physicians Cosmas and Damian grafted the leg of a deceased Ethiopian onto the body of a patient whose own leg was diseased. This act, of course, was regarded as miraculous, and by means of such wonders Cosmas and Damian converted many pagans to Christianity, an achievement for which they were later martyred.

The apparently miraculous character of transplants between persons would persist for a very long time. From a technological standpoint there were two major hindrances. First, the surgical techniques that would allow for the attachment (or reattachment) of living tissue would not be discovered until the early 1900s, when future Nobel laureate Dr. Alexis Carrel published his findings on vascular anastomotic techniques, first in France and later in the United States.[2] Dr. Carrel pioneered techniques that made it possible to graft together veins and arteries, establishing sufficient blood flow to support organ survival. He worked for a time in Chicago with surgeon Dr. Charles Guthrie, and the pair performed several important transplantation experiments on animals. These techniques, which are among the most important discoveries in medical history, led to Carrel's Nobel Prize in Physiology in 1912.

A second difficulty, however, undermined the early optimism that attended Dr. Carrel's discoveries. Although blood typing was discovered by Karl Landsteiner as early as 1901, it would not be until many years later that the mystery of why some blood transfusions "worked" and others caused the patient to die would be resolved. Carrel himself was able to transplant animal kidneys to different locations in the donor's own body with great success, but he found that transplants between different animals—even of the same species—generally quickly failed. Dr. Reuben Ottenberg performed the first blood transfusion utilizing blood "typing" in 1907, but many attempts at solid organ transplants were unsuccessful. It was observed that the patient would first develop a fever, and then the organ would fail within a relatively short time unless the donor was either the patient himself (termed an *autograft*) or the patient's identical twin (termed an *isograft*). Transplants between people who were less closely related, such as siblings or individuals with no blood relation to the patient at all (termed *allografts*), continued to be unsuccessful.

Thus, for some time, the only successful organ transplants involved skin grafts for burn patients, which involved using the skin from another location on the patient's body, and transplants between identical twins.[3] Research continued, however, and it became clear that the body's own immune reaction was responsible for the failures of most organ graft efforts. In the 1940s, the great physiologist Sir Peter Medawar embarked on a careful study of the factors influencing the success of skin grafts, a topic of great interest because of war wounds and the numerous burn victims produced by incendiary bombing. Medawar discovered that skin failed allografts, if repeated, would be rejected more quickly the second time. This phenomenon, termed the *anamnestic response*, suggested that the immune system could "learn" from its experiences, an important insight into its functioning. Medawar received the Nobel Prize for Medicine in 1960 in recognition of his pioneering discoveries on immune response, which provide the basis for modern transplantation immunology.

The first successful kidney transplant was performed between identical twins, the Herrick brothers, at Peter Bent Brigham Hospital in Boston, Massachusetts, by Dr. Joseph Murray on December 23, 1954. Dr. Murray did not need to use immunosuppressive drugs because it was established prior to the transplant that the twins were immunologically compatible by observing skin grafts performed for this purpose. His work then triggered many transplants between twins in the years to follow. Most patients, however, are not gifted by nature with a perfect donor, and successful transplants between genetically nonidentical people had to wait until advances in tissue and blood typing procedures were developed in the 1960s. These advances, combined with the development of far better protocols for the handling of organs from cadavers, made modern organ transplantation possible. With cyclosporin, prednisone, and other antirejection drugs gaining approval and wider distribution, it became almost routine to transplant kidneys, livers, pancreas, hearts, intestines, and even lungs in the United States, Europe, and South Africa.

More Recent Advances

Successful solid organ transplants rely on the twin technologies of surgical vascular grafts and immune suppressive therapy. Suppressing the immune system can be done in several ways, although drugs are the overwhelming method used today. However, early work by French physicians utilized radiation treatment applied to the patient's lymphatic system, which suppresses the immune response. This approach was also consistent with observations on the lack of immune responses among survivors of the atomic explosions in Japan. Unfortunately, this technique generally leads to excessive reduction in immunity, and fatal infections often follow transplants performed in this way.

Fortunately, advances in pharmacology would soon provide an alternative method to limit the chance of graft rejection. By the late 1950s and throughout the 1960s, new drug therapies were discovered, tried, and made a part of ordinary transplant practice. Among the first successful antirejection drugs was the steroid cortisone, which was initially used in the late 1950s. Scientists George Hitchings and Gertrude Elion discovered and synthesized azathioprine and several related compounds in the 1960s, and these drugs, combined with cortisone or prednisone, formed the basis of all transplant pharmacology until the late 1970s. At that time, the drug cyclosporin, introduced by Sir Roy Calne, was integrated into transplant medicine, and the results were astounding. Unlike previous drugs, cyclosporin offered the physician the ability to carefully control immune response levels with far less toxicity than previous treatments. One can safely say that cyclosporin, and those drugs that followed it, ushered in the modern transplantation era. Today, many newer drugs have joined cyclosporin, and long-term graft survival rates have greatly increased compared to earlier times.

The first liver transplant was performed by Dr. Thomas Starzl at the University of Colorado Hospital in 1963. Dr. Christiaan Barnard of South Africa, who worked with Norman Shumway, later stunned the world by transplanting a heart on December 3, 1967. The U.S. American Medical Association (AMA) adopted the first "brain death" medical standard in 1969, paving the way for greatly expanded deceased (or "cadaveric") donor organ transplant activity. In 1981, Dr. Bruce Reitz performed the first successful heart-lung transplant at Stanford University in California. Such "multiorgan" transplants, involving heart-lungs, kidney-pancreas, and other combinations, are today a routine and important part of transplant activity. (In the United States, over 600 multiple organ transplants are now performed each year.) Progress in immunosuppressive pharmacology and surgical techniques has continued unabated and new insights are changing transplantation at a rapid pace. Transplantation of limbs, and even the human face, is now feasible. Modern medicine has now succeeded, after 1,700 years, in replicating the miracle of Cosmas and Damian.

Outline of Organ Transplantation

It is difficult to quantify the extent of transplantation activity worldwide with any credibility, although it seems quite likely that the figure ranges between 60,000 and 100,000 solid organ transplants yearly, with kidneys constituting more than half of these procedures. About 25 percent of these transplants take place in the United States, although that share is declining. In any event, the great majority of transplants occur within regulatory and legal systems that evolved in a medical-technological environment wholly unlike the one in which we now find ourselves. Thus, a fundamental incompatibility between current technological realities and the regulatory apparatus of an altruistic related donor framework has emerged.

It is important to recognize that organ transplantation is not merely feasible, but it has become commonplace, and it is now the preferred treatment for a number of serious diseases. In the United States today, for example, approximately 100,000 people are living with functioning kidney grafts, almost 40,000 with liver grafts, 20,000 with beating donor hearts, and 5,000 breathing through someone else's lungs (UNOS, 2008). Years ago, such people would either be dead (liver patients, most heart and lung patients) or spending their days hooked up to dialysis machines (kidney patients). Internationally, transplantation has expanded rapidly throughout the world. The United Kingdom performs around 2,600 solid organ transplants per year, and transplantation in Continental Europe is at rates comparable to the United States. International organizations such as Eurotransplant and Scandiatransplant coordinate some transplant activities across national borders. Indeed, active transplantation programs exist in virtually all middle- and upper-income countries.

Types of Transplants

It is traditional to divide organ transplantation into several categories. The organs of the chest—the heart and lungs—are referred to as "thoracic" organs. Except in rare cases, these transplants require deceased, usually brain-dead, donors. Other organs transplanted include the kidney, liver, pancreas, and intestine. Kidney donations by living donors are quite common, and in some countries, such as Japan, where brain death is not generally accepted, living donors comprise the bulk of all suppliers of kidneys. Other cultures look with considerable suspicion or revulsion on the use of cadavers for any purpose, and they too rely heavily on living donations. Until fairly recently, livers were obtained solely from cadavers, but recent surgical advances, many invented in Japan, allow transplantation of a part of a functioning liver into a patient, thus allowing some use of living donors. Such procedures, however, are fairly rare: in Germany, for example, living-donor liver transplants are less than 5 percent of all liver transplants (Eurotransplant, 2008). Transplantation of the pancreas or intestine is fully dependent on deceased-donor organs.

Tissues and fluids are also transplanted, although these procedures are not the focus of this book. Grafts of skin, bone, corneas, limbs, and even the penis are feasible, and the first three are quite common. Blood transfusions are probably the most common of all transplants, followed by transplants of bone marrow, stem cells, and other bodily fluids as nonsolid organ transplants.

Although organ transplantation is often the best therapy available for many conditions (such as renal failure), all allografts will eventually fail. For various complex reasons, any transplanted organ will accumulate scarring over time, which limits, and eventually compromises, its function. For kidney transplants, the eventual occurrence of "chronic allograft nephropathy" is apparently inevitable. Thus, those receiving an organ transplant may need additional transplantation therapy in the future. However, it is also clear that the toxicity of the drugs that transplant patients take presents its own risks, often manifested in heart damage or, ironically, failure of the transplanted organ itself. Thus, once the patient survives the first critical months after the transplant, during which the risk of acute rejection episodes can be high, physicians often seek to reduce the use of immunosuppressive drugs to minimal acceptable levels. A fine balance is maintained, and constant monitoring of patients' blood chemistry is required in order to make appropriate adjustments to dosage and frequency. Patient cooperation in treatment and rigorous adherence to drug regimens are vital. The failures by some patients to abide by their doctors' advice are a constant challenge in transplant medicine.

Transplants are often categorized by the source of the donor organ. As mentioned above, autografts involve transplantation of material from one location in the body to another in the same body. Isografts are transplants between genetically identical donors. Allografts, which are our main focus here, indicate a transplant from a donor who is not genetically identical to the recipient, but, in contrast to a xenograft, is at least of the same species.[4]

In the case of livers, it is sometimes possible to actually divide a deceased donor's organ into two pieces and graft each into two different patients, especially children. Such "splits" are not generally done because the patients' outcomes are observed to be poorer. Equally rare, a "domino transplant" involves three individuals, in which an organ from one is transplanted into another, who in turn donates an organ to a third person. Heart-lung transplants sometimes generate "spare" hearts that may then be transplanted into someone else.

Sources of Donor Organs

Putting aside rare exceptions, organs for transplantation into human beings must be obtained from other human beings. These donors may be living or dead, depending on which organ is needed. Of course, many organs may be obtained only from deceased donors, since the organ is vital for life. The most important exception is the kidney, of which most people have two, and it is possible to have one kidney removed and live a normal, healthy life. Importantly, deceased or cadaveric donors must die under a specific set of circumstances that allow for the removal and transplantation of their organs. Only a very small fraction of deaths, perhaps 1 percent, qualify. Historically, the primary sources of deceased-donor organs have been motor vehicle accidents (head traumas), some stroke victims, and suicides. Generally, it is necessary that such patients suffer brain death in the hospital so that their vital functions may be maintained by medical intervention until organ removal can be performed.

The donors must be free of cancer, HIV, and similar diseases, since the organs will be transplanted into sick people who will then undergo powerful immune system suppression. Donors also should be of the appropriate age at death, and the organs must be in reasonably good condition. Donors who die under these stringent conditions are generally termed "standard criteria donors" and are the most desirable source of deceased-donor organs. Improvements in health care, motorcycle helmet laws, and better motor vehicle design, however, have had the unintended effects of severely limiting the potential supply of such donors.

Severe shortages of deceased-donor organs that satisfy standard conditions have led doctors to use less desirable donor sources, including "non-heart-beating" or "Donation after Cardiac Death" (NHBD or DCD) donors and "expanded criteria donors" (ECDs), for which the requirements are reduced, resulting in medically inferior organs and somewhat diminished patient outcomes. The advantage of such organs, and it is a large advantage, is that the potential supply is far greater than in the standard criteria case. Nonetheless, the understanding and handling of non-brain-dead donors and their organs have improved in recent years. Consequently, it is conceivable that eventually such donor pools may substantially alter the shortage situation.

Cadavers that meet the above medical criteria are ordinarily able to provide multiple organs for transplantation. For example, a deceased donor meeting standard criteria in the United States will, on average, provide about 1.5 to 1.7 kidneys, in addition to a liver, intestine, and so on.[5] However, not all families consent to donating all or any organs. In addition, of those organs donated, some are lost due to delay, disease, or other misadventures. Thus, the number of cadavers donated, the number of deceased-donor organs harvested, and the number of various organs transplanted into patients are all different. These points are important when one moves to examine the potential impacts of various sorts of remedies intended to reduce the shortage of organs for transplant.

Living donors comprised the original source of all solid organ donations. It was not until the late 1960s and 1970s that surgical procedures and immunosuppressive drugs improved to the point that deceased-donor organs were useful. Deceased donors, of course, arrive at random intervals. Consequently, transplant operations must be arranged in a hurried fashion, and tissue matching and other preoperative necessities must be done quickly and without room for error or delay. The longer the organ remains without blood flow (referred to as cold ischemic time), the worse its condition, and the lower the prospects for graft success. With living donors, however, surgery may be scheduled more freely, cold ischemic time is minimal, and organs obtained are generally in better shape. Such effects impact patient survival and morbidity. Therefore, from the recipient's point of view, a living donor is medically preferable.

Unfortunately, living donation is not without risks for the donor. In the case of kidneys, the chances of dying are very low (perhaps about 0.03 percent or less), but the hospitalization, loss of income and enjoyment, and other inconveniences are not negligible. Such drawbacks are, however, quite low when compared to the benefits obtained by the recipient. As compelling as this logic might appear, the medical communities in most of the world's nations have been reluctant to aggressively promote live donation, even when no compensation is involved. Other countries, however, such as Japan and South Korea, have relied almost entirely on living donations, while Iran, more or less uniquely, has gone almost entirely to compensated live donation under government control.

In the United States, European countries, Canada, Australia, and many other parts of the world, living donation has been largely family-based. In the absence of payments, the costs of donating a kidney are generally sufficient to discourage all but the personally interested from donating. In the United States, siblings, parents, and spouses comprise most live donations, although friends and sometimes strangers represent an increasing, if small, share of grafts. One drawback with this approach, of course, is that transplantation requires some degree of biological match, and one's willing relatives may not be compatible. In response to this problem, and in an attempt to increase the number of transplants using live donors, "paired-exchange" programs have recently been introduced, in which a potential recipient who has an incompatible, but willing, donor is able to "swap" that donor with another patient in similar circumstances. In this way, the pool of potential matches can be increased. The first U.S. paired exchange kidney graft occurred in 2001. Since that time, a few hundred of these exchanges have been performed, and considerable efforts have been applied to improving matching algorithms to facilitate expanded exchanges. Still, such programs are quite small in comparison with kidney transplant waiting lists.

For cadaveric organs that become available for transplant, most countries have instituted national clearinghouses that operate algorithms to propose and facilitate matching organs with recipients. This process must be conducted with extreme swiftness, as often organs must be physically transported great distances.[6] Some organs are typically lost due to delays in transplantation.

The Patients' Perspective

The Graft Process   Although the medical aspects of organ transplantation are not, and cannot be, the focus of this book, it is important to be familiar, if in a layman's sense only, with the barest outline of the graft process. To this end, we consider the case of a hypothetical kidney patient and his or her probable experience with the medical authorities.

First, our patient finds herself needing a transplant because her kidneys have failed, perhaps due to diabetes, hypertension (high blood pressure), or some other chronic disease. This patient, once kidney disease is diagnosed, will have been given medication to assist her kidneys to function adequately and control the hypertension. In addition, she is likely to have been encouraged to implement a long list of health care changes, possibly including weight loss, dietary changes that reduce kidney load, exercise, underlying disease control, and so on. If such measures proved inadequate, the patient is likely to have been referred to a kidney dialysis center, or "dialysis station," to obtain hemodialysis treatment.[7] This treatment involves blood filtration and fluid removal by a hemodialysis machine. Such filtration is achieved by inserting two large-gauge needles into the patient's access, which is surgically created, usually in the arm. The machine then pumps the patient's blood through an external filter, known as a dialyzer.

These treatments generally require three 6- to 8-hour sessions each week. The treatment is designed to mimic the functioning of the human kidney by removing fluid and waste products from the bloodstream. Dialysis can be extremely burdensome, leaving the patient with a "washed-out" feeling after each treatment. Moreover, there is evidence suggesting that dialysis increases suicide rates, among other indicators of extreme stress (Kurella et al., 2005). Most patients are unable to work. Dialysis is also very expensive and is publicly financed in almost all industrialized countries (for a review, see Winkelmayer et al., 2002). For the great majority of patients who do not receive transplants, dialysis therapy will be required their entire lives. Life expectancy on dialysis is less than that provided by a transplant (Kimmel et al., 2006).

The patient is likely, if she is willing and medically suitable, to be evaluated as a candidate for a kidney transplant. In virtually all developed countries, a set of fairly rigorous medical preconditions are applied in selecting candidates for the "active" transplant waiting list. In the United States, the transplant centers control access to the waiting list, applying various criteria. For example, many transplant centers will not accept patients for transplant who have any of a long list of diseases that make immunosuppressant therapy impractical, such as cancer, AIDS, and so on. Many also impose age cutoffs and a variety of more or less "subjective" requirements, such as the physician's perception of the patient's level of compliance with her prescribed treatment. As is inevitable, the doctors "play God" in their roles as gatekeepers of the waiting list. Thus, in most countries, the census of dialysis patients exceeds the kidney waiting list by some multiple. Further, admission standards may increase as the organ shortage worsens. Consequently, it is likely that published waiting lists understate by an unknown amount the number of patients who might, on purely medical grounds, benefit from a transplant, although not all wait-listed patients are actually viable transplant candidates.

If the patient is judged to be a viable candidate for a transplant, she will be added to the waiting list. Different countries use somewhat different criteria in determining a patient's order on the list and in selecting candidates for transplantation. In most cases, perfect matches will always be made regardless of queue order. For matches that are less than perfect (based on blood and tissue matching protocols), some combination of compatibility and time on the waiting list is generally applied. In most countries, any patient placed on the kidney waiting list faces an expected waiting period of over eight years, and often longer for those with more difficult compatibility requirements. The frequency of different blood types varies dramatically across countries, and even within countries, creating significant differences in waiting lists within otherwise similar regions. In some countries, such as the United States, transplant centers have considerable discretion in organ allocation and differ in their ability to obtain deceased-donor organs. U.S. patients will often register separately at different transplant centers, which causes a discrepancy between transplant "candidates" and patient "registrations." In countries with purely national listing, this is not advantageous.

Unless the patient is exceedingly lucky, or has access to a viable living donor, she begins a seemingly endless period of waiting. A packed suitcase is kept by the door at all times in anticipation of the call. In addition, blood samples are sent to the transplant center each month, and the patient stays in constant contact with the transplant authorities. If and when an organ becomes available, the patient reports immediately to the designated transplant center.

Kidney transplantation is a well-understood surgical procedure. The recipient is anesthetized, and a long incision is made on one side of the patient's abdomen. The donor kidney is transplanted into a location well below the existing kidney, which may or may not be removed, depending on the presence or absence of disease. The actual graft involves attaching the kidney's vein and artery to the iliac vein and artery to initiate blood flow.

The transplant operation places a foreign object in the patient's body. The success of the transplant then depends on the reaction of the host to this extreme intrusion. Ordinarily, the human body reacts to such intrusions with an immune response, in which case the kidney will be rejected and must be surgically removed. To avoid this outcome, the ability of the body to fight infections must be substantially reduced with the use of powerful, toxic drugs. Small rejection episodes are common, especially in the first few months after the graft, but these can often be overcome by adjusting the dosages of the immunosuppressive drugs. In almost all cases, the transplant patient with a functioning graft will need to take such medications as long as she has the transplant.

A patient receiving a kidney graft and appropriate follow-up treatment and medication is freed from dialysis for the duration of the graft. Many are able to return to work. The length of time the graft continues to function depends on myriad factors, including the type of donor involved and the health of the recipient. Those receiving organs from living donors do much better, all other things being equal (Davis and Delmonico, 2005; Gaston and Wadström, 2005). Further, many patients outlive their initial grafts and successfully receive another, so one must distinguish between patient mortality and graft survival.[8] Five-year survival rates for kidney grafts from standard criteria donors, however, are approximately 70 percent for industrialized countries, with grafts from living donors lasting five or more years in about 80 percent of cases (Eurotransplant, 2012; OPTN, 2012). It is common for kidney grafts to last ten years or more. Patient survival rates, of course, are higher.

Organ Shortages   The potential recipients of organ transplants are generally very ill, and the degree of their desperation depends on which organ is failing and the medical means available to treat them prior to transplant.

Although there are shortages of almost all solid organs for transplant in almost all countries, the prospects of obtaining a transplant depend on which organ is needed, the potential recipient's blood and tissue typing, and the recipient's location. Kidneys, for example, are far and away the organ exhibiting the greatest relative shortage, despite the facts that renal grafts can be performed using living donors, and deceased donors ordinarily provide more than one kidney. The problem of the kidney shortage is (ironically) made worse by another of medicine's major achievements: kidney dialysis. Kidney dialysis makes it possible for patients suffering renal failure to survive for periods that often stretch into decades, although not without some adverse health consequences. Worse, kidney failure is a common consequence of diabetes and hypertension, diseases that are prevalent in many wealthy societies and are increasing due to rising levels of obesity and aging populations. Thus, as we will document in a subsequent chapter, the waiting lists for kidney transplants are enormous compared to other organs, and thus expected waiting times are longer.

In contrast, those patients waiting for liver transplants, since no mechanical devices that mimic the function of the human liver exist, face shorter waiting lists, and a primary reason they die is the absence of an alternative treatment for their condition. Similar idiosyncratic factors affect the waiting lists for other solid organs. One important consequence of these relationships concerns our ability to reduce or eliminate waiting lists by increasing cadaveric and/or living donations. For organs that must be obtained from deceased donors, only increases in cadaveric donations or medical breakthroughs will help. Organs, however, are jointly supplied. As a result, any increase in deceased donors that benefits heart patients, for example, will automatically increase the (potential) supply of the other organs. On the other hand, policies that promote living donors will, again barring some change in medical technology, do nothing to help those needing solely cadaver-supplied organs. Complicating this issue even further are the large differences in direct and indirect costs and benefits associated with the transplantation of different organs. For example, kidney transplantation is, by far, the most cost-effective known treatment for renal failure for many patients, and the social return to kidney transplantation appears to be very high, as we discuss in Chapter 4. It is more difficult, however, to make that claim about some other organs, such as hearts. These matters, which affect both appropriate public policy and the politics of the organ shortages, are addressed in Chapter 5.

How We Got Here—Adoption of the "Altruistic" Procurement System in the United States and Abroad

The Family as the Procurement Organization

As just noted, the technological constraints under which the early (approximately 1955 through the late 1960s) kidney transplants were performed required the use of living related donors. As a result, all organ procurement activity at that time took place within the potential transplant recipients' families. If no such donor was available, the transplant operation simply could not be performed.

Importantly, in that environment, there was no need for an official organ procurement system or for any explicit payments to potential donors to encourage consent. The affection between closely related family members was generally expected to be sufficient to motivate donor supply. And where it was not, explicit (but unobserved by the transplant centers) payments and/or emotional coercion could be applied. Thus, during this early period, there were no organ procurement agencies, no waiting lists, and no apparent shortage.

In addition, at that time, dialysis technology was also in its infancy. And because the U.S. federal government had not yet begun funding dialysis treatments, the expense associated with such treatments was beyond the reach of most patients and their families. Consequently, in the absence of a suitable living related donor, most patients suffering renal failure died during this period.

Transplant Centers as Procurement Organizations

Two important developments soon changed that situation in the United States. First, the discovery of more effective immunosuppressive drugs and improvements in surgical techniques greatly expanded the pool of potential organ donors to include unrelated deceased individuals (during the mid- to late 1970s). Thus, transplantation of cadaveric organs became feasible. As a result, the scope for application of this life-saving technology was greatly expanded.

Second, in 1972, the U.S. Congress passed legislation creating the End Stage Renal Disease (ESRD) program. That program provides federal funding for both dialysis expenses and kidney transplants, thereby increasing substantially the effective demand for both of these medical services. Moreover, significant strides were made in dialysis technology, and, with the help of federal funding, numerous dialysis clinics were opened. This provision of third-party payment not only made kidney transplants available to a much larger population, but it also kept many more of these patients alive for much longer periods of time.[9]

In addition, during the mid-1980s, private insurance companies increasingly began to provide coverage for other, nonrenal organ transplants (hearts, livers, and lungs) as these procedures moved from the experimental stage to more routine medical practices.

The resulting increase in transplant demands quickly translated into organ recipient waiting lists and a more institutionalized system of deceased-donor organ procurement. Initially, the organ transplant centers shouldered the responsibility for deceased organ procurement activities, and these efforts were largely confined to the hospitals that housed these programs. And due, perhaps, to their prior experience with unpaid living related kidney donors, these initial procurement efforts adopted, without much analysis or debate, the existing policy of altruistic supply.

The Current U.S. Procurement System

The center-based donor system remained in place in the United States until the National Organ Transplant Act (NOTA), sponsored by Al Gore, was passed by the U.S. Congress in 1984. This Act replaced the rather informal center-based procurement system with a more structural, bureaucratic approach. Specifically, the Act contained two major provisions. First, the legislation created two new institutions: organ procurement organizations (OPOs) and the United Network for Organ Sharing (UNOS). The first consists of approximately 60 independent nonprofit agencies, each of which was assigned its own exclusive geographic collection region. (As of 2012, there are 58 OPOs in the United States.) These agencies then became responsible for all cadaveric organ procurement activities, coordinating with the hospitals located in their respective collection regions. They rely heavily upon the hospitals' cooperation in identifying potential organ donors. The second institution, UNOS, was assigned responsibility for distributing the acquired organs to qualified recipients on the various organ waiting lists. Toward that end, UNOS soon developed a computerized point system for organ allocation decisions, with points assigned for degree of match, time on the waiting list, and medical condition. Despite the national scope of UNOS's lists, most cadaveric organs collected have been allocated within the acquiring OPO's region under this system.[10]

The second major provision of NOTA was to legally proscribe payment of any sort to cadaveric (or living) organ donors or their families in order to sway the organ donation decision.[11] Specifically, the Act makes such payment a felony, with substantial penalties.[12] Thus, an organ procurement policy that was a natural component of a transplant system that, due to technological constraints, was limited to living related kidney donors was institutionalized into a system that now relies heavily upon cadaveric organs from unrelated and generally unknown (to the recipients) donors. Goodwin (2008) provides a detailed legal history of the U.S. experience.

Interestingly, NOTA was passed, in part, in response to a natural market re-action to the emerging organ shortages. Specifically, a Virginia physician named Barney Jacobs had begun to broker living unrelated donor kidneys in an at-tempt to help alleviate the growing shortage.[13] Apparently, Dr. Jacobs experi-enced some initial success in locating willing buyers and sellers and attempted to arrange the necessary transplant operations. Upon learning of these potential market exchanges that violated the existing donor policy, the medical com-munity expressed outrage and sought legislation that would forbid it. Resulting political pressure led first to state legislation and then the passage of NOTA. Similar legislative action soon followed in the remaining states. As a result, the system inherited from earlier times was firmly locked into place in the United States without any serious inquiry regarding its likely performance in the new technological environment.

Procurement Policies in Other Countries

Western Countries   Around the time that NOTA was passed in the United States, similar legislation was being adopted in many other countries. Cherry (2005)[14] lists 51 countries in which legal prohibitions on the purchase or sale of human organs for purposes of transplantation were enacted and reviews state-ments of opposition by various international medical associations. For the most part, these laws were passed during the 1970s and 1980s, as the patient queues were just beginning to form. While these acts can differ from one another in several important respects, they all have one provision in common: they all proscribe the purchase or sale of human organs used in transplant operations.

As in the U.S. experience, organ procurement policy around the world developed in response to both technological progress and, unfortunately, sen-sational news accounts of organ brokers, organ theft, and the like. While tech-nological advances drive and inform the policy debate, the ultimate regulatory and legal frameworks adopted often reflect the scientific frontiers of earlier years. As noted above, the U.S. NOTA law summarized a moral consensus that arose during a period in which all transplants involved living, related donors. As immunosuppressive therapy and the protocols for the handling of deceased-donor organs improved, medical communities in many countries embraced this newly viable resource, but they did so within a legal framework that was inherently incompatible with organ supply from strangers. Thus, the U.S. experience of increasing shortages, rising waiting lists, and increasingly desperate potential recipient populations is not unique.

However, the medical sectors of the world's countries differ dramatically in their levels of funding and technological sophistication, just as the world's populations differ dramatically in their moral and religious traditions, and especially in their attitudes toward the utilization of dead bodies and their understanding of death. As a result of these variations, it is quite inaccurate to portray the evolution of organ procurement policies worldwide as merely the U.S. experience writ large. In fact, the varied experiences of countries as disparate as Spain, Iran, and Japan, when properly understood, offer substantial insight into the sorts of potential policy changes that could go far in alleviating the global organ shortage.

Broadly speaking, organ procurement policy reflects the moral and economic circumstances of each country. Wealthy Western countries, such as the United Kingdom, Germany, France, Australia, and so on, have relatively similar systems: all prohibit payments to donors (even cadaveric donor families) and have largely or completely publicly financed procurement and transplantation programs. All also have shortages to varying degrees, although some, such as the Eurotransplant countries, have been able to stabilize their waiting lists. Spain is a special case that we discuss in a later chapter. In contrast, Asian nations, such as Japan and South Korea, have followed very different courses that reflect their ethical traditions. The concept of brain death is not accepted in many Asian societies, and this moral orientation is attributed by some writers to the different notion of the relationship of the human "soul" to the human body in Confucian and related traditions. In addition, the Western notion of "altruism" is not identical to that found in many Asian cultures where gift-giving is often viewed as a reciprocal activity. In contrast, countries of the Islamic world, while not homogeneous in their experiences, generally share a traditional aversion to the use of cadavers as donors, reflecting a long-standing tradition in Islam regarding the proper respect due to the remains of deceased persons. Thus, some Muslim scholars regard removal of cadaver organs for transplant as a sort of defilement, and some countries, such as Iran, rely primarily (but not exclusively) on living donation. In addition, middle- and lower-income countries often lack the medical infrastructure to support deceased-donor organ transplant on any wide scale, so a reliance on living donation, if ethically acceptable, is economically rational.

The development of transplantation in most of Europe mirrors developments in the United States to some extent, although Europeans, as is the tradition, are far more likely to embrace transnational organizations and give such entities real authority. For example, the organization Eurotransplant, which currently comprises the nations of Austria, Belgium, Germany, Luxembourg, the Netherlands, Slovenia, and Croatia (and is engaged in accession talks with others), was founded in 1969 and exercises authority in the transnational distribution of organs for transplant among member states. While historically an organ obtained by a procurement organization in a particular country is, indeed, more likely to be transplanted within that country, Eurotransplant has final authority on distribution, and such patterns reflect factual, rather than political, circumstances. Eurotransplant, headquartered in Leiden, The Netherlands, coordinates programs among the national transplant authorities, donor hospitals, and tissue typing laboratories. Eurotransplant creates and operates waiting list and transplant registries, and it created the allocation algorithm used in member political boundaries.

Scandiatransplant, an organization similar in mission and structure to Eurotransplant, is comprised of the countries of Denmark (where it is headquartered), Finland, Iceland, Norway, and Sweden. Thus, Scandiatransplant serves a population of about 25 million people. Scandiatransplant coordinates the operations of 12 transplant centers and 8 tissue typing laboratories. Founded in 1969 by Professor Flemming Kissmeyer-Nielsen, Scandiatransplant performs around 900 kidney grafts per year, with about one-third utilizing living-donor kidneys. Exchanges of organs among transplant centers in Scandiatransplant are relatively significant (on average, about 12 percent of organs are shipped away from the centers that obtained them), illustrating the impact of the organization.

Transplant activity in the United Kingdom is extensive, and the kidney transplant waiting list has been growing at about 10 percent a year for some time, reaching 7,877 persons in 2009. The National Health Service performs about 3,000 to 3,500 solid organ transplants per year. Desperation born of the length of the renal transplant waiting list moved the Labour government of Gordon Brown to propose a presumed consent law for cadaveric donations in late 2007, allowing public taking of cadaver organs in some cases, a dramatic turn of events for a country that is the historical source of the common law tradition. This issue remains a focus of debate in the United Kingdom.

Spain represents a very important case study for European transplant activity. In particular, Spain has routinely exhibited very high levels of donation, and the "Spanish model" has been the subject of extensive discussion among researchers interested in procurement policy and reform (Miranda, Vilardell, and Grinyo, 2003; Matesanz and Dominguez-Gil, 2007). Spanish transplant authorities have achieved yields from deceased donors on the order of 35 per million. (In comparison, typical donation rates per million persons currently are around 22 (France), 21 (Italy), and 19 (Portugal) (OECD, 2010).) Spain does not rely very much on living donation. Alone among Western countries, Spain has, in effect, eliminated the "shortage" when that is taken to mean they have stabilized, and reduced, the waiting list for kidney grafts. We return to the "Spanish Model" in subsequent chapters.

Other European countries, such as Italy and France, also have very active transplant programs and participate in transnational efforts, although these are less authoritative than Eurotransplant. In general, transplantation rates in Western Europe are often lower than in the United States, although European rates of end-stage renal disease are also generally lower. Importantly, however, the political evolution of procurement policy in most of Europe has shared the philosophical and ethical orientation of that in the United States, as have policies in Canada, Australia, and New Zealand. Specifically, organ supply is restricted to uncompensated donation only: payments to donors, or donor families, are generally legally prohibited and are regarded as ethically unacceptable.

This altruistic "consensus" has been overwhelmingly endorsed by the world's leading medical organizations, including the World Transplantation Society, the World Medical Association, the Nuffield Council on Bioethics, the World Health Organization, the American Society of Transplant Surgeons, the American Medical Association, and so on. This ethical view has been given force through legal prohibitions in the national laws of most wealthy countries, and the timing of these enactments mirrors the U.S. experience. For example, laws prohibiting payment for organs were enacted in Italy (1975), Denmark (1976), France (1976), Spain (1979), Austria (1982), Greece (1983, amended 1999), Finland (1985), Belgium (1986, amended 1997), United Kingdom (1989), Germany (1997), and elsewhere in response to these ethical concerns. (A more extensive list can be found in Cherry, 2005.)

The influential American medical ethicist Arthur Caplan (1984) and others provide useful summaries of the basic propositions underlying the moral claim that compensation for organs is unethical and should be illegal.[15] Although we examine these claims in Chapter 7, it is useful here to briefly state them, since they have broad and continuing implications for organ procurement policy in much of the world. First, the sale of organs would "commodify" the human body, reducing human beings to "things." Second, sales of organs would exploit the poor, who would be forced into selling parts of their bodies to rich transplant candidates. Further, any commercialization of organ procurement would adversely affect the quality and/or quantity of organs obtained through donation (as was claimed to occur in blood sales in the past).

Finally, if organs were economically valuable, patients would fear premature termination of care in an effort by physicians or others to obtain their organs for profit. Similarly, many medical commentators have been wary of living donation and have regarded living donation as a regrettable act that should be considered of last resort due to the (small, but real) risks to the donor. Thus, most Western countries have strictly prohibited payments to donors for organs, have publicly funded transplants, and have established public authorities to regulate and monitor transplant activity. Living donors are evaluated by official boards to guard against coercion by family members, lack of informed consent, hidden payments, and so on. Generally, living donation is allowed only between related or closely affiliated persons. Although sometimes honored in the breech, these principles have informed and shaped the current system.

Non-Western Countries   The experiences of non-Western societies have been quite different, although they have been shaped no less by ethical concerns and technical constraints. In poor countries, for example, the medical infrastructure is ordinarily insufficient to allow for any extensive use of cadaver organs. As explained early in this chapter, high-quality organs are obtained from brain-dead donors, whose breathing and circulation are maintained mechanically until the needed organs may be removed. The equipment and facilities to do this are expensive, and even in developed countries, only larger trauma centers are usually capable of obtaining usable organs. Lacking these resources, many countries have placed far greater emphasis on living donation, in which the donor's own body provides the "life support." Of course, such a policy essentially implies that only kidneys will be routinely transplanted, as many organs are vital and are thus available only from cadavers. A country need not be poor to follow this approach: Iceland, which is rich but quite small, performs only living-donor kidney grafts on its own soil, sending patients without living donors to Scandiatransplant partners such as Sweden.

Similarly, ethical traditions and the influence of religious authority vary widely among countries, and these factors can materially affect the evolution of transplant policy. In many Asian societies, such as Japan and South Korea, the medical concept of "brain death," which the American Medical Association (AMA) accepted in the late 1960s, remains very controversial. Although both countries have introduced laws defining brain death and authorizing the removal of organs from such patients, many people have been very slow to respond to the changes. In Confucian and related traditions, the human "soul" is not identified with the human brain, as is implicitly done in many Western discussions, but is regarded as widely diffused throughout the body. As a consequence, the continuing wholeness and integrity of the body are culturally important, and many families are reluctant to donate parts of their deceased relatives. Additionally, the Western notion of essentially "anonymous" donation of body parts to strangers is regarded as unusual, as it does not involve social interaction and reciprocity.

These considerations have had a profound effect in Japan, for example, where relatively few deceased-donor transplants are performed, the overall rate of transplant is low, and the age structure of the population has produced the highest rate of dialysis in the world, with nearly 190 hemodialysis patients per 100,000 persons in 2005. For example, Japan had only 859 kidney grafts in 2003, fewer than Poland or Canada. South Korea had 6,724 patients registered to receive kidney transplants on the national list in 2006, yet it performed only 263 cadaveric renal grafts that year. These circumstances have given rise to increased emphasis on living-donor procedures, and Japan, for example, pioneered the transplantation of a part of a living-donor liver. However, despite the wealth of Japan and South Korea, and the great technical ability both countries possess, long-standing cultural traditions and distrust of Western medical practices have limited the use of transplant therapy compared to many other countries.

In predominantly Islamic countries, the issue of organ transplants itself is often debated. Although generalizations are hazardous, it is probably fair to say that most Islamic scholars of southern Asia (e.g., India or Pakistan) generally reject transplantation on theological grounds, while those of the Middle East proper are less opposed, although they also impose stringent conditions on the practice. Most opposition stems from Sharia, or Islamic law, which is understood to hold the human body to be sacred and to prohibit mutilation. For example, the orthodox scholar Imam al-Marghinani (*Al-Hidayah—The Guidance*, circa 570, 4.39) reasons that "it is unlawful to sell the hair of a human as it is to take benefit out of it. . . . It is not permissible to disgrace any part of a human's body." Later, the Imam remarks, "If a person feared death due to hunger, and another person said to him, 'Cut off my hand and consume it,' or he said, 'Cut a part of me and eat it,' it would be unlawful for him to do so" (*Al-Hidayah*, 5.310). Many similar sentiments exist in commentaries and fatwas, and many refer to mutilation or describe the body as a gift from God that is not property.

In contrast, other scholars point to traditions that allow one to choose the lesser of two evils or to use what is prohibited in circumstances of grave need. Organ transplants are generally then held to represent such cases of grave necessity. Somewhat interestingly, almost no Islamic scholars have prohibited blood transfusions, and that practice is routine throughout the Muslim world. Thus, as with the rest of humanity, the issues of organ transplants have generated serious ethical debate within Islam.

One Islamic country that has acted quite energetically in promoting organ transplantation, at least for kidneys, is Iran, which is the only country with an active, public system of paid living donation. Iran, where many locations lack equipment to maintain the functioning of brain-dead potential donors, relies overwhelmingly on living-donor kidneys, although a small number of deceased-donor transplants are performed. The clerical authorities oversee the system, and donors and recipients are evaluated using criteria derived from religious tradition. The Iranian program began in 1988, and by 1999, it had eliminated the kidney waiting list, although one must remember that deaths among ESRD patients are high given the low number of dialysis stations. Although the Iranians recognize brain death, only about 166 deceased-donor transplants were performed in 2003, compared to 1,660 living unrelated donor grafts (Ghods and Savai, 2006).

Donor compensation in Iran, though low by Western standards, is over U.S.$1,000 and includes both a cash grant and health insurance benefits. Charitable institutions provide some of the payments to donors, and foreigners may neither donate nor receive transplants, except in special circumstances. Interestingly, while the Iranians appear to feel that the compensation they offer is at least ethically "tinged," they argue that the payments are "life changing" in size, thus substantially benefitting the donor and his or her family; other countries also use payments, but they restrict the payments to the other stages of the process. In any event, the "Iranian model" is very important for purposes of world debate.

The giants India and China have become significant actors in the transplant sector only fairly recently, and unfortunately not always in the best circumstances. Both countries have populations of potential recipients that vastly dwarf their available supplies of organs. However, both India and China have been identified as locations for transplant activities aimed heavily toward foreigners and allegations (in some cases valid; in others quite ridiculous) regarding how organs for transplantation are obtained. We examine these issues in Chapter 3. However, both India and China have developed rather extensive transplant facilities in environments of weak or unclear regulation. In China, for instance, the International Organ Transplant Hospital was founded in 1992, and it has aggressively advertised transplant services to non-Chinese, especially Japanese and Canadians. Their advertising promises maximum waiting times for kidneys of one month, with liver transplants requiring two months at most. Those patients with a compatible donor may receive a graft in a few days. Costs quoted by the hospital are less than half what one might pay in the United States. Particular controversy has arisen about transplantation in China because of the documented use of organs from executed prisoners, who are admitted to supply as much as 65 percent of organs for transplant as late as 2009 (*The Times*, August 26, 2009). As China's role in world affairs increases, it will be interesting to see the degree to which such policies are curtailed or abandoned.

Conclusion

Human societies are routinely challenged by technological progress. Improvements in science often bring unwelcomed stress when the scope of what is possible must exist within the legal and social constraints of an earlier time. This is clearly illustrated by the evolution of transplantation. Many observers, who developed their moral positions in the pre-cyclosporin era, have not abandoned their opposition to compensation despite the greatly expanded potential of transplant medicine to save lives and reduce costs. One could say, of course, that moral principles are not subject to revision based on current circumstances. That this moral rectitude has appeal we will admit. However, it is not reasonable to maintain this point of view in concert with an ignorance of precisely what "current circumstances" are. And current circumstances are dire indeed. These are the subject of the next chapter.

3

Consequences of the Current Policy

Introduction

In many countries, organ shortages are a fact of life, but this was not always the case. In earlier times, lack of effective immunosuppressive therapy limited most solid organ transplantation to persons sharing a close blood kinship. In this sort of environment, the issue of donor compensation was ordinarily a matter dealt with within the family. The introduction of more effective antirejection drugs, however, made transplants between unrelated people feasible and made deceased donors useful. The way donors were motivated, however, did not change in concert with the technology of transplantation. An ethical consensus, born of this earlier time, guided the creation of the national organ donor laws, and donor compensation was almost universally prohibited. It is unlikely that the architects of the current donor system envisioned the sizes and consequences of the shortages, although several commentators, including Dukeminier (1970), predicted shortages as early as the 1970s.

In this chapter, we document the consequences of our continued reliance on the current procurement policy. Under this policy, shortages, combined with progress in transplantation medicine, lead to growing waiting lists. As these waiting lists grow, expected waiting times increase commensurately. In turn, as the waiting times get longer, an increasing number of patients die because they are unable to obtain the needed organs in time. In addition, longer waiting times prolong patients' suffering and reduce the likelihood that the transplant will succeed. Moreover, as the situation becomes worse, patients, their families, and caregivers all experience growing desperation, which leads to increased reliance on substandard organs, a rising use of living donors, and an increase in black market activities.

This chapter examines the current state of the global organ procurement system and discusses the most direct consequence of the organ shortage: transplant waiting lists. Waiting list dynamics and the situations both in and outside the United States are analyzed. We examine the secondary effects of the shortage and analyze the increased reliance on living donors and the rising use of marginal donors. A third "secondary consequence"—the black market for kidneys—which we consider an especially dire effect of waiting lists, is treated at some length. Finally, we review the future prospects for the global organ shortage.

The Organ Shortage and Waiting Lists
A Digression on the Waiting List Dynamics

The most obvious "symptom" of the current failure in organ procurement is the "waiting list," which is a census of those patients hoping to obtain a transplant, those for whom a transplant is at some relevant time medically feasible, and those who qualify for a transplant and are admitted by medical officials to the queue. Waiting lists for many organs are maintained by medical officials in many countries, and such lists are often incorrectly identified as representing the extent of the organ "shortage." This is incorrect on several counts. First, such lists necessarily undercount those who might, on purely medical grounds, benefit from a transplant. Some patients fail to register, seek transplants abroad, or are discouraged from registering by harried physicians. Second, some researchers believe that waiting lists are, to some extent, "managed" by transplant authorities. For example, a patient needing a transplant might be admitted to the list only briefly, right before the transplant is performed. It seems probable that most transplant centers, which control registrations, would be reluctant to "turn away customers." Third, removals from waiting lists also arise for reasons such as inoperability and death. While such removals *reduce* the sizes of the lists, no one believes those reductions constitute progress. Fourth, many waiting lists, including those in the United States, contain both "active" and "inactive" sublists. Those on the inactive list may be too ill for a period to receive a graft. As expected time to transplantation increases, more patients on the list become too sick for transplantation, and patients may become inactive. Finally, the relationship between the lists and the shortages in their economic sense is often misunderstood.

It is important first to understand the economic definition of a "shortage" and how it relates to the observed organ waiting lists. By definition, a shortage is equal to the difference between the quantity of a good demanded and the quantity of that good supplied. This amount is to be understood *at a given price* and *during a specified time interval*—for example, one year. Therefore, shortages arise whenever the price of a product is held below its equilibrium, market-clearing level. Because the quantities along both the demand and supply curves are expressed as flows, the shortages are also flows.

Applying this definition to the organ shortage reveals that a waiting list, which is a stock, is not equal to the shortage, which is a flow. Rather, the waiting list is the accumulation of all past shortages, adjusted for deaths and other causes of removals from the list (e.g., too sick to transplant) other than transplantation. Assume, for simplicity, that these other causes for removal are zero. In that case, the waiting list at the end of period t, $WL(t)$, is simply equal to the waiting list at the end of period $t-1$, $WL(t-1)$, plus the shortage in period t, $S(t)$, minus the deaths in period t, $D(t)$. That is,

$$WL(t) = WL(t-1) + S(t) - D(t) \qquad (3.1)$$

Thus, the shortage is

$$S(t) = WL(t) - WL(t-1) + D(t) \qquad (3.2)$$

In other words, in this simplification, the shortage at time t is merely the *change* in the waiting list, plus deaths.

Thus, an elimination of the shortage would not mean that the waiting lists disappear but that the waiting list is stabilized, net of deaths. Therefore, in order to reduce (and eventually eliminate) the waiting list, it is necessary to implement a policy (or price) that will create surpluses (or "negative shortages") in each period. The length of time required to eliminate the waiting list then depends on the current size of the list, the magnitude of the surpluses that can be generated, and other removals. Because the current waiting lists have accumulated over many years of shortages, it will not be possible to eliminate them quickly.

Finally, it is worth noting that expected waiting times are directly related to the length of the waiting lists and not to the size of the shortage at any particular time. Therefore, the consequences for patients resulting from a continued string of shortages are directly related to the size of the relevant waiting list, not to a given period's shortage. As a result, although the waiting lists are *not* immediate measures of a shortage, they are of independent significance and are worthy of study.

Organ Shortages and Waiting Lists in the United States

Given the above understanding, we now turn to the evidence. Figure 3.1 shows the overall waiting list (for all organs) in the United States over the 1988–2009 period. Also depicted is the U.S. waiting list for kidneys over the same period. (The U.S. list for kidneys was 92,810 in July 2012.) Several important observations can be drawn from this figure. First, because both waiting lists have grown in every period for which we have data, we can conclude that a shortage has been experienced each year over this period. That is, there has not been a single year in which the market for transplantable organs has cleared. Second, because the overall waiting list is equal to the kidney waiting list plus the waiting lists for all other transplantable organs, we can immediately see that the shortage problem is more acute for kidneys than for other organs. And third, due to the magnitudes of both of these waiting lists, it will likely take a prolonged period of surpluses in order to bring these lists down to more tolerable levels.

As previously mentioned, waiting times for transplantations depend on the size of the relevant waiting list (among other factors). One may say that,

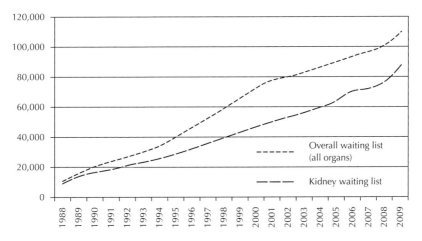

Figure 3.1 Number of persons on organ waiting lists, United States, 1988–2009
SOURCE: OPTN.

roughly speaking, the ratio of the number of patients on the waiting list to the number of transplants performed annually gives an estimate (albeit crude) of the "average" time patients must wait for transplantation. Such a calculation, of course, ignores deaths, other removals, the availability of organs of specific blood types, and the differential growth rates of the underlying series. Thus, medical authorities typically use more sophisticated techniques to make such predictions. There is a distinction to be made between the historical experiences of a cohort of ESRD patients entering the transplant waiting list during some past period and a valid statistical estimate of the likelihood a patient entering the list now will receive a transplant by some future date. The latter calculation is a statistical forecast, while the former is ordinarily irrelevant for current patients and their families. How deaths and other removals should be treated in the calculation is also problematic.

Despite these complications, it is clear that those patients awaiting renal grafts in the United States have seen their prospects dim substantially over the past decade. Raw OPTN data for cohorts joining the U.S. kidney waiting list from 1999 to 2000 show a median waiting time until transplant (ignoring deaths and other removals) of 1,255 days, rising to 1,316 by 2003 to 2004. For black patients, the median wait is longer still: 1,781 days in 1999 increases to 1,833 days by 2003. Such medians, which merely identify the time at which one-half of unremoved patient registrations have been transplanted, clearly grossly understate the reasonable expectation of a potential transplant candidate. For many blood types, and in many areas of the United States, kidney patients are routinely quoted time frames of ten years or more.

As one would expect, as waiting times have increased, the number of patients who have died while awaiting transplantation has also risen. The OPTN has kept track of such deaths since 1988. Beginning in 1995, that organization has also reported the number of patients who were removed from organ waiting lists because they had become too sick to undergo the necessary surgery. Generally, one can assume that most, if not all, of this latter group have died as well.

Figure 3.2 shows the series for kidneys. Three observations merit discussion. First, U.S. patient deaths have risen in tandem with the waiting list over most of our sample period. As noted earlier in this chapter, the adverse consequences of the organ shortage are driven primarily by the size of the waiting list rather than the actual shortage in any given year. That is, the suffering and deaths caused by the current organ shortage arise from the cumulative effects of persistent shortages that have occurred year after year. While eliminating the

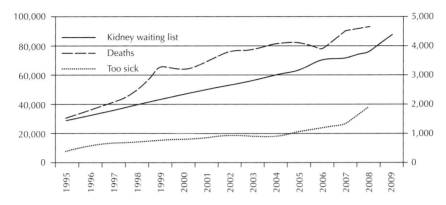

Figure 3.2 Number of persons on kidney waiting lists, removals due to death and sickness, United States, 1995–2009

SOURCE: OPTN.

shortage will stabilize the waiting list, it will take years of surpluses to ulti-mately cure the effects of that policy.

Second, while the U.S. kidney waiting list death rate has risen monotoni-cally over most of the sample period, it shows some sign of slower growth after 2000. This result appears somewhat anomalous as the waiting list has contin-ued to grow, albeit at a slightly reduced rate. There are several explanations for falling organ list death rates discussed in medical circles. First, the so-called MELD/PELD program was implemented in the United States for liver pa-tients on February 27, 2000. This program changed the allocation criteria for candidates on the liver transplant waiting list to more closely reflect the sever-ity of the patients' medical condition. Specifically, the revised algorithm uses a statistical model based on liver function tests that predicts the probability the patient will die while waiting. It then assigns priority to the most critically ill patients. Its implementation appears to have lowered the number of deaths on that list significantly. For heart patients, the left ventricle assist device (LVAD), a sort of "artificial heart," has greatly improved the conditions of many awaiting transplantation. This equipment helps to keep heart patients alive longer and, thereby, also reduces the number of deaths on the list. Neither of these devel-opments, however, has directly affected kidney patients.

Rather, as we document following, the shortage of kidneys of high qual-ity has led to an increasing use of marginal (or "extended criteria") donors (ECDs), and of non-heart-beating donors (NHBDs).[1] While the success rates of transplants using such donor organs are somewhat below those that use standard criteria donors (SCDs), the increased availability of cadaveric organs caused by this loosening of quality standards does get more patients removed from the waiting list prior to their deaths. This factor contributes to slowing death rates among U.S. patients.

Improvements in patient care and/or increased organ donor pools through reduced donor criteria have slowed the rise in deaths among various U.S. organ transplant populations. Whether they will be sufficient to permanently halt the growth in patient deaths, however, is an empirical question that cannot yet be answered. However, such an outcome appears highly unlikely unless the waiting list itself can be stabilized or reduced. What is clear is that the rising use of substandard organs is itself a consequence of the organ shortage, although some would say a desirable one (Howard, 2005). It can only be reversed by an increased supply of higher-quality, standard criteria cadaveric donors or further expansion of live donation.

Finally, it is important to note that Figure 3.2 shows only the *annual* U.S. death tolls attributable to the organ shortage and the procurement policy that has created it. A more accurate (and telling) indicator of the total human suffering this policy has caused is the cumulative deaths that have occurred over the years this policy has been in place. If we add the number of deaths over our sample period, we obtain a total loss of 107,502 lives in the United States.[2]

Deaths are only one way of measuring the burden of the kidney shortage. Many medical experts prefer *deaths per 1,000 patient-years at risk*, a statistical calculation reported by OPTN and many other transplant authorities. This measure equals the number of relevant events (e.g., deaths) that occur, divided by the "exposure" of the relevant population to the event. Since patients spend varying periods of time on a waiting list, this approach allows more reasonable comparisons to be made between patient groups. Looked at this way, deaths per 1,000 patient-years for kidney patients have exhibited slow improvement in the last decade in the United States and elsewhere, a consequence of several factors, including better care and more vigorous removals. In 2000, the United States showed around 84 deaths per 1,000 patient-years for kidney transplant patients on the official list, while this rate had improved to around 65 deaths by 2007. As a generalization, death rates per 1,000 patient-years are much higher for other organs and multiple-organ transplants.

Faced with a shortage of transplantable organs, patients will turn to any life-sustaining alternative treatment available. The principal alternative for kidney patients is dialysis. While considerable evidence shows that the quality of life is unquestionably lower on dialysis than with a successful transplant, this alternative

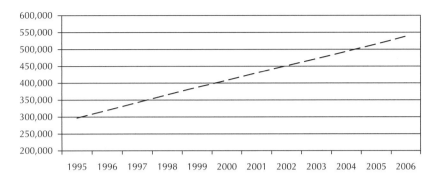

Figure 3.3   Number of patients on dialysis, United States, 1995–2006
SOURCE: OPTN.

treatment modality does keep renal patients alive, although the cumulative effects are dire: the probability of a patient at day 91 of dialysis treatment in the United States living five more years is about 33 percent, while the chances for ten-year survival are around 10 percent (USRDS, 2009). End-stage renal disease is diagnosed in around 110,000 people each year in the United States, and around 530,000 patients are being treated for it as of 2008 (USRDS, 2009).

Most patients on the waiting list for kidneys undergo dialysis treatments while they wait for an organ to become available. The converse, however, is not true: many patients who are on dialysis are not medically acceptable candidates for transplantation. (In the United States as of 2007, for example, around 370,000 people were being regularly dialyzed, although the kidney-only transplant waiting list amounted to about 76,000.) Moreover, dialysis is generally a much more expensive treatment for renal failure than transplantation (see Chapter 4 for a detailed analysis). In addition, the length of time on dialysis has been shown to cause a variety of adverse health consequences, and it has also been found to reduce the likelihood of a successful transplant.[3] Thus, dialysis is the less preferred treatment modality for many cases of ESRD, and the number of patients undergoing dialysis treatment is another indicator of the consequences of the organ shortage. Figure 3.3 shows the uninterrupted increase in the number of patients on dialysis in the United States. Within ten years, the figure has nearly doubled.

Organ Shortages and Waiting Lists Outside the United States

Circumstances outside the United States are, for the most part, similarly discouraging. However, several important points must be made in this regard. First, the United States has among the highest rates of dialysis usage, ESRD, and diabetes in the world.[4] This implies by itself that the demand for kidney transplants, at least, will be inherently higher in the United States than elsewhere. Additionally, the United States is a high-income country that lacks any comprehensive national health scheme or social insurance fund and spends twice the amount per capita on medical care as do many other high-income countries. Thus, it is clear that the U.S. experience will not be identical with that of other countries. Indeed, U.S. problems are, for the most part, worse, but it is quite inaccurate to say that the organ shortage is an American phenomenon. On the contrary, best evidence suggests that the shortage of organs, particularly but not exclusively kidneys, is a global phenomenon. Further, those countries with small or no waiting lists are ordinarily low-income nations lacking the dialysis stations and advanced medical facilities that permit ESRD and other very ill patients to remain alive while they await a transplant. Such a status can hardly be counted as a blessing.

Western Europe in Comparison with the United States   Western Europe, with its sophisticated public health systems and high incomes, presents an important example of the extent of the organ shortage outside of North America. In Eurotransplant countries (Austria, Belgium, Germany, the Netherlands, Slovenia, and Croatia), for example, the number of patients awaiting kidney grafts has appeared to stabilize in recent years, with the numbers cycling around 10,000 to 12,000 annually and Eurotransplant centers performing approximately 3,200 renal cadaveric grafts per year and about 1,100 living transplants annually (Eurotransplant, 2009). Deaths on the list are now relatively stable at about 450 per year. This performance, which suggests lower or even negligible contemporaneous shortages, has been made possible by a combination of factors, including a modest increase in cadaveric donation, larger increases in living donors, and no increases for many years in the numbers of new registrations to the list. This last factor strongly distinguishes the Eurotransplant environment from that seen in the United States, where both ESRD/dialysis populations and list registrations have increased relentlessly for many years.

However, the complete explanation of this record is somewhat controversial, and a number of scholars have suggested that transplants obtained abroad, combined with more changes in listing criteria, may offer a partial explanation. In any event, no one in Eurotransplant would characterize the performance of the procurement system as good or even adequate, and numerous measures aimed at increasing cadaveric organ supply are underway now. Taking the somewhat longer view, Eurotransplant's renal graft waiting list has increased, often at a very high rate, particularly from about 1985 through 2000. Total deaths on the kidney list from 1990 to 2006 amount to 8,959 persons.

Tables 3.1a and b and Figure 3.4 provide some recent statistics for Eurotransplant, including the country waiting lists for 2009, the evolution of various lists from 2001 to 2009, and waiting time on the renal list. We observe in the last case that more than one-quarter of kidney transplant candidates wait more than five years for their grafts. (The active kidney waiting list for Eurotransplant countries stood at 10,365 on April 1, 2010.)

The Netherlands, being part of Eurotransplant, is in one respect an exceptional case. It is the only country in Europe (not only within Eurotransplant countries) with a crossover donation program for living-donor kidneys (see, e.g., de Klerk et al., 2005; Busko, 2007). The Living Donor Kidney Exchange Program seeks to match two donor-recipient pairs that are both blood type incompatible with their respective partner. The program started in 2004 with the participation of all transplant centers in the country. Within two and a half years, around 50 percent of 150 individually incompatible donor-recipient pairs were successfully matched. A major limiting factor for such crossover donations is the (small) group of individuals with the O negative blood type: while they can donate to all other blood types, they must receive a donation from an O negative donor. In order to reduce that barrier, there have been discussions

Table 3.1a Number of persons on organ waiting lists, Eurotransplant countries, by organ, 2009

Organ	Austria	Belgium	Germany	Netherlands	Slovenia	Croatia
Kidney	801	806	7,652	901	52	321
Liver	102	166	2,083	105	15	54
Heart	61	50	920	58	18	14
Lung	72	92	617	183	0	0

SOURCE OF DATA: Eurotransplant.
NOTE: No separate data for Luxembourg. All figures relate to single-organ transplants (i.e., domino transplants are not included).

Table 3.1b Time spent on Eurotransplant kidney waiting list, 2003–2009 (percent of patients)

Waiting period	2003	2005	2007	2009
Preemptive transplant	1.9	2.5	2.5	3.1
Less than 1 year	24.9	23.4	22.0	22.0
2–4 years	48.6	48.0	48.3	45.6
5 years and over	24.6	26.1	27.2	29.3
Total	100.0	100.0	100.0	100.0

SOURCE OF DATA: Eurotransplant.
NOTE: All figures relate to single-organ transplants (i.e., domino transplants are not included).

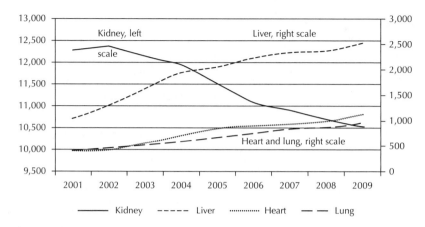

Figure 3.4   Eurotransplant waiting lists, by organ, 2001–2009
SOURCE: Eurotransplant.

in the Netherlands regarding donation to the waiting list (Living Donor List Exchange, LDLE) in exchange for a priority allocation of a kidney to the intended beneficiary of the donation. However, in many cases, the donor would provide an ubiquitous organ, while the recipient would require a rare one, a circumstance that would increase the waiting time for some patients on the list. Thus, LDLE is regarded in the Netherlands, as in most other countries, as contravening the national organ donation laws (Health Council of the Netherlands, 2007). We examine the issue of pairwise exchanges further in Chapter 6.

Individual European Countries   The United Kingdom faces challenges of a similar sort, although the performance of the British system is not as strong as Eurotransplant's. As of early 2009, the National Health Service (NHS) reported around 6,900 persons on the active kidney transplant list. In all, the United Kingdom performs about 3,800 total solid-organ transplants annually, with around 2,700 of these being kidney grafts (NHS, 2010). The NHS has managed to increase donor supply, although use of expanded criteria donors has risen significantly. The U.K. kidney waiting list is relatively stable, although growth in lists for other transplants, particularly livers, is showing double-digit figures.

The experiences of U.K. renal graft wait-listed patients are similar to those in other industrialized nations. For adults registering on the list between April 2004 and March 2005, after five years, about 62 percent can expect to be transplanted, about one-fifth will still be waiting, and almost one-fifth will die or be removed, primarily due to deterioration in their conditions (NHS, 2010). The

United Kingdom had around 26,500 living kidney recipients as of March 2010. According to the U.K. Transplant Center *Annual Report 2009–2010*, for the period 2007–2008, 298 of 779 living donors were unrelated to the recipient by blood or marriage, though this included a small number of paired exchanges.

The Scandiatransplant countries (Denmark, Finland, Norway, Sweden, and Iceland) have reduced their waiting lists in recent years for kidneys, but they have had less success with other organs. Tables 3.2a–c provide the sizes of their active waiting lists for four organs for the years 2004 and 2009. Unsurprisingly, Sweden and Denmark provide the most listings. Finland holds the distinction for being the least-reliant developed country with respect to use of live donors, a point we will return to later in this chapter. Scandiatransplant has successfully reduced waiting lists, but deaths on the waiting list for kidneys have risen: 54 ESRD patients died on the list in 2005, 87 in 2007, and 89 in 2009.

France has an active transplantation program, and French scientists have made important contributions to the medical techniques involved (specifically Dr. Alexis Carrel; see Chapter 2). The Agence de la Biomédicine maintains the national waiting lists for organ graft candidates, and recent years have seen steady growth in the sizes of the waiting list for most organs.[5] For kidneys, end-of-year registrations rose from 5,408 in 2003 to 6,152 in 2006, a jump of about

Table 3.2a   Number of persons on waiting lists, Scandiatransplant countries, by organ, 2004 and 2009

Organ	2004	2009
Kidney	1,656	1,558
Liver	85	118
Heart	72	70
Lung	120	135

SOURCE OF DATA: Scandiatransplant.
NOTE: All figures relate to single-organ transplants (i.e., domino transplants are not included). End-of-year values.

Table 3.2b   Kidney transplants, cadaver and live grafts, Scandiatransplant countries, 2007 and 2009

	Cadaver grafts		Live grafts	
Country	2007	2009	2007	2009
Denmark	115	141	50	90
Finland	168	174	5	6
Norway	174	188	86	104
Sweden	256	229	123	164
Iceland	0	0	7	7

SOURCE OF DATA: Scandiatransplant.

Table 3.2c   Persons on waiting list, death on waiting list, Scandiatransplant countries, 2007 and 2009, for kidney and liver

	Kidney			
	Persons on waiting list		Death on waiting list	
Country	2007	2009	2007	2009
Denmark	548	455	36	44
Finland	328	383	12	15
Norway	242	240	18	11
Sweden	505	480	21	19
Total	1,623	1,558	87	89
	Liver			
	Persons on waiting list		Death on waiting list	
Country	2007	2009	2007	2009
Denmark	21	32	2	4
Finland	n.a.	5	1	3
Norway	11	13	0	6
Sweden	38	68	7	8
Total	n.a.	118	10	21

SOURCE OF DATA: Scandiatransplant.
NOTE: Iceland: n.a.

14 percent. By 2007, the list had expanded to 6,491. Similarly, the Agency reports a rise in the number of patients seeking liver transplants from 449 in 2003, to 538 in 2006, to 575 by 2007. French kidney transplants have risen from around 2,500 per year in mid-decade to almost 3,000 today. The French additionally have a decade-old policy of giving priority in transplantation of organs from younger donors to recipients who are younger than 16 years old.

Spain represents a very important and special case, as the Spanish have been able, through a variety of reforms, to stabilize and reduce their kidney waiting lists. Further, Spain's achievements have not been dependent on high levels of living donors. As documented by Matesanz and Miranda (2002), Spain's national transplant authority, the Organizacion Nacional de Transplantes (ONT), began a program in 1989 seeking to greatly expand the supply of deceased-donor organs, especially kidneys, through the use of specialized teams, led by physicians who were kept informed of the status of all plausible donor patients in selected ICU facilities throughout the country. These "special coordination teams" receive significant public funding support and provide member compensation tied to donation successes. The result has been a documented increase in deceased donors, from around 550 per year in the late 1980s to over 1,300 per year by the mid-2000s. The shortage has been more than eliminated, and, thus, the renal graft waiting list has steadily declined. Further, most commentators do not attribute the success of the program to Spain's presumed consent donation law, which, as is often the case, is not always honored by physicians who are unwilling to go against the wishes of bereaved family members.

Spanish law, since at least 1979, has prohibited payment for deceased-donor (and other source) organs. However, Spanish procurement officials are allowed to offer monetary compensation to the families of potential deceased donors, and this procedure, which is not widely acknowledged, is regarded as legal. This is because the payments offered are presented in a humane and supportive fashion as either funeral cost assistance or as a grant to assist the family in repatriation of the donor's remains for burial. Rodriguez-Arias, Wright, and Paredes (2010) provide a bare description of this process and cite the relevant Spanish legal authority for the practice. Thus, the Spanish system does involve compensation, although it is neither universal nor transparent. The extent of this activity is not publicly known, so it is difficult to determine the degree to which the Spanish model's success is attributable to compensation.

It is undoubtedly true that the Spanish system also is efficient in the more conventional areas of expert training of procurement officers, good information sharing, and excellent coordination between emergency/critical care physicians and transplant surgeons. In addition, Spain has a presumed consent law, in force since 1979, but it appears that physicians still subscribe to the nearly universal practice of consulting with surviving family members. One can plausibly argue, however, that the presence of this legal framework makes the physicians' jobs somewhat easier. Further, Spanish procurement officials, who are highly regarded for their skill and effectiveness, receive additional compensation tied to their success in recruiting donors. At a minimum, the Spanish experience suggests that a good procurement system combined with relatively low dialysis populations (compared to U.S. levels) and available compensation can stabilize the renal graft waiting list. We return to the case of Spain in Chapter 6.

Other Countries   Organ transplantation programs in Canada have long been handicapped by Canada's almost unique lack of a comprehensive national organization to oversee organ procurement and distribution (Zaltzman, 2006). As researchers have noted, "Kidney transplantation in Canada is limited by the availability of organs, not by financial constraints" (p. 489). The Canadian Institute for Health Information collects statistics on transplant activity in Canada. Canada's waiting list for solid organ transplantation has been fairly stable at about 4,000 individuals since 2000. While the Canadians have obtained virtually no increases in cadaver donation in the last decade, living donation has nearly doubled, so they have been able to transplant over 40 percent of their active waiting list each year in recent periods. The need for renal transplants in Canada is significantly lower than in the United States. Nevertheless, over 200 patients on the organ lists die yearly, with kidney patients accounting for about 75 percent of that number (Canadian Institute for Health Information, 2007).

In Australia and New Zealand, the rate of transplantation of listed patients is much lower. Internal criticism of the Australian system is reviewed by Mathew, Faull, and Snelling (2005), who report more that four-year waits for cadaveric kidneys are typical today and are getting longer. Only about 7 percent of the waiting list for kidneys is transplanted each year, so the 2007 list stood at over 1,390 patients. New Zealand, with its large indigenous population prone to renal failure, had a list of nearly 330 persons in 2005. Australia and New Zealand closely coordinate their organ transplantation programs.

Large to severe shortages of organs for transplantation, and growing waiting lists, are reported for countries as diverse as Mexico (Luna-Zaragoza and Reyes-Frias, 2001), which performs perhaps 1,000 transplants per year, many for foreign visitors; South Korea (Cho and Kim, 2003), where many patients travel to China to obtain transplants; Brazil (Garcia, 2003), where transplants from living donors have grown substantially in view of the shortage of cadaveric sources; Kuwait (Oteifa, 2007), where the government has sought to implement a severe presumed consent law to lessen the shortage; and Israel (National Center for Transplantation, 2009), where a waiting list of over 800 persists despite widespread international travel by patients who obtain transplants in Eastern Europe, the Philippines, and even China. Oniscu and Forsythe (2009) wrote the article "Overview of Transplantation in Culturally Diverse Regions," and Jingwei, Yu-Hung, and Ching (2010) wrote about Asian countries. The World Health Organization has documented the global nature of the shortage and has recently introduced new guidelines and recommendations aimed at reducing the shortage, albeit by the usual, conventional means.

The case of Sri Lanka merits special consideration. On the one hand, the country shares a shortage of dialysis stations and of intensive care units with other developing countries. Thus, many ESRD patients die before they have made it on any "waiting list." On the other hand, the Buddhist culture of the country encourages altruistic donations, including those of organs. Postmortem donations of corneas and whole eyes have made Sri Lanka the second largest provider of such tissues and organs to other countries (after the United States). Altruistic donation of kidneys, both postmortem and living, is likewise encouraged, including nonrelated living donation. However, the success is much lower in this case. Evidence from media publications (e.g., LankaNewspapers.com, September 24, 2007) suggests that there exists a vivid black market in kidneys.[6]

Iran stands alone in offering a highly regulated, public system of paid living-donor compensation for kidney supply. The "Iranian model" was adopted in 1988 and had managed to eliminate the official waiting list by 1999. Ghods (2002) provides a detailed review of the Iranian experience. Iran lacks sophisticated trauma centers in many rural districts, so the utilization of deceased donors is not generally feasible. Further, Islamic teachings on respect due to the bodies of deceased persons are a significant barrier to cadaveric donation. Thus, living-donor kidney grafts are the focus of their efforts. Donors are ordinarily unrelated by blood or marriage, and, as critics of the program, such as the influential U.S. transplant doctor Francis Delmonico, like to point out, these donors are not from the highest income groups in Iranian society. On the other hand, the Iranians argue that their level of payment, which amounts to roughly U.S.$1,000, including insurance benefits and other nonmonetary rewards, is sufficiently great to materially improve the life expectations of those providing the grafts.

Further, in an interesting riposte to many Western critics, the Iranians point out that compensation for kidney transplantation is actually quite widespread internationally: physicians, hospitals, laboratories, and others all benefit monetarily from transplants. From the Iranian perspective, these activities are not less morally problematic than compensating living donors. Although recipients are asked to provide part of the donor compensation, in practice poor patients receive financial assistance from a well-funded group of Islamic charitable foundations. Further, the poor also make up the bulk of the recipient population, a consequence of untreated diabetes and hypertension.

The Iranian system has, by most accounts, been successful historically, increasing the numbers of transplants performed by 577 percent between 1988 and 2003. This result has been obtained within a bureaucratized framework in which religious judges examine potential living donors, looking for signs of coercion or mixed motivations. Great emphasis has been placed on continuing care for donors, with medical follow-up, insurance benefits, and so on made widely available, at least in principle. Foreigners may not donate or receive a transplant in Iran, except under special, rare circumstances. This latter practice has apparently gone some distance in allowing Iran to avoid the sorts of commercialization that would offend ethical sensibilities.

However, a recent lack of public funding seems to have undermined the past successes. Zargooshi (2008a, b) reports that the recent annual kidney transplant figure has decreased and now amounts to about one-tenth of the annual number of new ESRD patients. Obviously, the official public payment to donors of Tolman 1mio (around U.S.$1,000) has been eroded by inflation. Kidney vendors seem to ask for increasing private copayments from the recipients. The "market price" for a donation is now likely to be around three times the official public payment. During certain periods, it is reported that the public system was unable to pay any compensation to donors. Lack of public funds seems to have also eroded the formerly strictly regulated donor system, and today there is a tolerated "free market" in which recipient income status has become a major determinant in the acquisition of a kidney. Thus, although the Iranian experience strongly suggested the viability of compensated living-donor kidney supply in some settings, it also provides a cautionary tale regarding the consequences of underfunding for such systems.

Organ Shortages—A Global Phenomenon?   At the end of this section, we explore whether the organ shortage is a global phenomenon. It is true, of course, that many other countries have no shortages of organs, at least as we have defined the phenomenon. A shortage, in its economic sense, refers to willingness to pay and willingness to accept, and it is therefore not meaningful to talk of a shortage of kidneys, say, among people without the resources to obtain transplants. In economic terms, the demand for organs is a "derived demand": organs are of no use or value in the absence of the technical and material means to implant them. In the same vein, if hemodialysis is not available, then ESRD patients do not live long enough for any sizable waiting list to emerge. In strict economic terms, such circumstances would not qualify as a shortage.

Some critics of modern medicine and its orientation toward extending life beyond "natural" limits, such as Nancy Scheper-Hughes (2004), regard the entire idea of an organ shortage as a contrivance of modern medical practice. It is not the purpose of this work to address such claims. For our purposes, a shortage exists if there is an increase in the waiting list, appropriately adjusted for deaths, sickness, and the like. Thus, by necessity, we will ignore most speculation concerning the numbers of persons who, on strictly medical grounds of some sort, might benefit from a transplant. This latter number will always exceed the active waiting lists, perhaps by a large margin. Some opponents of market-based reforms in organ procurement have claimed that any increase in available organs will only trigger a flood of additional registrations, as physicians begin listing their patients under weaker and weaker criteria. Yet, even if abundant numbers of good organs were available for free, transplantation would remain an expensive procedure in absolute terms, so it will likely never be the case that transplants will be generally done on very thin grounds. In most or all industrialized countries, the general consensus is that those on waiting lists are, in virtually all cases, persons who would, in fact, benefit from a transplant in a meaningful and substantial way.

Thus, it seems quite fair to say that a global organ shortage does indeed exist. Although our conceptualization of this shortage means that we will pay too much attention to economically advanced countries, it must be emphasized that many middle- and lower-income nations would have shortages, as we define them, had they the resources. That is, on reasonable medical grounds, transplantation is the best therapy, and sometimes the only good therapy, for a variety of serious conditions, and these conditions are, unfortunately, prevalent throughout much of the world.

Secondary Effects of the Organ Shortage

It is important to recognize that the annual shortages of transplantable organs (the flows) are, by definition, generally smaller than the waiting lists in any given period (the stocks). The impacts on those patients in need of a transplant, however, are driven more by the cumulative effects of an extended period of annual shortfalls in supply (i.e., the waiting lists) than by any given period's shortage. Thus, as the organ shortages continue to remain unresolved, the adverse consequences tend to increase over time. Later in this chapter, we examine three different secondary effects of the organ shortage: the increased reliance on living donors, the rising use of marginal donors, and the expanded black market activity.

Increased Reliance on Living Donors

The Facts   Reliance on living donors has increased substantially in recent years in the United States and elsewhere. Because the kidney is the principal organ for which living donation is feasible and is, by far, the most frequently transplanted organ from that source, we focus first on kidney donations. Figure 3.5 depicts the number of deceased and living U.S. kidney donors over the 1996 through 2008 period. The deceased-donor supply has increased at less than one-half the rate of living donors. Although the medical risks of live donations are very small (see, e.g., Segev et al., 2010), kidney explantation is major surgery, and those undergoing it lose many weeks of work and face the attendant costs. Thus, the decision to provide a living kidney is not a casual one.

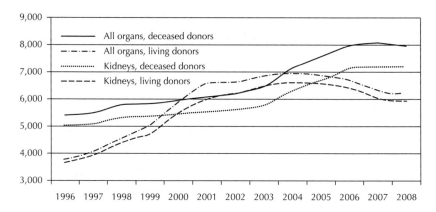

Figure 3.5   Number of organ donors, by organ and donor type, United States, 1996–2008
SOURCE: OPTN.

As a result of the costs of live kidney donation, most potential donors experience at least some trepidation, and many potential recipients are under-
standably reluctant to request (or even allow) such donation. Consequently,
the observed increased reliance on living kidney donors is a strong indicator of
rising desperation among potential recipients and their families. This phenomenon is especially significant given the relatively low rate at which potential
deceased-donor kidneys are harvested in the United States and many other
countries.

The degree to which countries rely on living kidney donors varies substantially, however, and the United States, due to its very high dialysis population, is
an outlier. Table 3.3 reports the ratios of cadaveric to living-donor renal grafts
for 17 countries in 2004, and orders the observations by decreasing reliance on
living donors. (In addition, the table reports the presumed consent status of the
nations in 2004 and the level of postmortem donations per 100,000 citizens.)

We see immediately that the United States relies on living donors to a very
great degree (in fact, in terms of the numbers of donors, rather than organs donated, living donors sometimes outnumber cadavers). There are many reasons
for these variations, not the least of which is the "demand" for transplantation
represented by dialysis populations. Although Japan and South Korea are not
included due to data gaps, both countries rely overwhelmingly on living donation, since both have cultural traditions that are not conducive to the medical
concept of "brain death." Moreover, they do not have presumed consent laws.
Thus, cadaveric donation rates are low in both countries.

Table 3.3 Reliance on living kidney donation, 17 countries in 2004

Country	Cadaveric grafts per live donor grafts	Presumed consent?	Cadaver donations per 100,000 population
United States	1.41	No	5.3
Australia	1.42	No	3.0
Canada	1.46	No	3.5
Greece	1.53	Yes	2.1
Sweden	1.62	Yes	5.8
Netherlands	1.69	No	4.1
Norway	1.78	Yes	5.8
Denmark	2.59	No	3.5
United Kingdom	2.93	No	3.0
Germany	4.04	Yes	3.0
Austria	9.16	Yes	4.7
Italy	11.94	Yes	3.0
Portugal	13.52	Yes	4.0
France	13.76	Yes	4.0
Belgium	18.60	Yes	3.7
Spain	34.83	Yes	5.2
Finland	38.40	Yes	3.7

SOURCE OF DATA: OECD, OPTN, and Abadie and Gay (2006).

Table 3.4 Living kidney graft rates, per 100,000 population, selected countries, 1995–2009

Country	1995	2000	2004	2009
Australia	0.53	0.95	1.22	1.77
Austria	0.15	0.46	0.47	0.84
Canada	0.76	n.a.	1.29	1.71
France	0.10	n.a.	0.27	0.35
Germany	0.10	0.42	0.59	0.72
Japan	0.48	0.59	n.a.	n.a.
New Zealand	0.65	0.83	1.18	1.73
Norway	1.38	1.71	2.07	2.16
Sweden	1.13	1.01	1.58	1.77
United Kingdom	0.26	0.58	0.77	1.00
United States	1.27	1.94	2.22	2.68

SOURCE OF DATA: OECD, OPTN, and authors' calculations.

Table 3.4 documents the evolution of the use of living-donor kidneys in 11 major countries. Although the reliance on living donors varies, as documented above, the trend in the use of live donors is common. In each country, use of living-donor kidneys for transplants has increased between 1995 and 2008–2009, often by multiples. Thirteen years passing saw the rates of live donation per 100,000 persons rise by 700 percent in Germany; more than triple in Australia, France, Austria, and the United Kingdom; and more than double in the United States.

Table 3.5 Number of transplants in Eurotransplant region, by organ and donor type,
2001–2009

	2001		2003		2005		2007		2009	
	Cadaver	Live	Cadaver	Live	Cadaver	Live	Cadaver	Live	Cadaver	Live
Kidney	3,154	619	3,385	655	3,406	866	3,728	1,032	3,590	1,148
Liver	1,114	124	1,264	133	1,364	121	1,625	101	1,691	98
Heart[a]	601	2	593	0	563	1	598	0	581	0
Lung	469	0	715	0	839	0	960	0	999	0

SOURCE OF DATA: Eurotransplant.
[a] Indicates a domino transplant.

Table 3.5 documents the recent utilization levels for living and cadaveric donors within Eurotransplant for the four primary solid organs (kidney,
liver, heart, and lung). Again we observe substantial increases over time in the
use of living-donor kidneys, although no similar result is seen for livers. On
the other hand, deceased-donor liver transplants have grown strongly, with a
52 percent rise over the decade. In contrast, Eurotransplant, despite its relatively
strong performance in comparison with the United States, has increased cadaver kidney donors by only around 14 percent during the same period, a fact
that helps explain the differential increase in living-donor kidney explantation
(Figure 3.6). Again, the suggestion is that living solid organ donation reflects
the serious shortages of deceased-donor organs, and, if cadaver organ supplies
should increase, one might see a discernible effect on living donation for those
organs for which that is feasible. We provide statistical evidence for this effect
in Chapter 5.

Possible Unwarranted Effects of an Increased Reliance on Living Donors   Increased
reliance on living donors is a plausible consequence of the shortage of cadaveric donations. Moreover, it seems to be welcome, at least at first sight, because
living donations increase the total availability of (mainly) kidneys and reduce
the average waiting time. However, possible negative effects should also be considered. Here we first consider the behavior of the medical staff with regard to
living versus cadaveric donation. Second, the behaviors of potential donors and
the bereaved are analyzed.

Behavior of the Medical Staff   For the medical staff, a successful deceased-
donor transplant involves a fight against the clock. Only a maximum of around
30 hours can pass between kidney removal and implantation. (For other organs,
the limit is even lower.) The greater the time that passes until implantation, the

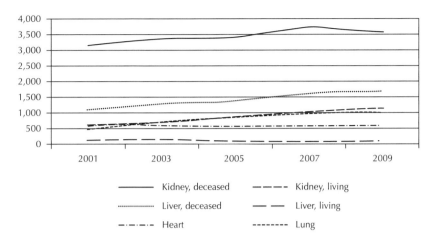

Figure 3.6   Number of organ transplants in Eurotransplant countries, 2001–2009
SOURCE: Eurotransplant.

lower the expected medical benefits of the transplant will be. A cadaveric transplant is also highly inconvenient. Many potential deceased donors are victims of traffic accidents. These accidents often occur at night and during weekends, when the clinic is not fully staffed. Cadaveric organ transplants are often organized so that surgeons in the receiving clinic also remove the organ. Thus, staff may have to travel long distances, at night, by small airplanes and in bad weather.

In addition to the severe time pressure and inconvenience, a deceased-donor transplant involves the delicate task of obtaining the family's permission for the donation of the deceased's organs. The applicable type of consent legislation is important. A policy of "presumed" (or even "implied") consent gives the medical staff more leverage to achieve consent for donation, and empirical evidence supports this conjecture (Abadie and Gay, 2006).[7] Moreover, it has been argued that the willingness of the bereaved to make a positive donation decision is itself influenced by the legislation (see, e.g., Wendler and Dickert, 2001). However, in practice, most physicians—under any type of legislation—seek the approval of the bereaved.

A fundamental challenge to hospital procurement officers seeking deceased-donor permission stems from the appearance of the brain-dead person: the deceased does not look dead. In order to facilitate organ donation, the cardiovascular system of the donor must be mechanically maintained. This means that the donor is seen to be breathing, has normal-looking skin, and is not cold.

Only the appearance of the eyes reveals the facts. In such a situation the be-reaved often do not believe that their family member is definitively dead, may assume that the clinic is not willing to do its utmost to save the person, and could suspect that the lack of effort is due to a wish to harvest organs.

A living kidney donation, by contrast, does not pose these problems for the medical staff and the clinic. The organ donor is provided by the patient. The explantation and implantation can generally be done "simultaneously," though this requires two operating rooms and can be scheduled for the convenience of the clinic. In contrast to a deceased donation, there is, in most Western coun-tries, one additional activity to be performed by the clinic staff: verification of altruism of the donation.

An additional difference between living and deceased-donor transplants re-lates to the remuneration of the explanting and implanting staff. While the remuneration for cadaveric transplant operations is paid in almost all countries by the organ procurement institution, it is often a health insurance fund, either public or private, which pays in the case of living donation. There are indica-tions that health insurance companies in many countries pay more than organ procurement organizations.

Behavior of a Potential Donor and the Bereaved   Altruistic donation, either by a potential donor considering a postmortem gift or a relative of a deceased per-son approached by hospital staff, is surely dependent on the degree to which the individuals involved see the organ procurement and distribution system as fair and uncorrupted. We can plausibly assume that the willingness to donate an organ after death in an altruistic setting—that is, free of remuneration—depends not only on the applicable consent legislation but also on how cred-ibly the (officially) altruistic setting functions. Specifically, the willingness of potential donors to actually donate is plausibly reduced if potential donors sus-pect that a substantial number of living donors are, in one fashion or another, compensated for their acts.

People may believe that the altruistic donation rule is incompletely enforced—implying that the rule is applied to them but not to certain others—for three reasons. One, of course, is the black market for organs. The number of living donations that are illegal is, of course, not precisely known. However, numerous media reports are probably sufficient to cause the general public to believe that illegal paid (living) donations are common. A second reason, arising from gen-eral life experience, is that living organ donations, even if officially approved as altruistic and legal, may appear implausible without remuneration of some sort.

A donation between related family members or spouses might settle an old obligation or may be based on a wish to bind the receiving partner to a marriage. In the case of living donors not directly related to the beneficiary, the possibilities for invisible remuneration are large and include later bequests. Unfortunately, acts of great generosity can be doubted given the cynicism of our world. A third factor may arise from the growing significance of living donations (see Tables 3.4 and 3.5), which focuses additional attention on the second reason.

If the behavior of the medical staff in clinics, as well as that of potential donors and the bereaved, is correctly hypothesized, then the high and growing importance of living donations may reduce cadaveric donations. This possible effect, which is termed "dirty altruism" (Osterkamp, 2006), needs to be carefully examined, although the results of Beard and colleagues (2010) do not offer much support for it in the United States. We empirically examine some of these links in Chapter 5.

Rising Use of Marginal Donors

As the shortages have persisted and the waiting lists have grown, the use of marginal donor organs has risen. Figure 3.7 shows the number of cadaveric kidney donors by category—standard criteria, extended criteria, and non-heart-beating—for the 1999 through 2008 period in the United States. These data reveal an increasing reliance on nonstandard criteria donors. While the number of standard criteria kidney donors has risen by only 14.5 percent over this ten-year period, the number of extended criteria donors has increased

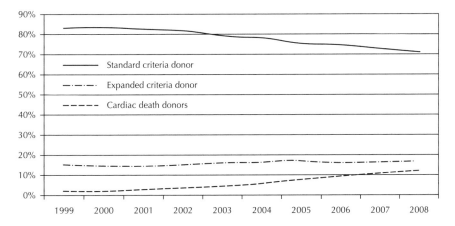

Figure 3.7   Deceased kidney donor characteristics, United States, 1999–2008
SOURCE: OPTN.

by over 59 percent, and non-heart-beating donor usage has risen by over 900 percent (from practically nil). Thus, the organ shortages have caused the U.S. transplant community to move along the quality/quantity trade-off in the direction of lower-quality organs.[8]

The use of lower-quality donor sources for organs is not limited to the United States, however, and it appears to be a growing phenomenon. In the Eurotransplant region, for example, the use of NHB donors has risen in recent years. Eurotransplant reports the use of 126 such donors in 2003, with the number rising to 155 by 2006 and 169 by 2008. (Such donors were not utilized in Germany during this period.) The growing reliance on lower-quality organ donor sources, which is a natural result of a continuing, serious shortage of standard criteria organs, has had both desirable and unfortunate consequences. First, of course, more patients are able to receive transplants. Given the severe risks of long-term organ failure, even substandard organs may well represent a tremendous improvement in quality of life and morbidity.

However, there are two widely observed consequences of these practices that are less welcome. First, it is well established in the medical literature that grafts performed using ECD and NHBD organ sources are associated with poorer outcomes, including lessened life expectancy, poorer graft function, increased rejection probabilities, and greater immunosuppressive drug reliance. In the United States, OPTN statistics illustrate this effect. Graft survival rates for ECD deceased kidney donors versus non-ECD deceased donors, as of 2007, are one year, 84.1 percent versus 91.3 percent; three years, 69.1 percent versus 81 percent; and five years, 54.6 percent versus 69.6 percent. Patient survival rates, of course, are higher, but even in this case, significant differences have been documented. Although the gross rates are deceptive (because the population of patients receiving ECD renal transplants differs somewhat from the transplant population as a whole), the five-year survival rate for patients receiving ECD kidneys is 68.8 percent, while patients receiving non-ECD organs can expect to live five years postoperation with a probability of 84.2 percent. Even if one corrected for the underlying conditions of the patients needing the transplant therapy, significant differences persist in almost every case. Evidence from the U.K. NHS provides a highly consistent picture. In 2004, the NHS reported five-year kidney graft survival rates of 89 percent (living donors), 83 percent (deceased heart-beating), and 73 percent (deceased NHB). Experiences are similar in Eurotransplant and elsewhere.

A second important consequence of the growing use of substandard donor sources involves the average numbers of usable organs such donors can typi-

Table 3.6 Number of kidneys transplanted per deceased donor, United States, 1996–2008

Donor type	1996	1998	2000	2002	2004	2006	2008
All categories	1.62	1.60	1.55	1.57	1.42	1.49	1.46
Standard criteria	1.73	1.73	1.71	1.73	1.67	1.69	1.65
Expanded criteria	1.16	1.11	0.98	0.99	0.87	0.93	0.95
Non-heart-beating[a]	1.63	1.55	1.57	1.76	1.56	1.67	1.62

SOURCE OF DATA: UNOS.
[a]Also called "donation after cardiac death" (DCD).

cally provide. As mentioned in Chapter 2, a deceased organ donor can ordinarily provide multiple organs for transplant, depending on the circumstances. However, in the important area of kidney supply, ECD and NHB donors are generally less productive sources of organs. Table 3.6 provides U.S. UNOS data on the numbers of kidneys transplanted per deceased donor by year for the three donor criteria.

Two facts are important in this regard. First, standard criteria donors provide more kidneys than other types. More seriously, the average numbers of kidneys harvested from a substandard donor have declined somewhat in the United States since 1996, especially for the ECD category. This trend is not the result of higher standards applied to organs removed from such sources, but all indications suggest a steady loosening of the definition of what is "acceptable" in the face of the shortage. Rather, the critical need for organs, and the growing numbers of patients who have languished on waiting lists for years, have led physicians to be less selective in evaluating organs for some patient populations. As a result, individuals are accepted as ECD donors who would previously not have been considered due to their ages or the presence of various diseases. Such individuals, however, are often found to have medical handicaps that preclude full utilization of their organs. Thus, even the quality of "low-quality" donors has declined.

Expanded Black Market Activity

The prevailing system of procurement and allocation of organs in rich countries can be termed a "market," at least in a wider sense. It is, in fact, a zero-price constrained market. Here, however, we turn to an analysis of illegal transactions for organs, primarily kidneys, where the prices paid are far from zero. Professional studies of the global black market for kidneys are rare, but public and media interest in this topic is impressive. A Google search for "black market kidney" produced 8,320,000 Internet pages; "selling kidney" produced 14,400,000 pages; and "buying kidney" returned 17,200,000 pages.[9]

The Market for Kidneys—A Diagrammatical Representation   Another indicator—besides long waiting time and the rising use of living and marginal donors—of the growing desperation of patients suffering organ failure is the increasing incidence of black market transactions. Such transactions occur when a potential transplant recipient pays a broker to arrange an illegal sale of an organ—usually a kidney from a paid (and generally poor) living donor. As the shortages continue to occur year after year, and as waiting lists and expected waiting times expand, the effective market demand grows. That growth, in turn, increases the demand price that some potential organ recipients are willing to pay and raises the profitability of illegal black market sales. As a result, black market sales increase.

Figure 3.8 illustrates the economic forces that drive these clandestine transactions. The figure shows the number of kidneys supplied and demanded in each period and the price per kidney. The demand curve for kidneys is given initially by D_1, while the supply of kidneys is represented by S. The demand curve indicates that Q_1 kidneys are demanded at a price of zero, and the supply curve shows that only Q_0 kidneys will be provided at that price. Consequently,

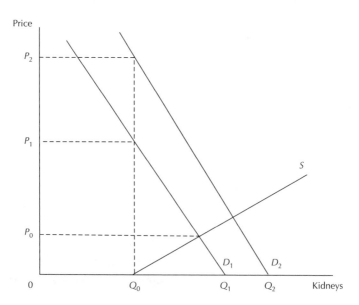

Figure 3.8   Shortages promote black market sales

under the zero-price policy, there is a shortage of $Q_1 - Q_0$ kidneys per period. Under these conditions, however, there are potential kidney transplant recipients who would be willing to pay at least P_1 for a donor organ. (In fact, some potential recipients might be willing to pay far more than P_1 because the supply available will not generally be distributed to those valuing it the most under nonprice rationing schemes.) This black market price is above the market-clearing price of P_0 if kidney sales were legalized. It is this widespread willingness to pay for a kidney that motivates the illegal sales.

Note, however, that the situation grows increasingly worse as the shortage expands. Suppose that the demand for kidneys expands to D_1 in the next period. The effect is to increase the shortage to $Q_2 - Q_0$ and push the black market price up to at least P_2. The higher price yields higher profits to those parties willing to break the law. And those profits, in turn, provide additional motivation for black market sales. Thus, the incentives that drive the illegal market are self-amplifying, and black market activity can be expected to increase over time.

Some Characteristics of the Market for Kidneys   The illegal market for organs is mainly a market for kidneys from living donors. Harvesting and transplanting of other organs are very difficult without cadaver donors available in a well-organized setting. Partial exceptions are the liver and the lung, parts of which can be harvested from living donors. Illegal trade in other body parts harvested from deceased donors has been reported, but our focus here is on the black market in kidneys from living donors, which constitutes the bulk of such activity.

Buying and selling of organs are forbidden in most countries in the world, with Iran being a notable exception. Due to the illegality of the industry, official statistics are unavailable. To our knowledge, there have been only a few professional studies of the trade in kidneys. One is Rothman and Rothman's (2003) study "The Organ Market," which mainly compiles evidence from journalistic reports. A similar approach, but in a more systematic way, has been followed by Shimazono (2007). We use both studies in the following description of some characteristics of the market.[10] Merion and colleagues (2008) conducted an econometric study on illegal kidney transplants, based on U.S. transplant statistics.

The shortage of professional studies stands in stark contrast to the wealth of journalistic reports, some based on extensive practical investigation. One

Table 3.7   Countries of origin of kidney sellers, buyers, and transplant locations

Sellers mainly from:	Buyers mainly from:	Main locations of transplant
Albania and other Balkan countries	Arab countries, oil-rich	China
	Israel	Czech Republic
Brazil	Japan	India
Caucasus countries	North America	Iraq (prior to 2004)
China	Western Europe	Israel
India		Philippines
Iraq		Romania
Moldova		Russia
Pakistan		South Africa
Palestine		Thailand
Philippines		Turkey
Romania		United States
South Africa		
Turkey		

SOURCE: Compiled from Rothman and Rothman (2003) and numerous other journalistic reports.

outstanding example is Michael Finkel's (2001) famous article "This Little Kidney Went to Market."

Table 3.7 lists several countries that are of importance in the trade as sellers, buyers, and locations for transplantation. The countries are arranged in alphabetical order, and not according to their—unknown—importance in the trade. All three columns must be regarded as incomplete. The list of countries of origin for sellers underlines what is plausible from the outset: sellers come mainly from poor countries, and they probably belong to the poorest strata of those poor countries. Buyers, by contrast, come from rich countries and are likely to belong to the elite strata there. The transplant operations are mainly performed in poor and middle-income countries where law enforcement and compliance may be weak. Moreover, while these countries may not offer a good health system for all, they do possess at least a number of well-equipped hospitals and well-trained surgeons.

China, India, Iraq, the Philippines, Romania, South Africa, and Turkey are, simultaneously, the origins of sellers *and* the locations for transplant operations. The United States, too, is listed as a location for illegal transplants. Some hospitals do not check for donor altruism when, for example, a wealthy Arab kidney patient presents a Palestinian or Moldovan donor as his "relative." In some Western European countries, such as Germany, the altruism checks at the hospital level seem to be stricter, but even they are surely not watertight. Sievers and Neitzke (2006), for example, presented a survey of the members of the Ethics Commission at German hospitals. They found that one-third of the respondents did not believe they could effectively differentiate between a legally permitted and an illegal living kidney donation. Even in wealthy countries with good oversight, we must expect that some "altruistic" transplants are, in fact, illegal "kidney deals."

The illegal market for kidneys is opaque to the buyer and the seller, as well as to the outside observer. On the demand side, a dominant role is played by so-called "brokers" who are approached by kidney patients. Brokers are connected to transplant hospitals in many countries of the world. On the supply side, willing sellers either directly approach transplant hospitals or are induced to do so by "pushers" whom hospitals or intermediaries send out to recruit sellers. It is reported that Turkish transplant hospitals keep long lists of willing sellers. This allegedly leads some sellers to bribe the hospital officials in an effort to move up the seller queue.

Usually, the buyer and seller do not meet and do not know each other. (During explantation, implantation, and recovery, they may, however, be only feet apart!) In most countries, not only is buying or selling a kidney forbidden, but it is likewise forbidden to be involved in such a business—for example, as a surgeon or a hospital official. Thus, transplant operations must be kept confidential, and they are often performed at night when most of the hospital staff is not on duty. Moreover, the illegality of the business makes political connections and political protection important.

To perform an illegal kidney transplant, a number of contracts are necessary. Usually, the contracts occur between a kidney patient and a broker, a broker and a hospital, a hospital and a surgeon, a hospital and an intermediary, and an intermediary and a kidney seller. But other constellations of contracts are also possible. For example, the kidney patient may conclude a contract directly with a surgeon of choice, such as one from his or her home country. It is important to note that, usually, no part of this chain of contracts exists in a written form but instead constitutes a purely verbal agreement. However, the buyer usually has to pay in advance, while the seller—as is often reported—will receive the agreed-upon price only after the explantation is completed.

The main risk for the kidney patient arises from the uncertainty about the quality and tissue fit of the organ. Due to the secrecy and intransparency of the market, a buyer cannot be sure that his willingness to pay a higher price would actually increase the quality of the organ and the transplant operation. The main risks for the seller are whether he or she will receive the agreed payment as well as the necessary postoperative care. News reports abound of betrayed

sellers who did not receive the agreed-upon payment or adequate postoperative care. But is it plausible that—even in an illegal market—betrayal of buyers
or sellers is the order of the day?

The market is, indeed, highly opaque, and claims against a contract partner
cannot be pursued due to the lack of written documents and the illegality of
the transaction. On the other hand, the market is highly competitive (there is
free entry on both sides), and kidney buyers as well as sellers probably share information within their respective groups. Brokers compete for kidney patients,
hospitals and surgeons compete for the brokers' clients, and hospitals vie for the
sellers of good-quality kidneys. Brokers, hospitals, and surgeons should value a
good reputation with kidney patients and potential sellers.

Kidney patients usually know many other kidney patients due to dialysis.
Most dialysis patients spend many hours each week in the company of others,
and discussions among them are often frank and personal. The experiences of
one would presumably be shared with others using the same clinics and physicians. Thus, information sharing is, at least in a parochial sense, very easy and
likely to occur.

Potential sellers are approached systematically by intermediaries and "pushers" acting on their behalf. The pushers go deep into the villages of the Indian,
Romanian, or Turkish countryside to recruit kidney sellers. It is reported that
in some Indian villages, a large percentage of adult citizens have sold a kidney.
This fact implies that the pushers concentrate their activities on villages where
recruitment has already been successful. One such village in India, as Zutlevics
(2001) reports, is Villivakham, a slum colony of Chennai (formerly Madras).
Due to the high number of people who have sold a kidney, the village is internationally known as "Kidney-Vakham." Fraud against sellers would surely
become known to the community, so outright betrayal, although possible, is
very unlikely.

The costs of an illegal kidney transplant depend on many factors and can
differ widely. For example, quality and tissue fit assurance, a top-quality medical
team, or a high-class hospital in a rich country would each increase the costs
substantially. On the other hand, the remuneration for the organ seller is usually
reported to be in a more narrow range—and the payment is often quite small
by Western standards. Table 3.8 provides some examples of total costs and selling prices compiled mainly from journalistic reports published between 2002
and 2008. The figures are neither fully comparable nor necessarily reliable. It is
reported that the advertised "all-inclusive costs" are usually divided as surgeons,
35 percent; hospital, 30 percent; seller, 20 percent; and broker, 15 percent.

Table 3.8   Costs of illegal kidney transplants, seller's remuneration

All-inclusive costs (in U.S. dollars), seller from the country of transplant operation		Remuneration to the seller (in U.S. dollars)
Operation in:		
China	12,000–30,000	n.a.
Iraq (before 2004)	20,000	1,000
India	35,000	1,000–2,000
Philippines	65,000–100,000	2,500–10,000
South Africa	100,000	n.a.
Turkey	150,000–200,000	3,000–10,000; seller from Moldova: 2,800
United States	250,000–500,000	100,000

SOURCE: Compiled from Rothman and Rothman (2003) and numerous other journalistic reports.

Political protection is not mentioned in the preceding revenue-sharing scheme, but that would also cost something. Uniquely, Israelis get a partial refund for a foreign (illegal) transplant from their national health system in the amount of around U.S.$32,000.

About the Size of the Black Market for Kidneys

Impasses in Assessing the Size of the Black Market for Kidneys   Although information on black market transplants in each country can be obtained from patients, nephrologists, transplant center personnel, and so on, aggregating this information into reliable statistics is largely impossible due to the clandestine nature of the activity. Because of these limitations, most discussions of the size of the black market for human organs rely on indirect approaches that are difficult to evaluate. It must be admitted from the outset that all estimates of the prevalence of brokered transplants must be regarded as speculative, and this caveat applies fully to the following estimates.

The Merion Study   In 2008, Merion and nine coauthors, mainly surgeons and staff members of transplant administrations, published the article "Transplants in Foreign Countries among Patients Removed from the U.S. Transplant Waiting List." The study covered the period from 1990 to 2006 and was able to detect 373 cases of removal from the waiting list due to a transplant abroad. During the same period, around 140,000 legal kidney transplants were performed in U.S. hospitals (OECD, 2010). The authors are convinced that the 373 cases "represent a minimum number of foreign transplants that underestimate the true extent of this activity" (p. 993). They mention two primary reasons. First, a number of patients may immediately opt for a transplant abroad without ever being on dialysis, being evaluated for a transplant, or being admitted to the waiting list. Their number is "entirely speculative" but "could easily outnumber . . . [the cases] reported here" (p. 993).

A second reason the study will underestimate the true number of foreign transplants is that the stated reasons for waiting list removals may be erroneous. The authors are of the opinion that "almost any one of the available codes [for waiting list removals] could represent additional occult cases of foreign transplantation" (p. 993). Moreover, "it is very likely that many more foreign transplant cases exist where the text field [of the removal codes] was simply left blank" (p. 993). The authors also conclude that the rate of foreign transplants is increasing.

The study goes on to assess the personal characteristics of the kidney patients who went abroad. Patients receiving transplants abroad, who are identified in the Merion study, can be classified by their age, gender, race/ethnicity, educational status, employment status, and primary source of payment (the last, for example, specifies private insurance, Medicaid, self-payment, etc.). Importantly, the Merion study comes to the conclusion that "those with higher levels of achieved education and the means to self-fund their transplant expenses" were "disproportionately [meaning more than proportionately] represented" (p. 991).

Another Approach Based on the Waiting List　We turn next to a speculative attempt to estimate the numbers of brokered kidney transplants arising among residents of some European countries by analyzing the Eurotransplant renal graft waiting list, although our approach differs from that of Merion and his colleagues (2008). The Eurotransplant statistics provide information on the annual ("active") kidney waiting list and the factors responsible for the annual changes. (Most of the figures are provided for 1990–2006, but delisting figures only relate to 1993–2001.) These factors are new and reregistration patient counts, transplantation (cadaveric and living—all, of course, legal), mortality on the waiting list, and delisting, sometimes specified as "delisting due to medical reasons" (for example, patient inoperability). Curiously, the table is inconsistent. The reported factors do not add up to the changes in the waiting list. Thus, either some factors that reduce the waiting list (transplantation, mortality, delisting due to medical reasons) should be higher or factors that increase the waiting list (new and readmission) should be smaller in order to make the accounting consistent. It is straightforward to assume that "delisting due to kidney transplants abroad" is the missing information that would make the waiting list figures consistent if this factor were reported.

We can therefore calculate what may be called "factual delisting, but not for medical reasons," and suggest that these delisting figures represent transplants abroad. The average annual value of this figure for Eurotransplant for the period 1991–2006 is 944. For the years 1991 and 1992, the figure averages 1,275. This estimate is much higher than the figures in the Merion study. However, we feel that it is again an underestimation for two reasons. The first reason, also mentioned by Merion and colleagues, is that a number of kidney patients may not register on the waiting list but may opt immediately for a foreign transplant. These transplants could not be inferred from changes in Eurotransplant's waiting list statistics.

The second reason for underestimation is that illegal (paid) kidney transplants may be recorded as legal transplants. The rapidly increasing number of living kidney transplants, especially in the United States, is a reason to be suspicious about the altruistic character of at least some of those "donations." In the Eurotransplant countries, the number of living transplants has grown faster than cadaveric transplants. Even higher growth is recorded for "unrelated living donation." This category includes donations by spouses, which is relatively unsuspicious. However, it also includes donation by "partners," which is less clear with regard to altruism. By far, the highest growth of living kidney "donations" in the Eurotransplant countries occurs in donors who are neither related to nor a spouse or partner of the recipient. The absolute figure is still relatively small, but it has grown from practically nil in 1996 to more than 10 percent of all living donations in 2006.

A (Simplistic) Attempt to Roughly Estimate the Size of the Global Black Market for Kidneys   We turn finally to a speculative attempt to determine, if only to order of magnitude, the number of brokered kidney transplants by evaluating the number of people of high income who are also ESRD patients. The idea here is that such individuals can, with high probability, be expected to seek transplantation by their own means rather than face the poor prospects offered by most transplant waiting lists. The OECD *Health Data* provides information on 30 OECD countries. For 21 countries, the number of dialysis patients is reported. The number of dialysis patients as a percentage of the total populations of the respective countries has risen steadily. In 1980, it amounted to 0.01 percent, but it had reached 0.10 percent by 2003, a tenfold increase. For our calculations, we use the latter percentages and apply them to the world population.

The question of affordability is less straightforward. No systematic information documenting the number of people in different income classes for the

Table 3.9 Number of wealthy adults in the world, 2000

Net wealth per adult (in U.S. dollars)	Number equal to or higher than
1,000,000,000	558
100,000,000	16,196
10,000,000	416,730
1,000,000	13,622,833
500,000	37,000,000[a]
250,000	100,000,000[a]
125,000	170,000,000[a]

SOURCE OF DATA: UNU WIDER project and Davies et al. (2007).
[a]Read from figure 6 in the publication.

whole world is available. However, figures on net wealth (assets minus debts) of adults, in U.S. dollars, are available. This information has been compiled and published by the WIDER research project of the United Nations University (UNU). We use James B. Davies and colleagues' (2007) publication "The World Distribution of Household Wealth." The data available are for the year 2000. The number of adults with specific wealth levels is shown in Table 3.9.

The first question is: How many people can afford to buy a kidney? The "all-inclusive costs" for a kidney transplant range from U.S.$12,000 to U.S.$500,000 (see Table 3.8). A common estimate is between U.S.$100,000 and U.S.$200,000. Given that ESRD can lead to premature death, dialysis is painful, and waiting times for a cadaveric kidney (if available at all) often amount to years, it is not implausible to conclude that even persons with a net wealth of "only" U.S.$125,000 might be willing and able to buy a kidney for themselves or a family member. One should also realize that such an adult is, more often than not, not alone. He or she may have a partner, and other adult family members might possess the wherewithal to pay for the transplant. In other words, buying a kidney is very often likely to be a family affair, with family-level financing. Unfortunately, statistics on such family wealth do not exist.

Such an assessment provides, of course, no proof and can only be regarded as suggestive. However, increased plausibility is gained by excluding the U.S.$125,000 class and by considering only the next-higher wealth classes: those that start at a net wealth of U.S.$250,000 per adult. About 150 million people are in these higher wealth classes. Now, we can plausibly assume that 0.1 percent of these persons suffer from kidney failure. This amounts to around 150,000 persons in the world who suffer from kidney failure and can, we assume, afford to buy a kidney. Implicitly, we also assume that they would prefer to spend the necessary money for the operation rather than go on dialysis and wait for a cadaveric transplant.

The 150,000 persons we have identified do not, of course, form the stock of rich kidney patients. Many of these patients will have solved their problems either by having been chosen to receive a kidney or by having bought a kidney. (Some, however, may be so sick that a new kidney would not help.) The annual turnover in the black market for kidneys is made up primarily of *new* kidney patients. What, then, is a plausible value for the annual growth rate of kidney patients? We do have available new and readmission figures for the official waiting lists. However, in the Eurotransplant countries, for example, the annual new and readmission figures are very high, amounting to nearly 50 percent of the stock of the active waiting list. This is not a plausible value for the annual growth rate of the ESRD population.

For simplicity, we make the assumption that the annual growth rate is 5 percent. This would mean that, annually and globally, 7,500 rich individuals with a newly acquired kidney failure might buy a living-donor kidney in the black market. In 2008, there were about 30,000 legal kidney transplants performed in OECD countries. Thus, the black market would, by this reckoning, amount to a sizable industry when compared to the annual volume of legal kidney transplants in Western countries.

The much higher figure of 15,000 illegal kidney transplants annually is a guess made by Nancy Scheper-Hughes (2008). By contrast, Shimazono (2007) provides a much lower "conservative" estimate. According to him, illegal kidney transplants may amount to 5 percent of the legal transplants. Our "guesstimate" of 7,500 is in between Scheper-Hughes's and Shimazono's estimates.[11]

How Do Countries Fight the Black Market in Organs?   In most OECD countries, it is illegal to be involved in organ "trafficking," as it is officially termed. This prohibition applies to medical staff and the intermediator (better known as organ broker) and, in principle, to the donor and beneficiary as well. In many countries, the legally imposed sanctions for organ brokers range between one and five years imprisonment and may involve a substantial fine. The legally prescribed punishment for medical staff is the withdrawal of the occupational license, sometimes combined with imprisonment. The punishment for donors and beneficiaries, although often mentioned in the laws along with penalties for medical staff and brokers, varies enormously. In Germany, for example, the German Transplantation Law states, "In the case of organ donors and/or

Table 3.10   Replies of Council of Europe member states to a questionnaire on organ trafficking, 2004

Question	Yes	No	n.s.	Member state
Question 5: Do legal provisions exist in your own state prohibiting the sale or the purchase of an organ:				
a. in your own country?	30	4	6	No: Bulgaria, Ireland, Lithuania, Malta
b. in another country?	18	11	11	No: Armenia, Austria, Denmark, Estonia, Georgia, Ireland, Malta, Netherlands, Norway, Poland, United Kingdom
Question 20: Are you aware of any allegations concerning the illegal removal of organs in your country?	5	31	4	Yes: Armenia, Estonia, Georgia, Russia, Turkey
Question 21: Are you aware of any allegations concerning the arrival into your country of organs removed illegally?	3	34	3	Yes: Albania, Armenia, Turkey
Question 22: Are you aware of any allegations whereby residents of your country have been traveling abroad to illegally sell or procure organs?	6	30	4	Yes: Albania, Belgium, Croatia, Cyprus, France, United Kingdom
Question 23: Have there been any official investigations, in the past, to ascertain allegations of organ trafficking?	7	29	4	Yes: Albania, France, Georgia, Germany, Russia, Turkey, United Kingdom
Question 24: Are there any official investigations, currently taking place, to ascertain allegations of organ trafficking?	3	33	4	Yes: Georgia, Germany, Russia
Question 25: Have there been any prosecutions for organ trafficking?	3	34	3	Yes: Germany, San Marino, Turkey

SOURCE OF DATA: Council of Europe (2004).
NOTE: n.s.: not specified. This table provides a selection of questions and answers only. The 44 member countries in the Council of Europe are Albania, Andorra, Armenia, Austria, Azerbaijan, Belgium, Bosnia-Herzegovina, Bulgaria, Croatia, Cyprus, Czech Republic, Denmark, Estonia, Finland, France, Georgia, Germany, Greece, Hungary, Iceland, Ireland, Italy, Latvia, Liechtenstein, Lithuania, Luxembourg, Macedonia, Malta, Moldova, Netherlands, Norway, Poland, Portugal, Romania, Russia, San Marino, Slovakia, Slovenia, Spain, Sweden, Switzerland, Turkey, Ukraine, and the United Kingdom. Four countries have not replied: Andorra, Bosnia-Herzegovina, Liechtenstein, and Moldova.

recipients, the court can dispense with a sentence, or can reduce the sentence at its discretion" (§18 (4)).

What do such legal provisions mean in practice? One answer can be derived from a questionnaire on organ trafficking that was distributed in 2003 by the Council of Europe, Steering Committee on Bioethics, to its 44 member states (with responses from 40 states and publication of the replies in 2004). A summary of the replies to some of the questions is provided in Table 3.10.

First, in a majority of European countries (30), sale and purchase of organs are prohibited. However, only in 18 countries does the prohibition also apply to trafficking in *foreign* countries (see Question 5). The United States, too, limits the prohibition to *domestic* trafficking. However, all U.S. federal states have prohibitions for their territories. Second, only a small minority of European governments admit to being aware of allegations that their citizens are involved in organ trafficking at home or abroad (Questions 20–22). Third, only in a (similarly) small group of countries are there active or recent official investigations, let alone prosecutions, against organ traffickers (Questions 23–25). Fourth, in the few countries just mentioned, the number of official investigations or prosecutions, past or present, is likewise low and usually ranges from one to three, with most of the cases being "discontinued" due to lack of proof (according to the notes provided with the replies to the questionnaire).

Official organ sale investigations and prosecutions seem to be very rare. When they do occur, they are a media event. Most of the few documented cases are exposed by journalists, not by official investigators. This happened in 2002 to a British medical practitioner, for example, who was naïve enough to frankly reveal to an undercover journalist that he could procure a kidney for him. The doctor lost his license (Savulescu, 2003).

Several spectacular cases of successful official investigations against organ trafficking have been reported from Turkey, South Africa, and India. In these countries, buying, selling, and transplanting kidneys almost appear to be an important industry. However, with political pressure from international institutions, the buying and selling part of this industry has been made officially illegal. In China, the sale of organs from executed prisoners has been banned recently. Similarly, Pakistan has introduced a law against organ trafficking. It is plausible to assume that the "successful investigations" occurred to demonstrate the commitment of the countries to the new (foreign-imposed) rules.

Donors and beneficiaries of organ trafficking are rarely prosecuted. From a human point of view, this is understandable, though donors and beneficiaries are identified in some legal codes as offenders, similar to brokers or medical staff members. However, it is noteworthy that transplant beneficiaries, upon their return from abroad, receive the customary package of long-term postoperative care, often financed by the taxpayer or the community of the insured.[12] On the other hand, most countries do not reimburse the costs of the illegal transplant abroad. A court ruling in Germany in 1995 denied the claim of a kidney patient for insurer reimbursement for a transplant in Bombay (Mumbai). The court argued that health insurance funds cannot be made to support "immoral treatment methods." By contrast, Israel is an exception in this respect. Israeli health insurers, including the public health ministry, provide some reimbursement for those returning from abroad after transplantation.[13]

Laws against organ trafficking exist. However, the efforts of rich countries against the black market are mainly directed at limiting the supply from abroad. Most governments claim ignorance of any allegations against their citizens for trading in the black market for kidneys. It is not surprising, then, that their domestic fight against the black market is halfhearted, in a double sense. First, the opportunities for reducing *demand* for foreign organs—for example, by fighting obesity—are not sufficiently used. Second, offenders can usually escape prosecution if they are not too naïve. This leads to the conclusion that the practical effects of the black market—reduced pressure on the waiting list and keeping a back door open for the rich—are regarded as welcome, or at least are held to be more important than prosecuting law violators. Häyry (2004) writes that high costs of transplantation and dialysis at home may be "likely reason[s] why certain governments 'close their eyes' when their citizens receive transplantations outside the country and after return gladly cover the costs of follow-up" (p. 267). Thus, the stances of rich countries can be called hypocritical, and their fight against the black market in organs seems to be duplicitous.

Future Prospects for the Global Organ Shortage

If our current predicament looks bad now, future predictions suggest things may become substantially worse. Although experience teaches that forecasting such phenomena is hazardous in the extreme, there are a variety of very strong reasons to be extremely pessimistic about the extent of future shortages if no material changes in policy and/or technology occur. While no such predictions can be precise, and while unexpected technological developments, such as cloning from stem cells, can alter the situation overnight, it is highly irresponsible to merely rely on such events, while ignoring trends and developments that could, if unchecked, affect the lives of many hundreds of thousands of people. Thus, we briefly examine here what little can be said about the future of the global organ shortage, with a particular emphasis on kidneys.

To begin, one may say that the degree of shortage, and the size of the waiting list, depends on the confluence of such factors as medical technology, diabetic and hypertension population sizes, disease management performance, the success of reforms in procurement, and so on. Each of these forces can be substantially affected by impossible-to-forecast scientific discoveries. For example, the development of drug therapies that allow the widespread use of inferior or poorly matched donor organs without substantial penalties would affect the supply of organs and the ability to perform transplants. In fact, successful kidney grafts are performed today with levels of antigen mismatching that would have been prohibitive in earlier times. Likewise, stem cell cloning of functional organs using genetic material from the patients' own bodies would allow each person with organ failure to become his or her own donor, with little or no rejection risk. Such advances will surely one day come about, but it is not responsible to rely on and wait for them, nor is it possible to forecast future conditions on such a basis. By necessity, then, our goal here will be much more modest.

It is indubitably true that many of the conditions that give rise to renal failure, such as diabetes and high blood pressure, are rising globally, to some extent as a result of rising levels of obesity, even in developing countries. The International Obesity Task Force (IOTF), a respected NGO with close ties to the World Health Organization (WHO) and the UN Food and Agricultural Organization, attributes about 90 percent of all Type 2 diabetes to overweight. The Commission of the European Union's (2005) report on obesity provides evidence of the rapid rise in obesity and its costs in Europe. The WHO suggests that 1.7 billion people worldwide were overweight or obese in 2000. James and colleagues (2001) documented the rising levels of obesity in rapidly developing nations in Asia, where, only a generation ago, malnutrition was the primary health challenge. Obesity leads to both diabetes and hypertension, which, collectively, probably account for about 70 percent of ESRD. These trends, if they continue, will increase the demand for kidney transplantation and exacerbate the shortage of organs.

In contrast to the grim outlines of the rising levels of global obesity, otherwise favorable developments, such as increasing life spans in many developing countries, can also increase organ shortages. As people age, their organs work less efficiently and, apparently, inevitably fail. Thus, societies with many elderly people will see greater demands for transplantation of kidneys, livers, and so on. This phenomenon is readily apparent today in Japan, which has among the oldest populations of any nation. Despite very low levels of obesity, Japan has the highest dialysis load of any country, with around 180 persons per 100,000 requiring regular hemodialysis, a result almost entirely attributable to the very high number of old people in Japan. The combination of longer expected life spans and low birth rates creates special burdens on organ procurement by simultaneously increasing the demand while reducing the supply. As other countries see their average age rise, the shortage of organs for transplantation will worsen, all other things being equal.

Forecasts of future organ shortages, or waiting lists, are sparse, although several simple models have been constructed for the United States. Beard and Kaserman (2006) provide a simulation model of the U.S. renal waiting list that provides short-range forecasts using relatively simple linear extrapolation rules and feedbacks. We examine that model in Chapter 4, so here we will limit our review to the very simple forecasting model of Beard, Jackson, and Kaserman (2008), which provides estimates of deaths and waiting list sizes for the United States. Their approach must be viewed for what it primarily is: an extrapolation that implicitly assumes no structural change in either the organ procurement system or the technology of transplant medicine. Both assumptions are, one hopes, entirely too pessimistic.

Given this, however, the results are sobering: by 2015, U.S. organ waiting lists will balloon to almost 160,000, with annual deaths increasing similarly. They calculate that, without fundamental change in the observed trends, lives lost to the kidney shortage will exceed 200,000 by 2015. These terrifying figures are only for the United States and, for various reasons discussed by the authors, understate the consequences of inaction. When one includes lives lost in the rest of the world, it becomes clear that 40,000 to 50,000 people per year will die on waiting lists (or be delisted for being too ill to receive a transplant) worldwide by the middle of the next decade, and the actual number may well be far higher as more countries obtain the resources necessary to operate organ procurement and transplant systems and dialysis becomes more widely available.

These estimates, of course, may be far too pessimistic, even in the absence of significant scientific advances and legal reforms. As discussed in the section on black markets, the continued existence of shortages leads inevitably to creative, and largely unregulated, responses by which desperate patients seek transplants. For example, Medscape Today (www.medscape.com) reported on new insurance policies available to some U.S. residents that provide funds to support travel abroad to obtain kidney transplants. Both the travel expenses and the expenses of the necessary organ procurement and surgery are partially covered. Thus, private enterprise can be expected to step in where government is unable or unwilling to act. As the organ crises worsen in wealthier, developed countries, we will see increasing patient travel for transplantation to poor countries, usually utilizing live donation. These activities will, of course, result in waiting list removals not attributable to death or illness and can attenuate the observed shortage. It seems unlikely, however, that such developments will be as desirable as fundamental reforms of the existing procurement systems in the wealthier countries.

On balance, demographic trends portend increased shortages of organs for transplantation, longer waiting lists, and higher numbers of patient deaths. The poor performances of the organ procurement systems of most countries, combined with relatively predictable increases in diseases and conditions associated with organ failure, strongly suggest that the future will look a lot like the recent past, only worse.

Conclusion

Two virtually ubiquitous characteristics of public policy decisions are that they are frequently adopted at the behest of politically influential interest groups, and they often have unintended and unanticipated consequences. The 1984 National Organ Transplant Act (NOTA), which codified into law the no-compensation organ procurement system in the United States, certainly exhibits the first characteristic mentioned above. The Act was passed in response to appeals made by various medical and transplant professional organizations to halt the emerging market in living-donor kidneys. There was no serious analysis of what that legislation would do to the organ procurement and transplantation system or, more importantly, its patients. No comparative evaluation of alternative policy approaches was conducted. Instead, a policy that was already in place, which had been inherited from an earlier technological environment, was carried over to the new environment without serious question. The experiences in many other countries mirror the U.S. example, and shortages and their associated pathologies are now widespread.

Around the world, shortages have triggered adjustments within the current system that reflect the strenuous efforts of those involved to ameliorate the consequences of the basic procurement model. We have seen expanded use of medically less-desirable organs. We have seen very large increases in the use of living donors, despite the failure to exhaust deceased-donor sources in many countries. And we have seen the emergence of a black market in organs, especially kidneys, that presents a dreadful appearance to the public at large, causing the challenge of convincing the public to accept donor compensation to become much harder. The irony of this circumstance is as apparent as it is unfortunate.

4

Social Costs and Benefits of Transplants

Introduction

As with any activity, organ transplants produce both costs and benefits. Unfortunately, while some of these costs and benefits are easily measured, others are much more speculative. As is usually the case in such circumstances, most of the available analyses tend to rely heavily on those financial magnitudes that are easily obtained. Yet, it seems quite probable that many relevant factors, especially on the benefits side, will be overlooked, and most cost-benefit calculations will be biased against transplantation. Fortunately, the financial case for the most common forms of transplantation, combined with a straightforward review of other relevant factors, is so strong that "perfect" calculation is unnecessary. This chapter outlines the (strong) case for public policies geared toward significant increases in transplant therapy. By necessity, our focus is on renal graphs, but we also examine literature on other organs.

Three Major Difficulties in Measuring the Costs and Benefits of Organ Transplants

In most countries, there are many more patients who could benefit from transplant therapy than there are organs available. This shortage has several implications for the analysis of the costs and benefits of transplantation. First, and most obviously, many thousands of people die each year while waiting for suitable organs. Such deaths are the primary and greatest cost of the current organ procurement system. Yet, those patients who do not die require very expensive and ongoing medical treatment. While most wealthy societies pay for most or all of this care through social insurance programs, both the patients and their families undergo various sorts of trauma. Kidney transplant candidates, for example, are often unable to work due to the time constraints imposed by dialysis or due to serious disability due to organ failure. The candidates' families often must schedule their daily routines around the unending demands of therapy. When living donation is possible, family members may voluntarily undergo costly and invasive surgery in order to provide a loved one with a transplant. Tests, hospitalization, lost income, discomfort, and the risk surgery imposes on the healthy donor are all potential costs of the current system.

Transplants, however, are not inexpensive, and it is difficult to quantify exactly how expensive they are for several reasons. First, the transplant operation itself is but a modest component of the costs of most transplantation therapies: pretesting and evaluation, organ procurement, organ allocation, physicians' services, hospitalization and skilled nursing costs, follow-up care, and immunosuppressant drugs are all expensive components of typical transplant treatments. Costs vary enormously, depending on the country where the graft is performed, the extent of any complications, donor organ quality, medical center experience, and so on. Although these so-called "direct costs" are the most easily measured, it is far too optimistic to claim that even these costs can be accurately calculated. Katz and colleagues (1999) provided an extended description and analysis of some of the issues arising in any attempt to measure direct medical costs from hospital billing records. In particular, a surprisingly weak correlation exists between billing records and medical records in many hospitals.[1] One hopes, however, that such errors are sufficiently unsystematic to allow valid generalizations to be made.

Second, in most countries, the majority of transplant costs and related treatments are paid for by third parties, typically government insurance programs such as Medicare in the United States, the National Health Service in Britain, and public and private insurers in Germany. Thus, the transactions being evaluated occur primarily in "nonmarket" settings, and the prices observed may not be equal to the true social costs of the services provided. For example, in the United States, the charges billed and paid by the publicly funded Medicare system for renal dialysis treatment (currently about $150 per session) are lower than the charges billed to private, third-party payers, such as insurance companies, for the same service. (Some informal evidence, in fact, suggests that private payments can be many times the public rate.) Yet, these latter charges are not generally made available as public record, and they are regarded as confidential by the parties involved. Complicating matters further, the service providers (in these cases dialysis clinics) are primarily for-profit businesses, although about one-third are nonprofit, and some are affiliated with transplant centers or major trauma center hospitals.[2]

Thus, when one analyzes the costs of various medical procedures, it is important to know that the cost figures used are primarily some form of administered, nonmarket prices arising either completely outside of markets or occurring in markets that are heavily regulated and subsidized. Public funds used in the provision of medical services are themselves raised via distortionary tax systems. This is not to say, of course, that the amounts actually paid for transplants by public authorities cannot be observed: such payments are generally public records, and private payments can also occasionally be observed. Yet, these figures should not be taken as equal to the social costs in general, since government payments for services often differ quite a bit from the prices that would prevail in private, competitive transactions. Clearly, some large degree of humility should attend any conclusions reached under these circumstances.

A third problem, which is severe in all economic analyses in medicine, arises because of the primary importance of inherently untradeable goods in the health area. Medical treatments that prolong or shorten life and cause or reduce pain create costs and benefits for which no market valuation is really available. As a consequence, health economists, physicians, and policy analysts have created a variety of methods to evaluate "cost" in such cases. This analytic richness often makes it nearly impossible to compare the findings of different studies even when they seek to address nearly identical questions.

Practical Approaches to Measurement

Most detailed economic analyses relevant to the issue of the social value of transplantation utilize one of several common methodologies. One (and the simplest) way is by counting the observable, direct accounting costs of various alternative treatments or policies and then selecting the lowest-cost alternative. This approach requires that one assume (generally appropriately) that one of a few acceptable options will contain the optimal choice. For example, one could compare in this way hemodialysis with kidney transplantation as a treatment for renal failure. Many studies have done exactly this, using public health spending records. It is also possible to include additional items to represent indirect costs or benefits, such as lost wages and so on.

Second, other studies have sought to incorporate the values of patients' health status more directly by utilizing so-called cost-utility analyses. This approach underlies the widely used Quality Adjusted Life Years (QALY) metric. In these studies, one focuses on the costs per QALY for different therapies, where utility factors, obtained from other sources, are used to standardize outcomes that are qualitatively different. For example, one might wish to compare an expected life span of ten years on dialysis treatment with an expected life span of eight years living with a functioning graft (these numbers are purely hypothetical). It may well be the case that, for the typical patient, eight years of relatively good health and freedom are more valuable than ten years of the demanding dialysis regimen and relatively bad health. Studies in this category look at the cost per QALY in selecting the optimal therapy. Closely related to this are studies that look at the cost effectiveness of different treatment modalities.

Economists, however, generally rely on cost-benefit analysis in which all outcomes are reduced to the common metric of money. This approach is presumptively the most general of all, since anything can be compared with anything else. The shortcoming, of course, is the necessity of valuing everything in monetary terms. The practical consequences of this requirement may be less than it would first appear, at least when one can construct a sufficiency condition that can be verified for a particular case. For example, it may be that option A dominates option B if one has the condition $x + y > z$. However, suppose that y is known to be nonnegative. Then, it is sufficient to argue that $x > z$ is true in order to show that option A is better. We will take this approach often, if only implicitly, in what follows.

Money Costs of Transplant Therapy

In the United States, the costs of renal transplantation and its main competitor, kidney dialysis, are primarily (but not exclusively) borne by the federal government through the Medicare and Medicaid programs, which fund the End Stage Renal Disease (ESRD) program. However, these public payers deal primarily with private service providers. Thus, careful studies of the costs to the government programs of various therapies for renal failure have been conducted. The total costs of these ESRD programs were around U.S.$26.8 billion in 2008. (With private spending included, it appears total U.S. costs for hemodialysis in

2008 were about U.S.$39.5 billion, so public participation accounts for about 70 percent.) It is useful to examine some of the recent findings.[3]

We begin with a brief review of the "costs of transplantation," which usually refer to costs attributable to performing the transplant, including preoperative and postoperative evaluation and drug therapy, ordinarily for a period of one year. A wealth of data that shed light on this issue are available, but often the data are restricted to payments made by social insurance funds, such as Medicare in the United States. These payments are generally *not* equal to the billings from providers, and the complexity of health care finance suggests caution is the appropriate attitude in analysis.

Although social insurance pays most costs for transplants in most countries, private payers also participate, and often under different terms. Medicare in the United States uses a "cost-based" methodology to reimburse transplant centers, and this differs from Medicaid, the U.S. insurance fund for those with low incomes or who have disabilities. In some states, Medicaid does not reimburse for kidney acquisition costs. Further, private payers do not ordinarily disclose their contractual terms and also tend to bundle the various components of transplant therapy—the graft procedure, drug treatments, and physician fees—into a single payment, unlike Medicare. As Abecassis (2006) stated, "Revenue depends greatly on contractual allowances that govern reimbursement rates. These, in turn, vary greatly, not only between payers but also depending on the specific cost center" (p. 1260).

For the U.S. Medicare program, which funds the majority of kidney transplants in the United States, the most recent evidence suggests the direct money costs of a transplant, given the extant patient population, is approximately $106,000 for the first year. This cost is composed of the costs of prescreening, the transplant event, kidney acquisition, follow-up, and physicians' fees. This figure has risen relatively less than one might expect in the last ten years: Yen and colleagues (2004) give a largely comparable figure of $87,400 for the year 2001. A variety of alternative estimates, which often differ somewhat in the patient populations being studied and the categories of costs included, are available in the review by Huang, Thakur, and Meltzer (2008). It is probably fair to say that $100,000 is a reasonable guess for the direct cost to Medicare for a renal graft and its immediate attendant treatment.

The Medicare figures do not reflect any private payments, nor is it certain that the levels of reimbursement equal the social costs of transplantation. Further, the cases of organ transplants other than kidneys are far more difficult to analyze, since fewer are performed and funding is far more chaotic. At the other

end of the spectrum, one may look at the charges for transplantation procedures, recognizing that these values will tend to exceed the amounts received
by providers.

The Milliman Research Report *2005 U.S. Organ and Tissue Transplant Cost
Estimates and Discussion* (Ortner, 2005) provides highly detailed billing figures
for transplants performed at a large, audited group of U.S. hospitals. These figures are derived from hospital-billed charges multiplied by usage levels obtained
from large public sources, such as OPTN. Table 4.1 gives a partial list of the
findings, calculated for the first year of the transplant (i.e., the figures include
only those preoperative costs occasioned by the transplant, such as evaluation
for surgery, the transplant operations, and subsequent treatment for one year).

Table 4.1 highlights several facts. First, hospitals in the United States bill
at rates greatly exceeding what Medicare actually pays them, something that
is well known to those in this industry. We see charges for a kidney graft that
are around twice the average reimbursement given by Medicare. The Milliman
figures have the advantage of reflecting both public and private pay patient
accounts, but perhaps they should be primarily regarded as providing useful
information on the *relative* costs of different types of transplants, rather than
absolute costs. In any event, transplantation is extremely expensive in absolute
terms. Further, costs rise dramatically for liver transplants ($392,800) and mul-
tiorgan transplants such as heart–lung ($640,800). Transplant therapy is among
the most expensive of all medical procedures. All of these operations are extremely expensive compared to corneal transplants, which are typically performed at total costs substantially less than $20,000.

Second, the large variations exhibited by these procedures are roughly inversely related to their frequency (in the United States). For example, kidney

Table 4.1 Estimated U.S. average first-year
transplant costs

Organ	First-year costs
Kidney	$210,000
Pancreas	$270,800
Liver	$392,800
Heart	$478,900
Lung	$299,900
Heart-lung	$640,800
Kidney-pancreas	$293,100
Intestine	$813,600

SOURCE OF DATA: Milliman Research Report (Ortner,
2005).
NOTE: All costs are in 2005 U.S. dollars.

transplants are by far the most common solid-organ transplant (over 16,500 were performed in the United States in 2008), and they are also the cheapest. At the other extreme, only 85 intestine transplants were done in the United States in 2008, at an average one-year billed cost of $813,600 (in 2005).

Finally, the large differences in procedure costs mask far less variation in the relative shares of costs attributable to the different areas of transplant treatment spending. For example, hospital charges, which include skilled nursing, in-hospital tests, operating room costs, supplies, and so on (but not physicians' fees), vary from a low of about 30 percent of costs (for kidneys) to a high of about 67 percent of costs (for intestine transplants, which require very long hospital stays). Immunosuppressive therapy typically ran $20,000 to $30,000 for the first year, regardless of the organ transplanted. Surgeons' and physicians' fees varied from less than $20,000 (again, for kidneys) to over $70,000 (for intestines).

Costs of Alternatives to Transplantation Therapy

The degree to which modern medicine provides therapeutic alternatives to transplantation varies widely by organ and patient health status. For many disorders, such as certain forms of liver disease and intestinal failure, the patient's prospects are very grim in the absence of a transplant. At the other extreme, ESRD patients can often (but not always) utilize dialysis therapy, and some are able to survive for decades (although not without some serious health consequences). These variations can be roughly summarized by looking at the death rates and illness removals on transplant waiting lists for various organs. (Such a calculation is indeed "rough," since the states of health the patients are required to have for various sorts of transplants are themselves variable. Thus, some waiting lists admit sicker people than others. Further, the rates of transplantation vary among organs.)

Table 4.2 provides indirect evidence on alternative therapies by showing the extent of waiting list removals for causes of death or sickness for several U.S. waiting lists in 2007, in addition to the ratio of transplants to waiting list size. As is clear, only about 7.7 percent of renal graft wait-listed patients died or became "too sick" to transplant during the year, while a quarter of those awaiting an intestine did so. The rates for livers (14 percent), lungs (16.6 percent), hearts (17.7 percent), and the other solid organs lie between these. Thus, one may conclude that therapies available in lieu of transplantation vary in their efficacies, with renal patients faring the best.

Table 4.2 Patients removed from waiting list in 2007, United States (in percent)

Organ	Removed due to illness and death	Removed due to transplant
Kidney	7.7	19.9
Liver	14.0	36.9
Kidney-pancreas	11.9	38.2
Heart	17.4	82.1
Lung	16.6	65.1
Heart-lung	22.0	28.6
Intestine	25.4	84.8

SOURCE OF DATA: OPTN.
NOTE: The percentages may add up to more or less than 100 percent due to other categories for removal (such as patient improvement) and the inflow of new patients over the year.

Renal dialysis, the mechanical imitation of a kidney's function using external filters, is the most important, and medically most successful, of all the alternatives to various organ transplants. In the United States, almost 500,000 patients were diagnosed with end-stage renal disease (ESRD) by 2006, and this figure rose to 547,982 by 2008, with total associated costs to the Medicare insurance funds of $26.8 billion (USRDS, 2010). For the majority (though not all) of these patients, dialysis provides the best available treatment short of transplantation. Not all ESRD patients receive dialysis, and not all dialysis patients are viable candidates for transplantation. Still, virtually all patients receiving kidney transplants were previously receiving dialysis therapy. (An exception is the small numbers of "preemptive" transplants.)

The growing prevalence of ESRD is attributable to several secular trends that show little sign of abating, either in the United States or elsewhere. As described in Chapter 2, kidney failure is often the result of poorly managed diabetes, and adult onset diabetes is often associated with obesity. Rising rates of obesity in most countries, even in developing areas, imply that the rates of diabetes and, consequently, ESRD can be expected to rise in tandem. As many public health analysts have pointed out, this problem may eventually become a sort of "perfect storm" for the health systems of many countries, presenting an almost unprecedented challenge in the areas of funding and the rationing of care.

Dialysis, one of the greatest medical breakthroughs of modern times, is also very expensive, and kidney patients who are not able to receive transplants ordinarily require continuing dialysis therapy. In the United States, these treatments are paid for by the federal Medicare program (about 75 percent of dialysis costs), Medicaid (about 15 percent), and private insurance (about 10 percent). It is generally believed that private payers are charged more per treatment than the government-funded Medicare system, although data on the private payment system are not reliable. Medicare ESRD costs, however, are readily observable, and they have grown rapidly.

The direct costs of dialysis treatment per Medicare patient can be readily calculated. In the United States, Medicare costs were $68,808 per person per year in 2005, with diabetic patients being more costly at $74,399. Older patients (those above 75 years at the beginning of 2005) were among the most expensive of all age categories at $74,637 per patient for one year of treatment. (Very young children were the most costly.) Thus, older diabetic patients, whose numbers will increase, can place exceptional burdens on the dialysis funding system, a trend that is unfavorable in the extreme. By 2008, continuous increases in dialysis costs and shifting patient populations have driven per capita hemodialysis payments by Medicare to $77,506. In an especially ominous trend, Medicare payments for those with chronic kidney disease (CKD) who have not yet reached complete kidney failure are rising very rapidly (USRDS, 2010).

A Review of Cost-Benefit Analyses of Organ Transplantation

Numerous studies have sought to assess the impact of organ transplantation on public insurance funds. Most of these studies have examined kidney transplants and have used the costs of dialysis treatments saved as a measure of the benefits accruing from transplantation. Because dialysis expenses are relatively continuous over time, while transplant costs are primarily a total amount up front, it is useful from the policy perspective to ask the question "How much time must elapse, on average, after a kidney transplant until the treatment payer has saved money?" In other words, how long must the patient be free of dialysis until the transplant has "paid for itself"?

It is clear that this question is a very narrow one, since generally no accounting is made for the improved economic circumstances of the transplant recipient, nor for the implicit costs of pain and suffering associated with dialysis vis-à-vis a transplant. However, if this question can be answered in a way that supports transplants, the case is strong, since all of the other effects of the transplant must weigh in its favor in any social accounting. Patients and their families benefit enormously from kidney transplants, and often recipients are able to resume work, earn an income, care for family members, and enjoy life to a degree that was impossible when they were undergoing dialysis. More significantly, transplantation is often life saving, and these benefits are ordinarily ignored completely.

Thus, it is legitimate and important to consider first the narrow "break-even" point of view, as we believe that findings of a positive social return to kidney transplantation using this approach are strong evidence of the social value of greatly expanding the numbers of such transplants generally and, in passing, constitute a powerful argument for fundamental reforms in the world's current organ procurement system.

Since our interest is focused primarily on recent experience, we do not review in detail earlier studies. As a generality, the cost effectiveness of renal graft therapy has improved over time, a reflection of improvements in drug therapy and patient management. A review of many earlier papers is offered by Karlberg and Nyberg (1995). Although the studies available are not really comparable in most cases, it appears that the break-even times for renal grafts in the United States have been falling somewhat in the last ten or so years. Evans and Kitzmann (1998) and Douzdijian, Ferrara, and Silverstri (1998) both find that transplantation is the most cost-effective treatment for ESRD patients under a variety of scenarios and assumptions about transplant success, recipient health status, dialysis cost, and so on. The widely cited analysis by Schweitzer and colleagues (1989) produced the estimates of a 2.7-year break-even period for the transplant population taken as a whole and an even more favorable 1.7-year payout for transplants using standard criteria donor organs given to relatively healthy patients.

Looking at the less desirable expanded criteria donors (ECDs), Whiting and colleagues (2000) find a break-even period of about 4.4 years, the longer time reflecting the elevated levels of complications in such cases. However, the authors do conclude that in the long-run, transplantation is virtually always less expensive than hemodialysis. Kasiske and colleagues (2000) found a Medicare break-even point of about 3.1 years overall using a patient cohort from the mid-1990s. Mullins and colleagues (2003) found very short break-even points of as little as 10 to 14 months for living-donor kidney transplants, although such analyses do not account for implicit costs borne by donors, whereas organ acquisition costs (i.e., payments to organ procurement organizations for transport, preparation, removal, and so on) are paid by Medicare and, for kidneys, run around $50,000 to $60,000 per organ. These costs do not apply in the case of living donations.

Nonstandard medical circumstances need not drastically alter conclusions on break-even periods for U.S. renal transplants. For example, Jassal and colleagues (2003) used a somewhat more sophisticated decision analytic simulation, combined with accounting cost data, to determine that transplants are economically beneficial even in somewhat older patients as long as the patients did not have to wait a long time for transplantation (and suffer dialysis while waiting).[4] This finding also illustrates an important point for all analyses that use current system statistics as inputs for cost-benefit calculation: the current situation of shortage has a variety of medical consequences that may elevate the costs of transplantation, producing a bias in the findings. For example, transplants using older patients and patients who have dialyzed for a long time are generally more costly because of additional complications and slower recovery. Yet, the current regime virtually ensures that a high proportion of recipients will be long-time dialyzers.

As described in Chapter 2, all transplants fail eventually, although modern treatment can often result in very long renal graft functioning. Patients who have had a graft that failed are therefore an important clinical population who present the physician with special challenges. Despite this, the results of Hornberger, Best, and Garrison (1997) suggest that the cost advantages of transplantation persist even for these patients. The authors offer a somewhat dated analysis, but, even given the technological capabilities of the mid-1990s, second transplants were economically attractive for many patients.

A useful and influential meta-analysis (synthesis of numerous published results) is offered by Winkelmayer and colleagues (2002) that evaluates dialysis in both centers and home settings versus transplantation. Their findings are important: transplantation offers costs per quality adjusted year of life gained that are well below any form of dialysis for many patient populations. Cost savings are substantial, and transplantation is the best treatment for ESRD for a majority of patients. Further, they argue that the costs of dialysis, which in real terms have been in the range of $50,000 to $70,000 per year for many years, may be validly used as a lower bound for society's willingness to pay for transplantation.

The study by Matas and Schnitzler (2003) addresses the hypothetical question "How much could society afford to pay for a living-donor vendor kidney?" The authors analyze the expenditure consequences of a living unrelated donor kidney transplant using a relatively detailed simulation on costs and medical outcomes. They maintain fairly conservative assumptions as to kidney distribution, treatment costs, and so on. Their analysis, however, does not include behavioral adjustment by most donors under a compensation regime.

Nevertheless, they find strong evidence for a substantial and immediate social return to fostering kidney transplants using living, unrelated donors. They note, "We have shown that if a vendor system were established for kidney donors, a significant payment could be made to the vendors without increasing the overall costs to the health care system. Further, cost-effective vendor payments of approximately \$250,000 are possible" (p. 220).

The value of a donor to society is also examined by Schnitzler and colleagues (2003) and Mendeloff and colleagues (2004). Schnitzler and his colleagues focused on life-years saved by deceased-donor organs and found that on average such a donor provides almost 31 life-years of benefit, shared among several recipients. Mendeloff and his partners looked at kidney, heart, and liver transplants arising from cadaveric donation and found a highly favorable return: 13 QALYs are produced per donor at an average medical cost of around \$16,000 per QALY. If, as some authors have suggested, we should value a QALY at around \$100,000, then society's willingness to pay for another deceased donor is presumably over U.S.\$1 million each.

Huang, Thakur, and Meltzer (2008) offered an extensive review of several studies. Their findings provide a fitting summary of the overwhelming medical and public health opinion regarding transplantation and ESRD:

> Renal transplantation, especially living-donor renal transplantation, is the most beneficial treatment option for patients with end-stage renal disease, and is highly cost-effective compared to no therapy. In comparison to dialysis, renal transplantation has been found to reduce costs by nontrivial amounts while improving health both in terms of the number of years of life and the quality of those years of life. These findings have been consistent over three decades and across nations. (p. 31)

The situation with solid organ transplants other than the kidney, however, is more difficult. In these cases, simple cost comparisons appear unlikely to be as informative, for several reasons. First, the costs of other organ transplants are generally much higher than for kidneys. Second, because the failures of organs other than the kidney often lead to a more rapid and painful death, the social benefits of such transplants are going to involve intangible or untraded components in greater proportions. (An exception is the pancreas, which makes insulin. Synthetic insulin is a medically strong substitute for a functioning pancreas.) Finally, and perversely, the relative shortages of these "other" organs are far smaller than for kidneys, reflecting a host of medical factors including, but not limited to, the lack of alternative therapies to prolong life. Thus, one must approach social insurance spending analyses of other organ transplants with even greater caution.

Most studies to date on organs other than the kidney have focused primarily on the accurate measurement of the costs of transplantation, since no obvious therapy, such as dialysis, exists whose costs can serve as a reasonable measure for the benefits obtained with the graft. However, some truly "economic" analyses are available. Sagmeister and colleagues (2002) evaluated both deceased-donor and living-donor liver transplantation and found that an average of six quality-adjusted years of life were obtained at a cost of about 23,000 euros per year. Both cadaveric and living-donor transplantation were deemed cost effective, with living-donor grafts having a marginally higher cost. Longworth and colleagues (2003) provided a detailed analysis of the cost-effectiveness of various treatments for liver failure arising from alcohol liver disease, primary biliary cirrhosis, and primary sclerosing cholangitis in England and Wales. They found that liver transplantation was effective in prolonging life and improving its quality in all three cases, although the cost per quality adjusted year gained was extremely high for alcohol liver disease patients, with an upper confidence limit on cost per year of life gained of £83,000 (about U.S.$125,000). They conclude that liver transplantation may not be cost effective for these latter patients.

Analyses of lung, heart, pancreas, and multiorgan transplantation therapies are relatively sketchy, and many published findings seek to answer the most basic questions, such as the financial effects of such procedures on the transplant centers and the approximate costs of such transplants. Evans, Manninen, and Dong (1993) offer a somewhat dated study of pancreas transplants, focusing on their costs. Lung transplantation was addressed by Anyanwu, Rogers, and Murday (2002), who tried to determine the relative cost effectiveness of transplantation compared to conventional medical care for end-stage lung disease in the United Kingdom. They found average benefits of around two to three quality-adjusted life-years for lung or heart-lung transplantation, producing net costs per year gained of between about $30,000 and $48,000. Later work by Enckevort and colleagues (1998) found additional life years costing the Dutch social insurance fund almost $90,000. Very high levels of recipient mortality and morbidity, combined with high transplant costs, suggest that this therapy may not be cost effective (given the nature of costs included in the analysis.) In a related study, Anyanwu and colleagues (2002) found three-year graft survival rates in the United Kingdom for transplants performed between 1995 and 1999 to be 74.2 percent (hearts), 53.8 percent (lungs), and 57.2 percent (heart-lungs). Egan (2002) provides some cautionary notes regarding Anyanwu and his colleagues' findings, again illustrating the extreme difficulty in performing such studies when patient selection into the transplant pool, and the severe shortage of suitable organs, materially affects the statistics of the existing system.

The primary problem with transplants other than kidney, pancreas, and liver arises from the extreme hardship surgery imposes on patients and organs. This effect is made relatively obvious by an examination of the graft survival rates such transplants offer. Five- and ten-year unadjusted graft survival rates for the intestine, for example, are only 36 percent and 25 percent, respectively. As of May 2008, heart transplant graft survival rates in the United States were at 72 percent and 53 percent, respectively. For a lung transplant, only about one-half of grafts survive even five years. In contrast, kidneys from living donors are still functioning for almost 60 percent of patients after ten years (OPTN/ SRTR, 2010). Only 584 patients are reported to be living with functioning intestine transplants in the United States as of 2006, and current figures are almost surely very close to this. These facts, combined with the extremely high direct costs of many of the more "exotic" transplants, suggest that such procedures will be far more difficult to justify on purely financial grounds.

It is therefore unlikely that strong consensus over the social benefits of solid organ transplants other than kidneys, livers, and pancreas will emerge in the near future. Such calculations are extremely difficult for many reasons. Some operations, such as multiorgan transplants, are rare. The quality of immunosuppressive drugs and available organs is critical. Further, patient condition will often determine whether a given procedure is socially beneficial, so it is impossible to generalize and state unambiguously that "such and such a transplant is (or is not) socially worthwhile." Rather, some operations will be socially beneficial for some patients under some, possibly limited, set of circumstances. In contrast, it is safe to say, as many authorities have done, that kidney transplantation is in very many cases a social good. The surgery is so often successful, the quality and quantity of life improvements are so great, and dialysis is so expensive that virtually any sensible expansion in renal graft numbers is desirable. By implication, then, current policies that limit organs available for transplantation impose large social costs.

Stabilizing the Waiting List through Compensation: A Simulation

While kidney (and some other forms of) transplantation creates net social benefits by almost all reckonings, actual organ procurement policies are complex, and changes in policies are likely to involve costs and benefits beyond those ordinarily considered in the microlevel cost-benefit analyses reviewed in the previous section. For example, one may sensibly ask if performing an additional kidney transplant would produce net savings for some national insurance fund. The answer, which is presumptively in the affirmative, does not by itself establish that some particular proposal, such as paying compensation for cadaveric donations, is socially beneficial. The change to a compensation mechanism will generally introduce a number of factors, including the probable price paid to cadaveric donors' families and the possible effect of increased deceased-donor organ supply on uncompensated living donation, which must be evaluated if a valid recommendation is to be made. Such "economic" responses to changes in regulation require the introduction of behavioral modeling components unneeded in the simpler cost analyses. It would not be in society's interest to introduce compensation into organ procurement if such a policy actually reduced the numbers and average quality of organs obtained.

Thus, it is sensible to restrict the analysis to a very focused question. Suppose that one introduced a procurement policy reform that had the (modest) effect of stabilizing the waiting list for kidneys by compensating cadaveric donors. Even this "simple" plan would have multiple effects, including (for example) an impact on live (uncompensated) donation. In order to provide some insight into the magnitudes of the costs and benefits involved, we utilize a very simple model by Beard and Kaserman (2006), which allows for some dynamic effects and feedbacks, but ignores more difficult supply-side questions. This model is calibrated to U.S. experience and inputs, but the basic approach is not parochial in that sense. Our goal is merely to suggest what sorts of cost savings a modest reform might produce.

The Beard-Kaserman model considers only kidneys and is explicitly designed to understate the benefits of a change in procurement policy. The model is based on a simple difference equation describing the evolution of the U.S. renal transplant active waiting list. First, the change in the waiting list from period $t - 1$ to period t, $(WL(t) - WL(t - 1)) = \Delta WL(t)$, is given by the equation:

$$\Delta WL(t) = A(t) - D(t) - L(t) - \mu C(t) + E(t) \qquad (4.1)$$

where, conventionally, we take $WL(t)$ to refer to the waiting list size at the end of period t. Thus, the waiting list at t equals the waiting list at $t - 1$, with a number of adjustments. Define $A(t)$ as an "exogenous" component representing, among other things, the arrival of new ESRD patients suitable for transplantation. $D(t)$ represents waiting list deaths and delistings for illness during period t, $L(t)$ represents living-donor transplants, $C(t)$ represents donor cadavers made available in period t, μ is a given value (less than 2) that represents the number of kidney transplants made possible per cadaver, and $E(t)$ represents other factors, such as random variation.

The model is made operational by specifying the functions A, D, L, and E, and selecting a value (or values) for μ. The structure can be readily generalized by allowing functions such as C to be vector-valued, where the different components refer to cadavers of differing medical usefulness, such as ECD and so on. In fact, the model can be made multivariate by defining all state and exogenous variables as vectors, which allows modeling the joint supply of cadaveric organs.

The framework given in (4.1) is essentially uninformative by itself: useful conclusions are obtained by a careful analysis of the underlying series. To illustrate an especially simple application, consider the Beard-Kaserman parameterization. First, the exogenous process is taken to be given by the linear trend $A(t) = a + At$, for unknown constants a and A. The value of μ is taken to be 1.47, which is the final year's average for the U.S. kidney waiting list data for the years 1995 to 2002 used in the simulation. $E(t)$ is taken to be a normally distributed, possibly autocorrelated error process. Next, living-donor transplants were observed to be roughly proportional to the size of the contemporaneous waiting list, so $L(t) = (0.12)WL(t)$ is used as a simple representation. This approach has the advantage also of implying that policies that actually reduce waiting lists will also decrease living-donor grafts. Deaths on the waiting list are nearly proportional to the size of the list over short intervals, and Beard and Kaserman take the value $D(t) = (0.067)WL(t)$, which is adequate for very short (i.e., one year ahead) forecasts.[5]

Cadaveric donations $C(t)$ are assumed to be exogenous of the waiting list (but see Osterkamp, 2005), with the process given by $C(t) = b + B * t + e(t)$, where b and B are parameters to estimate, and $e(t)$ is a normally distributed, possibly autocorrelated disturbance. Estimation of the relevant parameters and application of the observed empirical proportions for deaths, living donations, and kidney yield per cadaveric donor produces the simple difference equation:

$$\Delta WL(t) + (0.067)WL(t) + (1.47)C(t) + (0.12)WL(t)$$
$$= 15{,}646 + (772)t \tag{4.2}$$

where the number of cadaveric donors in each period is $C(t) = 4,974 + (97)t$ if there is no change in U.S. organ procurement policy. Changes in proposed procurement policy, then, are represented by changes in the specifications for the processes for $C(t)$ and/or $L(t)$.

Although this parameterization of the model is so simple as to offer little more than an example, it is fairly accurate in its short-term predictions of U.S. kidney procurement and transplantation. Data used to calibrate the model came from the 1995–2002 period. Using observed values and forecasting grafts one year ahead (i.e., to 2003) yields a prediction of 14,944 U.S. kidney grafts and 3,625 deaths on the waiting list. In fact, 2003 saw 14,857 grafts performed and 3,874 deaths, so the simulation is somewhat more optimistic than the reality. (More accurate predictions are obtained by introducing more realistic representations for the underlying processes.)

The primary goal of the Beard-Kaserman simulations was to place a lower bound on the net social costs of maintaining the current policy of organ procurement, as opposed to introducing some mechanism for increasing organ supply through compensation for cadaveric donations. The direct medical cost savings are not controversial; even the harshest critics of compensation proposals agree that more transplants would be beneficial, all other things being equal. More controversial, however, are the issues of (1) the numbers of organs obtainable under a compensation capable procurement system; (2) the effect of compensation for donation on altruistic donation, especially (though not exclusively) among living related donors; and (3) the prices that will be paid for donor organs.

Suppose, then, that a compensation system is implemented for deceased organ donors and no compensation is offered to living donors who are, in most cases, close relatives of the recipients. The supply target for the hypothetical program is relatively modest: enough compensation will be offered to produce sufficient organs to stabilize the waiting list.[6] Further, the analysis includes a negative feedback effect from cadaver organ supplies to living-donor supply through the waiting list itself.

Given this scenario, Beard and Kaserman calculated that such a policy would result in the following outcomes. First, kidney grafts would rise to 18,413 per year, an increase of 3,469 transplants compared to the case of no change in procurement policy. Further, living-donor grafts are projected to be lower under the reform: only 6,102 persons would donate a kidney under the compensation system, compared to an estimated 6,492 under the baseline case. Total cadavers obtained are larger under the reform by 2,625, although this increase would, of course, have to be paid for. Finally, waiting list deaths are lower under the reform scenario: 3,407 versus 3,624.

Given these modest results, what value might one then assign to a compensation mechanism that could produce them? The four critical magnitudes are the value assigned to 3,469 additional grafts; the value assigned to 390 fewer living-donor transplants; the value assigned to 218 fewer waiting list deaths; and the net cost anticipated, if any, in moving from the current procurement system to the one described, including payments to donor families.

Beard and Kaserman borrow illustrative values for the first and the third values listed above and ignore the second and the fourth ones. Using U.K. NHS figures, they calculated an average net savings over a mean graft survival horizon of nine years to be about $343,800 per patient. Similarly, they used a value of $686,430 per life saved, this value reflecting a life-expectancy-adjusted, organ-specific statistical life calculation provided by the health economist Phillip Held.[7] Using these figures, one concludes that a social valuation of the first and third items is about $1,342,000,000 for one year.

To this figure, one may add whatever value seems appropriate for the implied reduction in living-donor transplants. Although living donation of a kidney is not particularly high risk, this operation does impose some costs. Becker and Elias (2007) suggest that an equilibrium price for a living-donor kidney would be perhaps $15,000, although using that figure would surely understate the benefits, since those who donate under the current system are relatives of patients, not the lowest-cost, most willing donors one would obtain under their market proposal. Yet, it seems unlikely the social value of reducing living donations will be determinative, since even at 100 times Becker and Elias's value, the resulting figure is far less than the benefits of discontinuing dialysis for thousands of patients. Thus, we ignore this benefit in what follows.

Finally, the issue of the cost of implementing a compensation system must be considered. It is very likely, however, that the costs of obtaining kidneys, including the compensation, will actually be far lower than they are under the current regime. First, although the current U.S. system is based on donations, it is in no sense low cost. According to the Milliman (Ortner, 2005) audit discussed earlier, first-year costs for kidney procurement in the United States in 2005 were $50,800 per organ. These costs represent payments to U.S. OPOs for obtaining, removing, testing, transporting, and delivering the organ. Many of these costs, of course, are unavoidable, but these fees are used to fund the organ procurement system and thus include costs attributable to recruitment of donors and other costs. In a sense, the question is, is it cheaper to beg for something one will not pay for or to pay for it in the normal way? If one successfully begs for something, one need not, by definition, pay the donor. This does not imply, however, that begging is a low-cost way of obtaining goods. The proof of this is that for-profit businesses virtually always find it cheaper to pay for their inputs rather than beg for them. Thus, it is an open question whether a reformed system that could offer compensation would on net impose any additional costs; it may very well be much cheaper.

The price to be paid for the deceased-donor organ also must be considered. Many studies suggest that such prices are likely to be fairly or very low, although Wellington and Whitmire (2007) is an extreme exception. The important study by Harrington and Sayre (2006) provides insight into this problem. In the United States, payment for organs is prohibited by federal law. However, it is legal to compensate families for whole body donations. Often, this compensation takes the form of a "funeral expense "or "cremation allowance" of several thousand dollars or less. This program has resulted in a debilitating glut of donated cadavers at medical schools, which are often forced to dispose of them when medical training has no use for them. Empirical evidence provided by Harrington and Sayre suggests that relatively small payments are sufficient to induce entire bodies to be donated, and the supply curve of these cadavers has a conventional, upward-sloping appearance. They state, "We present evidence that families respond to financial incentives in making whole body donation decisions. Surely if modest payments can coax families to donate whole bodies, similar payments would also coax families to donate organs . . ." (p. 19).

The basic template used in the Beard-Kaserman simulation approach is tautological, and so it is not objectionable per se. However, one may certainly dispute the specifications of the underlying processes generating the series C, L, D, and so on. In particular, critics of compensation schemes, such as the influential Institute of Medicine in the United States, often claim that the introduction of compensation will fail to materially increase, and might even decrease, the supply of organs for transplantation. We discuss these issues in Chapter 8, but clearly such feedback, if true, can be incorporated into the approach outlined here.

It is also important to note that the illustrative calculations performed above will probably drastically understate the social value of a policy allowing compensation for cadaveric donation. For example, it is quite possible that a compensation system could do far better than the mere stabilization of the waiting lists. After all, the number of additional cadaveric donors needed to stabilize the U.S. kidney active transplant list may be below the estimated number of potential viable cadavers for some years, although not forever. If better results are feasible, then the social benefits will grow apace. Second, we have completely ignored the potentially large effects of the joint supply of organs. Any increase in cadavers providing kidneys will also increase the availability of livers, hearts, and so on. Although it may prove difficult on purely financial grounds to show that increases in some types of transplants are beneficial, that is probably not the case with livers. Liver transplants also have a greater impact in reducing mortality, since there is no therapy as effective as dialysis for end-stage liver disease. Third, we have largely ignored the potential benefits of better antigen matching and shorter waiting times, which a larger supply of organs for transplant will provide. These qualitative improvements could be very valuable. Finally, increases in legal transplant activities will reduce black market and gray market transplantation and its attendant social and political consequences.

Conclusion

In the case of kidney transplantation, there is overwhelming evidence that transplants more than pay for themselves from the standpoint of public insurance funds. This, in turn, suggests that, when all the costs and benefits are properly accounted for, reforms that increase transplants, including those that permit compensation, will be highly desirable. Even when one restricts attention to the case of cadaveric donor compensation, it appears extremely probable that fundamental reforms would save billions of dollars/euros annually. More ambitious proposals, such as compensating the supply of kidneys and/ or livers from living donors, are not evaluated here, but they surely hold the promise of further benefits.

5

Economic and Political Causes
of the Shortage of Organs

Introduction

When the current organ procurement policies of most of the world's countries were being set in place, it is unlikely that the decision makers involved correctly foresaw the extent of today's shortages and their dire consequences. Although a number of economists and legal scholars did warn of the likelihood of inadequate organ supply, organ transplantation was, in many ways, still unusual, somewhat experimental, and relatively rare.[1] Until solid organ transplantation became heavily subsidized under various national social insurance funds, the great majority of ESRD patients, for example, lacked the financial resources to pay for transplants and the related drug therapy. In the cases of organs other than kidneys, such as hearts or lungs, the very high costs of transplantation put such treatment well beyond the reach of any but the wealthy.

Public funding of transplant therapy, demographic changes, improvements in anti rejection drugs, and rapidly rising income levels in many countries have led to very large rises in the demand for transplantation. This secular increase in demand is so striking that a number of critics of modern transplantation medicine, following in the intellectual tradition of Ivan Illich and others, describe the resulting organ shortages as contrived. Nancy Scheper-Hughes (2000), for example, remarks, "This scarcity, created by the technicians of transplant surgery, represents artificial need, one that can never be satisfied." While we strongly disagree with this sentiment, it is certainly true that the shortages we observe exist precisely because it is possible to save thousands of lives through organ transplants. How, though, have we come to this point? The simplest answer, of course, is that the quantities of organs available for transplants have consistently failed to keep pace with demand for them. One can credibly argue that this would not be the case had we not made the collective decisions to fund transplant medicine and renal dialysis. Very low-income countries have no shortages and no waiting lists; the bottom line is, patients with ESRD die.

It is not the purpose of this book to evaluate the wisdom of the public funding of transplant medicine. Rather, we accept the conclusion of physicians that transplants are very often the best, and in some cases, the sole, means of treatment for a variety of serious, often fatal diseases. We also accept at face value the evident intent of many societies that this form of treatment should be made available to all those who can benefit most from it, independent of their income or wealth. Given these premises, however, one is immediately impelled to ask: Why must those awaiting organ grafts often wait so long, and, in many thousands of cases each year, "too long"? If societies are intent on using these life-saving treatments, why does the current shortage persist?

This chapter examines several primary causes of the shortages of organs, especially kidneys, beginning with the most basic economic explanation: the prohibition on compensating organ donors. Although economists are unlikely to quibble with this point, human organs are, for very many people, not appropriate articles for "commerce," and this fact has led many critics to suggest that, should compensation be introduced, the results will not be satisfactory. Whether due to a loss of donations, public revulsion, or expansions in the waiting lists, human organs are viewed by some as very poor candidates for economic transactions.

Additionally, though, there are several other contributing forces that appear to exacerbate the organ shortages in most countries. These factors, which include the institutional structures of organ procurement organizations, weak incentives at some intermediate stages in the transplant process, and substitution behavior among donors under uncompensated systems, are, in our opinion, of second-order importance, but they still deserve evaluation. We consider them as well in what follows.

A Zero-Price Market for Organs

Because all early transplants occurred between closely related, living donors, the problems of donor incentives were "solved" within the family unit. As it became technically feasible to use organs from strangers and cadavers, many governments, fearing the specter of an "organ bazaar," instituted laws that prohibited payments for organs, even those obtained from deceased donors. These policies established what economists term a "price ceiling" on organs, with the legal price mandated to be zero. As all principles of economics textbooks explain, shortages of any product or service arise when the price is effectively held to a level below its equilibrium, or market-clearing level. In other words, by prohibiting donor compensation, the current policies cause the quantity of organs offered for transplantation to be below the numbers that willing and able "buyers" wish to obtain.

This simple description, however, is not acceptable, even as a metaphor, by many intelligent people. This widespread resistance to the market interpretation of the shortage of organs arises from several independent sources. First, some critics suggest that human organs are, for various reasons, totally unlike goods one could successfully trade in a market setting. Possible reasons for this stifling heterogeneity could include the role of third parties in the financing of transplantation, the short "shelf life" and idiosyncratic character of organs, and the revulsion some people feel when contemplating such markets.[2] Second, a number of critics suggest that the "supply" and "demand" for organs cannot be assumed to have those characteristics these terms ordinarily imply. For example, the "demand" is "created" by public intervention through the financing of transplantation and, should the availability of organs improve, there would be concomitant increases in "demand" (i.e., waiting list registrations) as a direct response. Similarly, the "supply," which now owes much to altruism, could actually shrink if compensation were offered due to the erosion of the altruistic impulse. Finally, of course, many persons object to compensation for ethical reasons.

That many intelligent people are persuaded by one or another of these points is obvious. We think, however, that these objections lose their power to convince when some mischaracterizations of the notion of a "market," as understood in economics, are eliminated. Thus, in what follows we want to stress the point that, in our economic usage, a *market* is, as Hubbard and O'Brian (2010) define it in their book *Microeconomics*, "a group of buyers and sellers of a good or service and the institution or arrangement by which they come together to trade." In the case of human kidneys for transplantation, for example, it is neither necessary nor realistic to assume that the "buyers" will literally be the ESRD patients themselves, nor that the market will resemble the stereotypical commodity market with its chaotic interactions and cut-throat rivalry. "Sellers," in turn, might be either potential living donors or the families of potential deceased donors. Finally, the "arrangement" by which the providers and recipients of human organs "come together" will by necessity reflect the exceptional character of the transactions at issue. Our specific proposals in this regard are presented in Chapter 8. Here, however, it is useful to consider and briefly review the "basic model" of the organ shortage, as often represented by economists (e.g., Barnett and Kaserman, 2002; Becker and Elias, 2008).

A Stylized View on a Zero-Price Market for Organs

For purposes of analysis, it is quite useful to summarize the "market for organs," as it is now organized, with the relatively conventional diagram shown in Figure 5.1. To begin, we ignore the potential "joint supply" of organs from cadavers and focus instead on a single organ: the kidney. We also abstract here from the real differences in the qualities of kidneys made available for transplant, and we ask the reader to assume that all kidneys are of a given, acceptable quality. The numbers of (postmortem) kidneys traded in the market (during a given period) are measured along the horizontal axis, while the vertical axis measures the price paid. The supply curve for kidneys, labeled S, has a somewhat unconventional appearance: as many as Q_0 organs are provided, even at the price of zero. To obtain more organs than this, prices above zero would be required. At point Q_3 we draw the S curve as vertical, indicating that price becomes

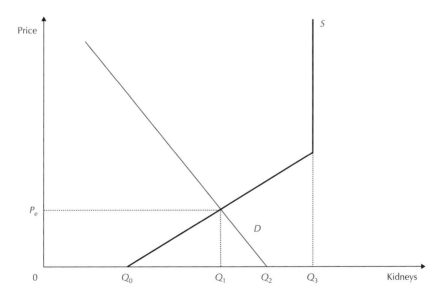

Figure 5.1   The organ market and the shortage, a conventional view

ineffective in soliciting supply past some limit. The demand curve, labeled D, looks more conventional, and it is drawn quite steeply as a metaphor for the very poor quality of the substitutes for kidney transplants, such as dialysis, or for the fatal consequences of renal failure.

We also label several significant points on Figure 5.1. Q_1 refers to the hypothetical equilibrium quantity of kidneys, and P_e to the corresponding equilibrium, or market-clearing, price. In the absence of the price cap, the presumption is that we would in fact observe this price and quantity pair, other things equal. The quantity Q_2 indicates the number of kidneys for transplantation that would be desired if cost were no object. Similarly, Q_3 indicates the maximum number of cadaveric kidneys that society might obtain under voluntary exchange.

In economic terms, the restriction of price to be zero results in a notional "shortage," given in the figure by the distance $(Q_2 - Q_0)$. The continuous accumulation of these shortages produces the waiting list, with adjustments made for deaths and similar reasons for removals from the list. Elimination of the price constraint, all other things being equal, would then be assumed to result in an equilibrium in which Q_1 organs would be supplied at price P_e. Thus, in this very simplified conceptualization, the zero price constraint is the "cause" of the shortage, and its removal would eliminate the shortage.

What assumptions lie hidden in this scenario? The answer is quite a few, of course, although the basic finding remains valid despite the complications and qualifications. To begin, kidneys are obtained from both deceased donors and living donors. The demand for cadaveric kidneys is directly affected by the supply of living-donor kidneys, and vice versa. Further, living and deceased-donor organs differ in quality, so their prices would typically also perhaps differ in equilibrium. If one contemplated paying only for postmortem kidneys, then it might be that Q_3 would lie further to the left, which could cause prices to be less effective on the margin in bringing forth additional supply. Also, little can be said about the magnitude of market price P_e.

No shortage would arise if Q_2 were less than Q_0: this is apparently the goal of conventional reform efforts, to be achieved by moving the supply curve with Q_0 rightward and/or reducing the demand for "legitimate" reasons—in other words, shifting the demand curve and Q_2 leftward. It is also clear that one must carefully define what constitutes the "demand" in this diagram. In almost all countries, kidney transplants, including the costs of procuring organs (about $50,000 for a kidney in the United States) are paid by public authorities with tax revenues. Thus, the "price" being measured here must refer to the price paid to the kidney donors and not to the prices being paid for kidney "acquisition, typing, and transportation" by these public authorities.[3]

Similarly, those who point to the roles of government funding and physician decision making in deciding who receives transplants would claim that any increase in the supply of organs (given by a rightward shift in the S curve) would trigger a coincident rightward shift in the demand curve. Hence, although more transplants would be performed, the shortage, as we defined it, would not decrease; it could even grow.

Thus, several important "unknowns" are concealed by Figure 5.1. Is Q_3 larger or smaller than Q_2? To what extent does the demand curve D depend on the waiting list? More generally, how should one interpret the demand curve D, and in what operative sense can the government be said to "demand" kidneys or other organs? What would an equilibrium, market clearing price be? Is the supply of cadaveric organs alone likely to be sufficient to reduce waiting lists over time, or must living donors also be used, as argued by Becker and Elias (2008), Breyer and colleagues (2006), and other scholars? Since the price will (we suspect and recommend) be determined in a market with a single, public buyer, how should this buyer set price offers, and when could it know its price policy was efficient? It is unlikely these questions can be precisely answered without well-designed trials.

A Market for Organs in a Wider Context

Despite fears of reduced total supply due to less altruistic donations and fears of increased demand caused by increased supply, it seems fairly clear that the existence of the nearly universal zero price constraint is a profound handicap and that it should receive the great bulk of the blame for the shortage of organs for transplantation. To see this, one need merely examine the organ procurement system in its broadest outlines and compare it to other systems that use market mechanisms to facilitate exchange of valuable, scarce goods. This is easiest to see in the case of cadaveric organ supply. As critics of a compensation system are wont to point out, thousands of cadaver donors are obtained each year worldwide without providing any compensation to the donor families (or to the donors themselves, premortem). Yet, this fact need not imply that organs are utterly unlike other goods (for which compensation is almost universally paid), but rather that cadaveric organs have an extremely low opportunity cost, so low in many cases that they are provided for free, merely at the request of ("begging by") others. The alternative use of these organs, in fact, is burial—in other words, destruction. The fact that in the United States, compensation for entire cadavers, legally permitted, leads to an abundant supply at less than $5,000 each (the compensation being relabeled as "funeral assistance") does not suggest that body parts are so unlike other articles of trade that no market is possible. Rather, we would argue that we do in fact have a market for organs, but one that is burdened by the most extreme possible form of regulation if the goal is to increase the number of transactions.

Indeed, can you think of any other "things" of such vital significance and evident utility for which begging, in effect, is the only allowable means to influence potential providers? Organ transplants require an entire sequence of actions by various persons. The number of transplant operations that finally occur depends on the incentives provided at each stage in the process. Each stage is necessary for the transplant to happen, and any stage can become a limiting factor. No one has seriously proposed that any stage in the process besides initial organ donation should be free of provider compensation. Without the surgeons' skills, patients would die just as they do when organs are unavailable.

Given the nearly unique nature of the ban on compensation for organs (even from cadavers), it is difficult to find particularly useful analogies from which one might draw a reliable policy lesson. However, the medical field itself offers perhaps the most cited examples. The market for blood and blood products has been much discussed in this context. Many critics of compensation proposals feel that Titmuss's (1970) famous and controversial analysis shows that, because of the (apparent) uniqueness of the human body and the complexity of human relationships, voluntary provision outperforms crude commerce. For a variety of reasons, however, the Titmuss claims have not been broadly supported by subsequent analysis. First, Titmuss focused on the blood market during a period prior to the general introduction of screening tests for hepatitis and similar diseases, so much of Titmuss's criticism of the quality of blood obtained from paid donors is not relevant today.[4]

More importantly, it is likely that Titmuss's position represents an ideological reading of facts that do not really indict the price mechanism. For many years, psychologists and sociologists have noted that material compensation for certain behaviors can, indeed, reduce that behavior. Frey's (1993) analyses are often cited in this regard. Titmuss (1970) claimed that first, such compensation actually undermined the altruistic impulse, and second, it led to inferior outcomes. The first point is now understood differently, as suggested by Gneezy and Rustichini's (2000) paper "Pay Enough or Don't Pay at All" (see also Bénabou and Tirole, 2006). Very small amounts of compensation may indeed reduce supply: When consumers wish to signal their altruism to others by donating, paying donors undermines that effort. There are many favors one might consider doing for friends, or even strangers, that one would decline to do for a small payment. This circumstance reflects the fact that almost all actions have multiple motives and that over some ranges of incentive these motives can conflict. This proves only that, should compensation be offered to living kidney donors, for example, it should not be of trivial magnitude.

The U.S. blood supply system attacked by Titmuss no longer exists. While some analysts strongly disputed many of Titmuss's factual claims, or the implications of those claims (Drake, Finkelstein, and Sapolsky, 1982; Schwartz, 1999), others, such as Arrow (1972), accepted much of Titmuss's evidence but did not accept the ethical interpretation. The results of Goette and Stutzer's (2008) case studies, for example, strongly support the claim that valuable consideration (e.g., lottery tickets) provided to donors increases blood supply. Hippen and Satel (2008) offer a careful review of most of the subsequent discussion. In any event, the United States now collects whole blood only from uncompensated donors and pays for plasma. It is also the case that the United States exports plasma and plasma products to Europe, while whole blood is frequently in short supply, and summer blood drives are a perennial feature of the public landscape. These circumstances hardly form an indictment of compensation.

There are several important cases in which human body materials are routinely sold, and there is far less discussion of these cases by critics of market organization proposals, presumably because they do not exhibit any useful pathologies. For example, the sale of human eggs is legal in the United States, and compensation ranges from $5,000 to over $15,000 for particularly desirable donors.[5] Payment to U.S. bone marrow donors is now considered legal (*New York Times,* December 1, 2011). Surrogate mothers are paid rates similar to those paid to egg donors, in addition to medical expense allowances, insurance, and the like. Sales of semen and many other body materials are legal.[6] These markets have allowed thousands of people to have children when they otherwise could not. Scandals in such industries do not appear more frequent than in other commercial markets.

We note finally that those national organ procurement systems that do use compensation of donors are generally much more successful than those that do not. The primary examples in this regard, as noted in Chapter 3, are Iran and Spain. In the Iranian case, significant levels of compensation for living kidney donors at one point eliminated waiting lists, although one must view the Iranian success within the context of that country. In Spain, the documented use of compensation, represented as assistance for funeral costs and the like, is carefully combined with a well-funded, nationally coordinated procurement system in the "Spanish model." It would be unfair to say that compensation is the sole reason for Spain's results (Rodriguez-Arias, Wright, and Paredes, 2010). It is likely that, for most potential donors, motives will be mixed, and financial compensation will represent only a part (though perhaps a large part) of their decision. Yet, the ability of donor recruitment officers to offer such compensation, along with the ethical and social arguments available now, would surely result in a substantial improvement in organ supply.

The Institutional Structure of Procurement

Although the greatest part of the blame for the shortage of organs, and the sickness and deaths it causes, must surely lie with the prohibition on donor compensation, it would be incorrect to say that this prohibition is the only factor that affects supply. The structures of the organ procurement systems in most countries reduce the incentives of many participants in the donor process, suppressing transplant activities even further. Although these factors must pale in comparison with the zero compensation rule, the high costs of losing even a relatively few additional organs make them worth examining.

Territorial Monopsonies and Not-for-Profit Entities

In the United States, as in other countries, the procurement of organs for transplantation is a public function, entrusted to monopsonistic, nonprofit authorities. Among the provisions contained in the 1984 National Organ Transplantation Act (NOTA) in the United States, for example, is one that created a set of regional organ procurement organizations (OPOs) and established the market structure under which they would operate. (The German equivalent, the *Deutsche Stiftung Organtransplantation*, has a very similar structure, although it is nationally unitary.) From the economic perspective, these structures exhibit two important characteristics. First, each of the 58 U.S. regional OPOs is assigned an exclusive geographic territory within which it could conduct its activities. These territories vary considerably in size, both in geographic scope and population served. For example, large OPOs serve parts of California (One Legacy Transplant Donor Network in Los Angeles, 17.5 million persons) and multiple states in New England (New England Organ Bank, 11.1 million persons), while smaller, sparsely populated states are often serviced by much smaller networks, as in New Mexico (New Mexico Donor Services, 1.8 million) or Nebraska (Nebraska Organ Retrieval System, 1.6 million). These assignments of exclusive territories provide each OPO a "monopsony" (monopoly on the buyer side of the market) over all organ procurement activities within its region. As a consequence, competition among procurement organizations in primary donor recruitment is limited.

The NOTA also established the financial incentive system under which these monopsony OPOs must operate. In particular, these organizations are legally (private) nonprofit entities. This status has several practical implications under the laws of the United States and most other countries. First, the OPOs do not have ownership rights that are tradable, implying that there cannot be a conventional market for the residual rights to income of the organizations. Hence, OPOs are not subject to market-launched "takeovers," nor is it necessarily a simple matter for outsiders to judge the performance of an OPO management.[7] Additionally, the selection of managers is made by volunteer boards whose incentives and abilities to evaluate OPO performance may be weak.

A detailed review of these features of the U.S. organ procurement apparatus can be found in Barnett and Kaserman (2002), so our treatment here is brief and generic. Nevertheless, these features are informative because, with few significant exceptions, they are duplicated in all the other countries.

Consider first the geographic monopsony feature. Due to this structure, the pressure to improve performance (i.e., lower costs and/or increase output) that is normally found in the competitive setting is eliminated. While a few organs are transported between OPOs, there is no head-to-head competition among OPOs at the acquisition stage. In terms of Figure 5.1, this means that the factual quantity Q_0 may be lower than some maximum feasible number that could be acquired—even at the zero price. That this is indeed the case is overwhelmingly supported by a variety of evidence from numerous sources. For example, the Organ Donation Breakthrough Collaborative (ODBC), discussed at greater length in Chapter 6, is itself predicated on the existence of such inefficiencies, which it seeks to eliminate. Plainly, OPO organ procurement rates (defined with respect to hospital deaths, for example) vary greatly in the United States, sometimes by a factor of ten. These differences are analyzed at length by Beard, Kaserman, and Saba (2005), who show that such variations are significantly related to variations in OPO efficiency. Thus, U.S. OPO performances vary dramatically, a result not inconsistent with the lack of any sort of ordinary competition among these organizations.

The existence of scale economies in procurement operations may provide a partial justification for the monopsony structure imposed on procurement by the NOTA, but this seems quite unlikely. Beard, Kaserman, and Saba's analysis attempted to account for such effects, if imperfectly, and they found that scale economies, while real, were small. So, while efficiency concerns imply that OPOs should be of a certain minimal size, the cost consequences of size differences appear trivial compared to the variations in performances. More generally, the role of geographic monopoly in OPO scale economies is conceptually unclear: scale economies are obtained by harvesting more organs over a larger set of potential donors, and it is not apparent why this is best achieved by restricting OPOs to geographic monopolies. One could envision a small number of large OPOs that share some common territory but are still of sufficient size to benefit from cost savings. The existing technology of communication and transportation would appear to allow such a structure.

The forms of organ procurement organizations found in the EU and elsewhere follow the U.S. pattern in most respects (e.g., geographic monopsony, nonprofit status), but most are explicitly public authorities rather than private nonprofits. Countries with national insurance funds invariably have public procurement agencies that are parts of the national health services. The practical consequences of this are not clear, but they are probably relatively minimal. In particular, variations in transplantation activities across countries are not explained by the private nonprofit versus public authority distinction.

The nonprofit status of U.S. OPOs imposed by the NOTA implies that any "profits" such organizations might earn would, by necessity, be a sort of common property shared by groups of persons who may have very different goals. The economic literature on nonprofit organizations, and the efficiency consequences of such organizations, is voluminous, and it is beyond the scope of this book to review it all. However, the role of nonprofits in the health care industry is substantial, and many health economists have researched the situation and have attempted to discern the consequences for society. Results have been variable. Wilson and Jadlow (1982) studied the nuclear medicine business in the United States and found that for-profit organizations were more efficient—that is, they had lower unit costs. In contrast, Burgess and Wilson (1996) found no such differences for hospitals, although the complexity of hospital goals and outputs makes the problem challenging. Numerous authors have looked at nursing home performance (e.g., Nyman and Bricker, 1989; Sexton et al., 1989; Rosko et al., 1995), and results have been mixed.

A complication of great importance is the presence of public organizations in addition to private nonprofits. In general, public organizations (which are nonprofit by definition) are found to be less efficient than private, for-profit firms, but the comparison between private for-profits and private nonprofits is less definitive. DeWar (2010) provides discussion and analysis on this point. After all, profit maximization is merely a form of utility maximizing behavior within a specific context, and it is not sensible to think that people stop behaving in a privately advantageous manner merely because they work in a nonprofit organization. The difference presumably arises from restrictions on the sorts of contracts they can enter into and with whom they can make such contracts.

Secondary Disincentives to the Procurement of Organs

Among the most common complaints heard at conferences or workshops about procurement and transplantation organizations are the low levels of reimbursement for transplantation.[8] The issue of inadequate recompense for hospitals is examined in some detail in Breyer and colleagues (2006), which focuses on Germany and Eurotransplant. Similar complaints are often voiced in the United States, although few detailed studies have been conducted of this issue. Complicating any analysis of this kind, many transplant centers in the United States and elsewhere simultaneously operate, or are affiliated with, dialysis clinics.

The complete financial impact on the transplant center/hospital arises not only from the reimbursement scheme applied to the transplantation and follow-up itself but also the possible loss of a dialysis patient. On the other hand, the rate at which dialysis clinics were compensated in the United States has been inappropriate and even harmful, since a fixed payment was given independent of run times.[9] The obvious and documented results of this crude sort of contract—reduced run times and higher patient morbidity and mortality—were direct consequences. (See Himmelfarb and Kliger (2007) for a review of performance-based compensation for dialysis.) Most recently, the Medicare Improvements for Patients and Providers Act (MIPPA) has sought to prevent clinics from overusing certain drugs for which providers may bill separately, thereby evading attempts by Medicare to limit ESRD program costs. It is likely that the financial consequence to a transplant center of the transitioning of a patient from hemodialysis to living with a functioning graft is quite complex. However, the great majority of dialysis patients in both the United States and Europe do not dialyze at clinics associated with transplant centers.

Interactions between Donor Types

Although we discuss procurement reforms, both proposed and actual, in Chapter 6, it is obvious that any efforts to reduce the shortages will presumably involve increases in organs for transplantation. (Demand reduction, although possibly critical in the longer term, does little to assist existing patients.) In the important case of kidneys, organs are obtained from both living and deceased donors, ordinarily in the latter case through the agreement of their surviving family members.[10] In both cases, the technical availability of organs is not the limiting factor, at least under current levels of utilization. Rather, people's decisions determine whether organs are supplied for transplantation. Since economic/material incentives are (presumably) not allowed to influence these choices, it is plausible that other factors, which might be safely ignored in a compensation-based system, become quite important. Evidence shows that these forces could undermine many sorts of reforms.

Cadaveric kidneys for transplantation are obtained primarily from accident victims, suicides, and those who die from strokes.[11] In general, the agreement of family members is sought, and is in fact determinative, in these decisions. If the family says "no," ordinarily no donation is possible, regardless of the expressed wishes of the potential donor. Although there is a fairly large body of work examining these decisions at the microlevel, little evidence exists as to the way in which the supply of deceased-donor organs varies in a "macro" sense. In particular, Osterkamp (2006) suggested that publicity surrounding payments made to living donors under sham arrangements may discourage families from consenting to altruistic deceased donation. This phenomenon, termed "dirty altruism," implies the potential existence of a link between living donation at one time and cadaver donation at a later time. If families believe that some percentage of living donations are, in fact, compensated, then they might become less willing to participate under the altruistic system.

Similarly—although less controversially—one can imagine a link between cadaver donations at time t, say, to living donations at time $t + 1$. The logic of this link is simple: donations by living persons are usually made to relatives or very close friends. It is the welfare of these friends or relatives that motivates the gift (in principle at least). However, a living donation is not something to be done lightly: it is irreversible and carries a small, but nonzero, risk. Thus, it is plausible that the numbers of such donations are affected by the numbers of the alternative, cadaver transplants (relative to the size of the need—i.e., the waiting list). One might call this phenomenon the "donor substitution effect."

Beard and colleagues (2010, 2012) evaluated the existence and size of this effect for the United States, using quarterly data on living and deceased-donor transplants and the renal graft waiting list for the fourth quarter of 1992 through the second quarter of 2006. The authors used a sophisticated time-series analysis of the evolution of U.S. waiting and donation statistics that combines cointegration (i.e., the positing of a long-term, equilibrium relationship between donations and the waiting list) with a vector error correction model in order to rule out certain alternative explanations for their results. Both long-run and short-run effects were evaluated. In less technical terms, the analysis allows the authors to investigate the immediate, intermediate, and long-term consequences of an increase in deceased-donor kidneys (as would occur under a number of reform proposals) on living donation and, thus, on the numbers of transplants performed.

The econometric results are both strong and discouraging. First, deviations from equilibrium, in the short run, are corrected primarily through adjustments in the levels of living donation. A significant donor substitution effect exists even in the short run: a 1 percent increase in cadaveric donation levels results in about a 0.2 percent decline in living donation immediately. Over time, the authors find that "the long-run substitution effect is substantial as (living donation) decreases further, leading to a 0.703 percent decrease in the long run, which is significant" (Beard et al., 2012). In terms of the consequences for transplantation rates, the authors conclude that "an increase of 106 postmortem organ transplants (representing around 70 additional deceased donors using historical values) will result in a decrease in equilibrium living donors of around 42, amounting to a net increase in transplants of only 62 (using 2008 transplant figures from OPTN)" (Beard et al., 2012).

Although Beard and colleagues found that increases in the waiting list led to more living donors, on balance the ability of policy makers to ameliorate the kidney shortage in the United States by raising the "yield rate" for deceased donation or increasing transplants performed with lower-quality organs is limited by "crowding out" living donations. On the other hand, little evidence exists that living donors crowd out deceased donors, so presumably efforts to increase living donation do not operate under a similar handicap. However, many reforms, such as the ODBC in the United States and the Spanish model, are primarily or exclusively focused on increasing deceased donation. We examine these issues in more detail in Chapter 6.

Reasons for the Resistance to Organ Donation Reform—A Political Economy Perspective

We turn now to an important and perplexing question. Given the apparently very strong case for reform, how does the "altruistic" model in its present shape survive? Its inefficiencies have been dealt with in earlier chapters of this book, and to repeat, there are mainly three. There is a serious underutilization of the potential for cadaveric organ donation (at least in most countries, Spain being a notable—and noble—exception). Almost every country is seeing a quickly growing and, in some countries, already a considerable amount of living donation—which would not be necessary if cadaver donations were more fully used. And there is a black market for organs with all its repugnant effects. (The latter two phenomena may render systemic reforms less urgent because they reduce the pressure on the waiting list.) But the tide against reform, obviously, is still strong. Even as of late 2008, influential international organizations continued to call for "preserving the nobility of organ donation" (see the "Declaration of Istanbul")[12]—which implies that they strongly oppose donor compensation.

Although proposals for reforms come (and go) with some regularity, resistance to compensating donors persists. While the moral aspect of this problem is, for many people, a fundamental stumbling block, cynics might believe that the failure to see widespread reform stems from the behavior not of philosophers or theologians but rather of politicians and businesspeople. From the economic perspective, if the current system persists, then it must be in some powerful people's interests that it does so. Although this problem is somewhat beyond the scope of this book, it is useful to briefly consider the relevant interested parties and where their interests might lie. To this end, we consider the roles of patients, the medical community, politicians, and insurance funds.

Patients

It is difficult to imagine how patients in need of transplants can oppose major reforms unless they believed these reforms would make matters even worse. Patients, however, are often desperately ill, so their ability to organize as a political force is nil. Their families, on the other hand, although burdened with their care, could do so. We are unaware, however, of any family or patient groups that oppose compensation as an organizing principle. On the contrary, groups such as the American Association of Kidney Patients (AAKP) have generally supported compensation.[13]

The Medical Community

The concept of donor compensation strongly divides the medical community, and several prominent transplant surgeons have historically opposed compensation in the strongest terms.[14] Many international medical organizations have made strong public statements against compensation. On the other hand, numerous prominent physicians, such as Arthur Matas in the United States, are open to reforms that include elements of donor compensation.[15] Those opposing compensation mechanisms emphasize perceived ethical defects and the undermining of the solidarity implied by the donor system. Those in favor of monetary incentives emphasize the dire shortage of organs and the deaths of patients who cannot obtain transplants. The pages of many leading medical journals have featured these debates for many years.

From the economic perspective, it is difficult, but not impossible, to rationalize medical opposition to compensation on financial grounds. Barnett, Beard, and Kaserman (1993) provide such an analysis, finding that a profit-maximizing monopsony, selling a service at a fixed price, and with a positive supply of a necessary input (e.g., kidneys) at a price of zero, *might* oppose the introduction of a market even when it raised the number of transplants performed. However, the conditions required, which include a significant reduction in uncompensated donor kidneys with the commencement of payment, are probably implausible. Somewhat ironically, medical opposition to compensation on self-interest grounds does appear to require that compensation undermine uncompensated donation. It appears, though, that the opposition of physicians to compensation is *not* primarily motivated by financial interests.

A possible exception to this reasoning arises from a consideration of the interests of dialysis providers. Here one sees perhaps the group with the strongest financial interest in a continuation of the current system. Although not all dialysis patients are suitable candidates for transplants, even if only one-half were freed of dialysis via transplantation, the consequences to dialysis providers would be on the order of many billions of dollars or euros per year.

Politicians

Politicians want to be reelected, and they are always looking for opportunities and trying to avoid any types of controversy. Thus, they may have many concerns when it comes to organ donation reform.

A reform of the present system would greatly benefit most patients on the organ waiting list, as well as dialysis patients not (yet) on the list. Moreover, it would be beneficial for future patients as well. However, the only voters on this list are current patients with organ failure—and they are only a small group. On average in the OECD countries, these persons make up a mere 0.10 percent of the population, and not more than 0.15 percent of the voters. In the richest OECD countries, the percentage is only slightly higher. Even if one takes into account the family members of the patients, the number of potential affected voters would remain low. In contrast, a reform initiative would risk losing many voters. With a fundamental change in the system—introducing donor compensation in a state-regulated framework—opposition from a large group of voters is plausible. Even a weaker proposal, such as a "club solution," might represent a significant liability to the politician backing it. Thus, one observes here the case of a small minority of persons—seriously ill and often quite poor—who might greatly benefit from a policy change, at odds with another group, a thousand times larger, who might be only somewhat opposed to it but who are aided by a small, highly educated and influential group of medical and academic critics of compensation. The mechanism by which the politician is likely to suffer for supporting reform is public criticism from this small group of experts.

Health Insurance Funds

In most countries, with the partial exception of Spain, cadaveric donation is considerably below its potential. Generally, one would expect health insurers to strongly support initiatives to redress this situation, particularly in light of the evidently very large financial benefits from doing so. However, and surprisingly, their role in the public debate about increasing cadaveric donation is very small. Why is this so?

Obviously, insurers may be reluctant to promote reforms because they want to keep their distance from a sensitive public issue in which morals, politics, and economics are so intermingled. At second glance, however, it is clear that more kidney transplants would reduce medical costs, presumably saving insurance companies money. Why, then, do health insurers not do more to promote campaigns and laws that contribute to increased cadaver donation rates?

While the cost of a kidney transplant is low compared to other solid organs (except corneas), *and* kidney transplants eliminate dialysis costs, transplants of the other organs are much more expensive *and* do not reduce costs of alternative treatment (since there is practically none). This suggests a hypothetical possibility: expansion of cadaver kidneys will necessarily increase the availability of other organs, such as hearts or lungs, for which the financial benefits are far less favorable. If this expansion of organ supply led to (pressure for) increased transplants of these "expensive" organs, the net effect on the insurance company might be deleterious. This explanation is extremely speculative, but a brief look at the costs involved seems warranted.

In our discussion, we assume a once-and-for-all increase in cadaver donation levels of 1,000 cadavers per year. An additional donation of 1,000 cadavers is about 10 percent of the current annual donation figure in the United States and the Eurotransplant countries. We examine costs and cost savings over time, but we only consider the direct money costs and money cost savings incurred by health insurers and ignore all the other benefits of a transplant. (For a discussion of the results of more inclusive cost-benefit analyses, see Chapter 4.) Our analysis is limited to three organs: kidneys, hearts, and livers. It is assumed that each cadaver permits the harvest of 1.5 kidneys, 0.8 hearts, and 1.2 livers (livers can be partitioned). The resulting potential additions of 1,500 kidney and 1,200 liver transplants are much below the U.S. shortages. In contrast, 800 heart transplants exceed the U.S. shortage, which is taken to be 318 (Kaserman's (2006) medium "S2" measure of shortage, to be discussed in Chapter 6). We use this lower figure for the calculation. Furthermore, it is assumed that 80 percent of the kidney transplant patients have formerly been on dialysis. We calculate the additional costs and cost savings that occur as a result of the hypothetical increase of cadaver donation levels. The cost figures relate to the United States and are mainly drawn from the Milliman Report (Ortner, 2005), which is also discussed in Chapter 4.[16]

The following variables enter the calculation:

- Total additional transplant costs per annum compared to year 0—that is, before the increase in cadaver donation occurred. These costs include postoperative care for one year.

- Total additional postoperative costs, which are assumed to occur only in the second year after transplant.

- Additional organ acquisition costs. It is assumed, first, that the average acquisition costs per organ (usually calculated per kidney) are identical with the average cost per acquisition/harvesting act and, second, that the increased acquisition has no effect on average costs.

- Cost savings. The most relevant factor here is dialysis, but diseases leading to transplants of other organs also cause pretransplant costs that are avoided after the transplant takes place. To simplify the calculation of the cost savings, it is assumed that all transplant activities in a year take place at the beginning of that year.

The simulation uses as inputs three assumptions on costs and benefits. First, we assume organ acquisition costs, under the expansion of cadaver donation, of $55,000 per cadaver. This is the current U.S. cost per cadaveric kidney under the UNOS system. Second, and in a similar vein, our assumptions for net per

Table 5.1 Additional costs and cost savings after an increase of 1,000 postmortem organ donors, over 10 years, for the United States (in thousands of dollars)

Year	Kidneys only			Kidneys, hearts, and livers		
	Additional costs	Cost savings	Net cost savings	Additional costs	Cost savings	Net cost savings
1	370,000	89,279	−280,721	993,650	101,639	−892,011
2	394,000	178,558	−215,442	1,057,550	203,278	−854,273
3	394,000	267,836	−126,164	1,057,550	304,916	−752,634
4	394,000	357,115	−36,885	1,057,550	406,555	−650,995
5	394,000	446,394	52,394	1,057,550	508,194	−549,356
6	394,000	535,673	141,673	1,057,550	597,473	−460,077
7	394,000	624,952	230,952	1,057,550	686,752	−370,799
8	394,000	714,230	320,230	1,057,550	776,030	−281,520
9	394,000	803,509	409,509	1,057,550	865,309	−192,241
10	394,000	892,788	498,788	1,057,550	954,588	−102,962

SOURCE: Authors.
NOTE: Transplant costs are from the Milliman Research Report (Ortner, 2005). Harvest rates per postmortem donor: 1.5 (kidney), 0.8 (heart), 1.2 (liver). Organ acquisition costs: $55,000 per cadaver. Synthetic insulin costs: $5,000 per year, per liver patient. Postoperative drugs and care costs: $16,000 (kidney), $50,000 (heart), $20,000 (liver) per year, per patient. Dialysis costs: $74,400 per year, per patient (UNOS, 2005). Heart transplants truncated at 318, liver transplants at 3,200 (Kaserman, 2006).

patient postoperative costs ($16,000 for renal grafts; $50,000 for heart transplants; and $20,000 for livers) are on the lower side, "stacking the deck" in favor of transplant expansion. The assumption that 80 percent of transplant patients were previously on dialysis is likewise low under current conditions, where almost all previously dialyzed, but might be more realistic in an environment with expanded transplant activity. Third, we also ignore cost savings associated with the early deaths of patients needing livers or hearts. From the standpoint of an insurer, a patient with a largely untreatable and rapidly fatal illness is much less costly than a transplant patient who will live much longer but will require relatively high levels of medical care throughout his or her lifetime. Thus, by ignoring these monetary incentives for insurers to resist cadaver supply expansion, we again introduce a bias toward expansion. Table 5.1 contains the results of the calculation.

Table 5.1 shows the financial consequences of a permanent increase of 1,000 postmortem donors for two different cases: when only the kidneys are used for transplants (column 2, 3, and 4) and when kidneys, hearts, and livers are used (columns 5, 6, and 7). In the "kidney only" case, the insurer can realize net cost savings from the fifth year onward. In the tenth year, the annual net cost savings amount to U.S.$500 million. By contrast, when all three organs are used for transplants, there are additional net costs instead of net cost savings during the whole ten-year period considered.

Hence, for the health insurers, a low level of postmortem organ procurement acts like a finger in the dike, because removing it could have grave financial consequences for them. Thus, it is quite realistic to expect that they will play a muted role in the public debate about how to increase cadaveric donation. It is simply not in their (financial) interest. By contrast, an increase in *living* donation *is* in their interest because it is usually limited to one organ only (the kidney). Unlike other organs, kidneys "pay for themselves," even from the strictest financial viewpoint, and while expansions in kidney transplantation levels are good in almost any reckoning, the same cannot be asserted for the other major organs.

We must stress the speculative nature of these calculations. Presumably, cost increases for insurers trigger increases in revenue (if only with a lag). However, the reluctance of insurance companies to qualify new procedures or to finance "experimental" treatments suggests that they are incompletely compensated for such cost shocks. Additionally, there is likely to be an important difference between the United States, where much health insurance is private, and many other countries that have national social insurance funds.[17]

Conclusion

If something is not going to be paid for, and it is useful to obtain and trouble to provide, then there will almost surely not be enough of it. Such is the case with solid organs, especially kidneys. Most national kidney donor laws, such as the NOTA in the United States, strictly prohibit compensation to donors or their families, even in the case of deceased donors. This nearly universal restriction impels almost all national authorities to resort primarily to moral suasion to obtain donor organs, and this is indeed a profound handicap. Somewhat curiously, this state of affairs was not strictly envisioned when the laws were being formulated, at least in some cases. Michele Goodwin (2008) points out that the chairman of the U.S. group that studied the relevant legal issues surrounding organ supply in connection with the Uniform Anatomical Gift Act (UAGA) of 1968 remarked, "The matter [of payments] should be left to the decency of intelligent human beings."[18]

Although the illegality of compensation to donors or their families is almost surely the primary reason for the shortage, several other factors appear to contribute to it. These factors include wide and documented differences in donor conversion rates between jurisdictions; the historical lack of an effective mechanism for correcting these inefficiencies; strong apparent crowding out, both in the short and long runs, between deceased-donor organs and living donors; and perhaps the complex political economy of the special interests involved and the high costs of transplant medicine.

Even (perhaps especially) those who are most opposed to donor compensation are consistent advocates for reforms of the organ procurement process, albeit mainly *within the current paradigm*. Thus, many prominent critics of payments for donation, such as Dr. Francis Delmonico in the United States, have put great effort into reforms that have some promise but do not use monetary incentives. These reforms are the subject of the next chapter.

6

Reforms Short of Open Donor Compensation

Introduction

The loss of life caused by the organ shortage has convinced even those most strongly opposed to compensation to propose various other means to increase organ availability. A large number of innovations have been discussed. Some of these ideas have been tried, although most remain to be tested. The overall track record is mixed, but several recent initiatives, such as the Organ Donation Breakthrough Collaborative (ODBC) program in the United States, have produced impressive results. Any discussion of organ procurement policy cannot ignore the experiences these reform programs have provided, and it is the purpose of this chapter to review this record.

We are concerned here only with those reforms that, in a significant sense, fall short of donor compensation. This distinction, however, cannot be entirely precise. Many reforms aimed at increasing the willingness of potential donors, or their families, to offer their organs necessarily involve some sort of inducement, if only a psychic one. Other proposals come closer to actual compensation schemes, such as when those who sign organ donor cards are given higher preference on transplant waiting lists should they need such therapy in the future. Financial assistance for funeral or cremation costs, travel accommodations, lost wages, and so on, though often taking a disguised form, involve direct payment to individuals with some say over the decision to donate and are, therefore, materially equivalent to compensation.

Broadly speaking, policies to reduce waiting lists within the existing procurement framework fall into three categories, although many individual programs involve components of several categories simultaneously. First, many efforts are aimed at influencing the behavior of potential or actual organ donors. Public service advertising, appeals to people's moral decency, and propaganda efforts clearly fall into this category. Programs aimed at increasing donation through changes in donation consent rules and procedures may be an effective tool. Most countries apply the "informed consent" rule, whereas "presumed consent," with the possibility to "opt out," is less widespread.

Weak forms of compensation to donors that fall short of direct payment also qualify. Interestingly, such weak incentive schemes need not be public functions. Private clubs, such as the LifeSharers program in the United States, offer members priority in the event they need an organ in the future in exchange for their commitment to donate to another club member under appropriate circumstances. Despite widespread verbal support for organ transplantation and donation, donor card signature rates remain low in most countries. Thus, proposals and experiments have been initiated to increase donor card signatures (and cadaveric donations) using specific forms of compensation that fall short of undisguised payment to donors. Similar proposals have been made for increasing living donation.

A second type of program aims to increase the extent to which the existing pool of potential organ donors is realized. These programs, such as the Organ Donation Breakthrough Collaborative in the United States and the "Spanish model," provide hospitals with both incentives to actively pursue donations and additional resources to support such efforts. By identifying and spreading best practice procurement techniques among transplant centers and hospitals, it is hoped that the average level of practice can be significantly raised. Such approaches, of course, are limited by the potential supply of donors.

Efforts such as the increased utilization of substandard donors (either those without heartbeats or with other medical deficits such as old age, hepatitis, and so on) also fall into this class. Such donors exist in relative abundance already, whereas standard criteria donors comprise perhaps only 1 percent of all hospital deaths. In a related vein, so-called "paired exchange" programs, in which living donors are "swapped" among patients in order to produce acceptable tissue and blood type matches, are in use in the United States and elsewhere. A number of authors have offered very sophisticated algorithms to facilitate matching patients to living donors so fewer organs are wasted and outcomes are better. Proposals for anonymous living donation to the waiting list also are considered here.

A third category of possible reforms short of compensation has received, somewhat surprisingly, little attention so far: the effort to reduce the need for transplants—what economists might term "demand-side management." Many individuals who need kidney transplants, for example, suffer either from poorly managed diabetes or untreated hypertension that can lead to organ damage. Programs that effectively treat these preconditions would almost surely be economically efficient when the costs of ongoing dialysis and transplantation are considered. Although not all dialysis patients are reasonable candidates for transplantation, it is not too misleading to say that every potential ESRD patient who is eliminated by preventive measures is as socially valuable as a living kidney donor.

Public Awareness Campaigns

Perhaps the least controversial approach to increasing organ donation involves public service advertising aimed at encouraging donation. A specific aim of such campaigns is usually to induce people to sign organ donor cards. It is not surprising that such efforts are, at current collection rates, relatively ineffective. This rather pessimistic finding, however, is inescapable, and it is made even more discouraging by the high level of support for organ donation found in most public surveys over the last 30 years. Although the public generally supports the concept of organ donation, they often do not agree to it when the time comes for an actual decision.

Evidence that the public claims to support organ donation is not difficult to find, although attitudes have evolved over the years. Manninen and Evans (1985) reported on attitudes toward donation in the United States and found considerable misunderstanding and some opposition in the early 1980s. Further, and perhaps indicating the immaturity of public views on transplantation during that period, they find that resistance varied among organs and that donor cards were not widely used or supported. In contrast, a decade later, Klenow and Youngs (1995) provided survey results for the United States that showed a greatly increased level of support for donation and transplant medicine. Donor cards are now widely known and supported, and required request rules also receive public support. The survey "The National Survey of Organ and Tissue Donation: Attitudes and Behaviors," conducted in 2005 for the Health Resources and Services Administration (HRSA) division of the

U.S. Department of Health and Human Services illustrates the triumph of the donation narrative, with 95.4 percent of adults claiming to support transplantation. More than half (51.4 percent) report that they are very likely to donate their organs after death. Almost two-thirds say they would donate while living to a family member.

Attitudes toward donation in Europe are more difficult to discern due to the wide variation in national regulations and substantial differences in observed donation rates. The Eurobarometer surveys of attitudes toward organ donation typically find wide support for the general idea, but national differences are large. For example, among Western countries in Europe, Spain often is reported as having the least favorable attitude toward donation, although Spain has donation rates that are among the highest. Eastern Europeans have less enthusiastic attitudes, explained perhaps by their historic experiences with many government-based programs. Nonetheless, public support for donation is generally similar to that in the United States. Unlike the United States, however, some European countries, such as the Czech Republic, have relatively strict presumed consent laws enacted by democratically elected governments.

Asian nations have cultural and social traditions that create special problems for the use of transplant therapy. In particular, Confucian tradition can discourage the use of deceased-donor organs due to long-standing taboos regarding desecration of the human body. Because many organ transplants, including hearts, intestines, and pancreas, rely on cadaver donors, such procedures raise difficult social and religious issues. The concept of "brain death," as defined in Western medical practice, is not recognized in some Asian societies, or it is viewed with suspicion.

In South Korea, for example, Kim Dongjin's (2003) study documented the failure of the Organ Transplantation Law of 1999 to lead to increases in the use of brain-dead donors. In particular, this law was enacted precisely to encourage the use of such donors by, for the first time, defining and legalizing the notion of brain death for purposes of organ transplantation. However, the author identifies "a traditional view of the human body" as a significant factor in public attitudes toward transplants. He adds, "There are some cultural differences between Korea and the West, which may explain the reluctance to donate organs. So, it is not enough that the system and technology of organ transplantation have been imported; a cultural and ethical background transplant is also needed in Korea" (p. 135). We find similar issues in Japan, which, while having the world's highest rate of dialysis therapy, exhibits a low rate of transplantation and organ donation.

In contrast to the strong apparent support for donation in many Western countries, there is a widely noted gap between perceived support on the one hand and the rate at which families actually agree to donate a deceased relative's organs on the other. In the United States, for example, a typical study of this issue would find that about one-half of families approached "*do not respond in such a manner*" that the organs are eventually taken for transplant. The rather curious wording is intentional: despite required request policies virtually everywhere, the ability of the request to overcome the family's resistance is not observed with any precision. The mere fact that a request is made means almost nothing. There is the famous anecdote where a surgeon asks the family of a brain-dead patient, "You don't want to donate any of his parts, do you?" In the case of the death of a single or widowed person, one can easily imagine a variety of inconsistent responses coming from surviving family members. For example, suppose that, in fact, 75 percent of all people support donation. Also, suppose that donation cannot occur without unanimous consent of family members. Then, if the "family" consisted of three people, the probability that at least one of them would say "no" exceeds 50 percent. While substantially oversimplified, such disadvantageous probability compounding is not unrealistic, and it reminds us that obtaining unanimous consent from groups of people can be quite difficult.

Attempts to alter public attitudes, and thereby get family members to say "yes" more often, have been widespread. Verble and Worth (1996) discuss a variety of reasons why public appeals are unlikely to be effective given the nature of the organ donation decision. However, the authors suggest that educational messages aimed at medical professionals are more likely to work but offer no empirical evidence. Beard, Kaserman, and Saba (2004) used a Freedom of Information Act (FOIA) request to obtain organ procurement organization (OPO) financial data for a large sample of U.S. OPOs. Using these data, the authors sought to determine the link, if any, between public and professional educational spending and the adjusted rates of deceased organ donors recruited during the mid-1990s. Their approach allowed for controls for a host of OPO region demographic factors, including racial composition, income/poverty, college educational attainment, population size, and regional effects. They sought to determine the effect of each type of advertising spending on donations obtained per thousand hospital deaths, thereby partially controlling for variations in this latter figure. The authors find no evidence of any significant effect arising from such educational spending. Rather, statistical results suggest that, inter alia, demographic factors, such as racial mix and per capita income, are the primary determinants of recruiting success.

All studies that seek to determine the effects of persuasive activities such as advertising are empirically challenging, and the absence of evidence is not necessarily evidence of absence. As Lester Telser (1964) remarked, "No business practice causes economists more uneasiness than advertising." However, even if one accepts that persuasive advertising might affect attitudes toward organ donation, which is plausible, isolating and measuring this effect are likely to be difficult for many reasons. For example, advertising, if it works, is often thought to produce a "stock" of goodwill that depreciates over time, in much the same manner as physical equipment. If so, the impact of advertising spending during a single period of time will not be a good proxy for the cumulative effects of advertising unless such spending is indicative of long-term efforts. The study by Beard and his colleagues mentioned above is unable to account for complex dynamic phenomena of this sort, and a careful analysis of pro-donor advertising remains to be done.

Changing Consent Rules for Organ Donation

In virtually all countries (except perhaps China), deceased organ donation is voluntary and ordinarily involves both the prior consent of the donor and the later consent of the donor's relatives, if any. There are several reasons for this. First, in the United States, Britain, Australia, and other nations with common law traditions, the body of a deceased individual is actually considered property belonging to the deceased's estate and/or family.[1] It is generally believed that, at least in the United States, the introduction of any policy that allowed the government to remove organs without consent would be a "taking" and, therefore, a violation of the U.S. Constitution. Thus, in some countries, significant legal changes would be required to drastically alter the current system of voluntary donation.

Another factor, which appears regularly in surveys of public opinion on organ donation, highlights many people's fears that, should they agree in advance to donation, medical personnel would fail to provide them with adequate care in order to hasten their deaths and collect valuable organs. This belief is occasionally bolstered by news accounts in which surgeons are charged with murder, ostensibly for the purpose of recovering the organs of the deceased for transplant. The French anthropologist Veronique Campion-Vincent, in her studies reported in her book *Organ Theft Legends* (1997) and her article "Organ Theft Narratives" (2002), provides a complex sociological explanation for the continuing currency of stories about such events that, for practical reasons, are probably quite rare.

Family refusal is a significant factor in the loss of suitable organs from brain-dead donors.[2] In the United States, perhaps 50 percent of families refuse the request to donate, although the ODBC program may materially alter this probability. Results are similar for the United Kingdom, but France and Spain are far more successful, with refusal rates below 30 percent.[3] As a logical matter, there is no direct link between presumed consent and family agreement, and surgeons may or may not consult with family members regardless of the consent law in force. As a practical matter, however, the issues are closely related because of the unwillingness of most physicians to act against survivors' wishes. This means that, in practice, physicians tend to obey the "required consent" rule.

In many European countries, such as Germany, there are laws that require citizens to render assistance to others in distress. Thus, it is legally possible to imagine the implementation of much stronger rules governing consent, in which persons would be required to "opt out" through some sort of premortem statement if they wished to avoid being donors. Breyer and colleagues (2006) performed a very careful study of possible reforms for Germany, and among their final conclusions is that such opting-out (or "presumed consent") rules could be implemented and might work. Their reasoning also highlights the rather different legal constraints faced in the European Union:

> Looking at the experience of countries such as Austria and Spain, a good many reasons can be found in favor of the assumption that the introduction of the opting-out ("presumed consent") rule would lead to a considerable increase in the number of available donor organs. Removing the burden from the next of kin of brain-dead patients could also lift an important psychological barrier for hospital staff. The expectation of solidarity inherent in the opting-out system is reflected in the fact that (initially) every individual is given the status of an organ donor. This attribution is a manifestation of an assumed moral obligation to donate. (p. 6)

The effects of presumed consent rules have been the subject of extensive studies in recent years. Many countries that have no common law tradition have implemented some form of presumed consent law. Austria, France, Greece, Hungary, Norway, Portugal, the Slovak Republic, Spain, Sweden, and many others have opting-out systems of varying degrees of rigidity. The practical difficulties from the point of view of evaluating such programs is that such countries exhibit substantial observed variation in donation rates and the implementation of presumed consent varies widely. Indeed, in many countries, the practical effects of the opting-out rule are greatly reduced by the de facto practice of surgeons continuing to request family approval for organ removal. The medical condition termed "brain death" can present great difficulties for family members, and not all cultural traditions even recognize this concept. Thus, studies seeking to evaluate the results of presumed consent rules face an unavoidable qualitative residual that makes conclusions tentative.

The best studies conducted to date, however, all suggest that presumed consent is associated with improvements in organ supply, although differences emerge over the magnitude of the effect. The widely cited study by Abadie and Gay (2006) looked at organ donation in 22 countries over a ten-year period, and their analysis gives a microeconomic framework within which variations in donation performance and its relationship with consent law may be understood. The authors view the behavior of a potential donor, either by opting out or failing to do so, as a signal of his or her desires. The family is consulted before organs are removed, and they take account of the observed choice of the potential donor.

Two consent rules are considered. Under informed consent rules, where a potential donor must affirmatively register, registration is a strong signal of intent. Because registration is costly, however, some potential donors fail to register. On the other hand, in presumed consent or opt-out regimes, those who strongly oppose donation can signal this by registration. In either case, families observe any public choice made earlier by the donor, and they combine this information with a private, noisy signal of donor intent. Under certain plausible conditions on the distributions of the underlying variables, one can show that family consent to donation will occur more often under presumed consent. While such an outcome is not the only one possible, the authors credibly argue that this is to be expected, and certainly casual empiricism supports this claim.

Abadie and Gay's (2006) analysis provides evidence that presumed consent rules increase donation rates. Because countries that have implemented presumed consent rules are not highly similar (in terms of income, religion, and similar factors) to those nations that have not, there is the typical problem of determining treatment effect in a valid way. Abadie and Gay examine eight specifications that differ in their variable lists and the inclusion of Spain in the sample. Problems of the potential endogeneity of presumed consent policies are addressed through the use of a "proxy" variable (in this case, blood donation rates), which one can argue are correlated with social preferences for organ donation, a potential source of presumed consent support. Specification testing is also undertaken. They conclude the following:

On the whole, our empirical results suggest that presumed consent laws may greatly increase the supply of cadaveric organs for transplantation. However, it would be erroneous to interpret our results as evidence that presumed consent is the sometimes-portrayed silver-bullet for organ shortages. First, it is unlikely that a 25 to 30 percent increase in cadaveric donation would eliminate completely the organ shortage problem in some countries, like the United States, although it would help considerably to alleviate it. . . . Moreover, it seems likely that an increase in the supply of cadaveric organs would be followed by a reduction in the supply from living donors. . . . Finally, many questions remain unanswered about how to implement a legislative change of this type.

Healy (2005) provides a straightforward econometric analysis of the effects of presumed consent among 17 OECD countries for the period 1990–2002. His analysis suggests that the effect of the laws, per se, is small in the absence of simultaneous strengthening of the procurement process, and evidence from Italy and Spain supports this view. More broadly, Healy sees organ procurement within a sociological context, in which the nature of the organizations charged with obtaining organs is critical. This view suggests that it will be quite difficult and, possibly, not very useful to identify the effect of presumed consent legislation. Howard (2007) provides a careful discussion of the presumed consent issue and notes that questions of interpretation are difficult.

While the problem of consent regimes remains an issue awaiting a final resolution, it seems likely that presumed consent rules do result in some measurable increases in cadaveric donation rates. The whole issue highlights the basic outline of the problem of cadaveric donation as usually practiced: regardless of the donor's wishes, clearly expressed or otherwise, the family's consent is ordinarily required. Scholars of this problem, such as Friedrich Breyer of Germany, have noted this critical aspect and have proposed steps to reduce or eliminate the role of family in the donation decision. Such systems are often termed "primary donor" rules, and they are based on the idea that only the deceased should have a veto-proof ability to dispose of their organs in the event of their death. If such an approach were combined with a presumed consent rule, it seems possible that substantially more deceased-donor organs would be available for transplant.

A step beyond presumed consent is conscription: organs of a deceased potential donor would belong to the public, represented by the government. Many of the advantages and difficulties with conscription-type systems are reviewed by Spital (2005), who points out, along with Jonsen (1988), that harm to a cadaver is a materially amorphous notion, whereas death on a waiting list is, in contrast, quite concrete indeed. If death is taken to be the ultimate harm to a person, and if needless death is the ultimate violation of a person's autonomy, then it is difficult to rationalize the moral case for burying organs that could save thousands of lives merely because interested third parties object to their removal after the donor's death. After all, as Spital also notes, we draft living persons into military or national service, and that seems far more intrusive than removing the kidney from a dead body.

However, the potential effect of "conscription" on broad public attitudes toward transplantation and organ donation is worrying, but this may be more a short-term problem, since evidently the public has grown to accept numerous examples of coercion in other spheres. Spital evaluated the Harris polling organization survey attitudes toward organ conscription in the United States. The results, despite the moral arguments just cited, are probably not surprising: 66 percent of respondents opposed the practice. Somewhat surprisingly, college-educated respondents were less supportive than their less-educated fellow citizens. One can conclude, with the author, that a strong conscription regime, either through presumed consent without family notification or actual confiscation, is unlikely to be accepted in the United States at this time, not least due to constitutional limits. Other countries, however, may have better prospects.

Presumed consent rules and conscription of deceased-donor organs lie at the tail end of a spectrum of reforms to the consent process that have been implemented nearly universally throughout the world's transplantation systems. Because the earliest transplants involved live donors who were closely related to the recipient, the notion of donor consent was inherent in the process from the earliest times. As organ shortages worsened with the widespread use of cyclosporine in the 1980s, required request laws were introduced in the United States in 1987. These laws mandated that families be asked for donor consent. Such requests, however, were often ineffective or poorly done. As a result, "required referral" was introduced, which sought to make hospitals refer potential donation opportunities to appropriate regional authorities, such as the OPOs in the United States, and designated national authorities in most other countries. Further reforms, such as the Spanish model and the ODBC in the United States, replace regular hospital personnel with specifically trained expert teams who make requests of family members, relieving hospital workers of this difficult and unwelcome task.

Donor Clubs

While a donor club may be thought of as a sort of in-kind compensation mechanism provided by a private association, the idea is of enough independent significance to merit a separate treatment. In a "donor club," as defined here, individuals are offered membership that simultaneously requires that they agree, should they become a brain-dead patient and a suitable donor, to donate in a directed fashion to another member of the club in exchange for the privilege of receiving such a targeted donation should they themselves need a transplant. The club members increase their chances of obtaining an organ, if need be, in two ways. First, there are no "free riders" in the club, contrary to the situation in the public procurement and donation system. Second, club members are permitted to remain on the public waiting list, which (ironically) makes them free riders themselves because they have agreed to only donate to other club members.

The most famous donor club is LifeSharers, a U.S. organization that had over 14,000 members in 2010 but that has not yet facilitated a transplant to our knowledge. David Undis, the founder and director of LifeSharers, is direct about the benefits of joining: "We offer people a great trade: if you agree to donate your organs through LifeSharers after you die, we'll increase your chances of getting a transplant should you ever need one to live" (LifeSharers.blogspot). The morality of joining is vouched for by clinical ethicist Katrina Bramstedt of the California Pacific Medical Center, who states, "In the case of organ scarcity, it is appropriate to favor fellow organ donors over free riders" (LifeSharers.blogspot).

Donor clubs are theoretically similar to the mutual insurance pools of Schwindt and Vining (2003), in that they can be viewed as partial responses to a moral hazard problem inherent in most organ procurement systems. Generally, "free riding" plagues voluntary donation efforts, since those in need of transplants and those who provide them are different people. A patient needing an organ graft is usually not penalized for his or her previous lack of willingness to be an organ donor. Donor clubs, therefore, allow those who wish to increase their prospects of receiving a transplant, should the need arise, to do so by signaling their willingness to donate themselves in some binding fashion. Of course, such insurance-type programs have their own incentive problems, and some means must be found to prevent those who are most likely to need transplants from registering, in the same way that life or health insurance companies with open enrollment policies must limit excessive participation by sick people. In the case of LifeSharers, enrollees face a limited benefit period after enrollment during which they are ineligible to receive a directed transplant through the organization.

Obviously, donor clubs and similar mechanisms do provide valuable consideration to potential donors and would thus appear to be donor compensation schemes. The legal status of such organizations remains unclear, at least in the United States, although this status is at least partially the result of the lack of practical impact such groups have had to date. Even 14,000 members, as LifeSharers reported to have in 2010, is a comparatively small number given the extreme unlikelihood of any individual person actually becoming a donor. Perhaps 1 to 2 percent of hospital deaths occur under conditions allowing donation under current standards, and the probability of somebody dying in a given year is also generally very low until that person is quite old. Further, a "coincidence of wants" is necessary, since a donor club member would have to be a potential recipient—that is, compatible medically. This sequence of (low) probabilities, then, renders the likelihood of an actual transaction extremely low. (However, see Howard (2007) for a review of the probabilities involved and the financial impact of registrations.)

Although the LifeSharers organization is a private, nonprofit organization, the basic principles it uses could possibly be applied to larger, publicly sponsored organizations. For example, a national organization, with government funding, could be created to enroll potential organ donors under the primary donor policy. Enrollment would imply binding consent for donation under appropriate conditions. Those enrolling would receive first priority for available organs in the case of need. Those not enrolling would not be barred from transplantation de jure, but would receive second priority. If the enrollment levels were large enough, significant attenuation of the shortage could perhaps be achieved. All such proposals, however, are limited by the numbers of potential cadaveric donors.

Hidden and In-Kind Compensation

A variety of other innovations in the process of obtaining consent and encouraging donation deserve at least brief discussion here. To begin, organ donor registration can be advocated in public campaigns and made as easy as possible for the signatory. In some countries, donor cards allow for restricting donation to specific organs, and even to specific beneficiaries—for example, members of a donor club. These programs are an attempt to make a premortem statement of donor consent inexpensive and easy. Lacking legal force, such statements serve primarily as a tool for organ procurement officials to use in attempting to convince family members of the deceased's wish to donate. Some U.S. states have recently tried to use the presence of such cards to indicate consent regardless of the family's wishes. Evidence is reviewed by Mocan and Tekin (2005).

Several authors agree with Schwindt and Vining (1998), who suggested that registration as an organ donor should provide the registrant with priority to receive a transplant, should that need later arise. Such proposals, which they call a "mutual insurance pool," emphasize the reciprocal nature of transplantation and are thus more likely to appeal to those who might also favor stronger public claims to deceased-donor organs. (This idea is very similar to the donor club.) Howard (2007) questions the usefulness of such arrangements, since they introduce nonmedical considerations into the transplantation process and do not address the issue of family permission. On the other hand, the ability of such methods to "punish" free riders is quite appealing. Nonetheless, proposals such as this amount to a sort of in-kind compensation.

Strict economic logic implies that "compensation is compensation," that is, if the organ donor or the family receive valuable consideration (in the legal sense), then we have a violation of the standards imposed by NOTA in the United States and by similar laws elsewhere. Thus, discussions of compensation clothed as "funeral assistance" in Pennsylvania in 1994 were ultimately dropped when it was concluded such payment would be illegal.[4] Similarly, Georgia experimented with a reduction in driver's license fees for those electing to be organ donors, although this practice caused some concern about the motives of signees. Whatever the payment or waiver is called, if it is valuable consideration in the legal sense, then it is presumptively illegal, a conclusion applicable to the vast majority of countries.

Perhaps the most relevant example of monetary payments, classified as "funeral assistance" or assistance to fund repatriation of the donor's body, occurs in Spain. Rodriguez-Arias, Wright, and Paredes (2010) state the following:

> The Spanish *Real Decreto* 2070-1999 forbids any person from obtaining any kind of financial compensation for human organs and frames organ donation as a voluntary and altruistic act. Nevertheless, in some areas of Spain, basic funeral expenses and costs of repatriating of the bodies of foreign donors can be reimbursed to families if they do not have insurance to cover these sums. This process is regulated and funded by regional health authorities. (p. 1110)

The authors also believe that the use of these practices is debatable.

We previously touched upon the issue of giving waiting list preferences to organ donors. Donor clubs and many of the rules adopted by organ procurement organizations fall into this category. When living donors are included in the analysis, a very large number of potential benefits, short of money payment, are possible. Health insurance benefits, priority for future transplants or other medical care, reduction in terms of imprisonment or satisfaction of national service obligations, and many other types of compensation are conceivable. For the most part, such proposals have not been implemented anywhere outside of Iran, which also makes direct cash payments for donation. (Iran also provides health insurance and transplant priority.)

Although economists generally argue that direct monetary incentives are more efficient (i.e., achieve the outlined goal at the least cost) than other forms of compensation, there is one sense in which various sorts of in-kind or similar compensation might have a practical advantage. This advantage could arise from the ability of such forms of compensation to maintain public support for organ donation or to reduce the loss of solidarity, for example, that payments might cause. If such forces were strong, then donors could receive recognition through award of a package of benefits, of which direct money payment might not be the largest part. In such a case, of course, the economic logic would in fact require compensation mechanisms of this sort, since they would prove to be the most efficient.

Proposals to link organ donation to criminal penalties are unlikely to be morally acceptable anywhere, although China may obtain the majority of its organs for transplant from executed criminals (Bellagio Task Force, 2009). This practice has garnered widespread international censure, and it is almost certainly true that such programs reinforce many fears people have regarding organ donation. In this sense, it may be that China's practices generate a negative externality for donation in other countries because of its lurid character.[5] Living donation, too—although problematic from both medical and moral points of view, as long as the potential for cadaveric donation is far from exhausted—might be encouraged by certain forms of compensation that fall short of "buying an organ." Such a procedure could compensate costs and disadvantages actually incurred by the donor—for example, lost income and pain during transplant and recovery. In the United States, minimal assistance of this sort is permissible under the Organ Donation and Recovery Improvement Act (ODRIA). Such assistance, however, is targeted toward poor donors and is not guaranteed as an entitlement.

Reforms of the Organ Procurement System

Many proposals receiving serious support from policy makers in Europe and the United States, such as the Organ Donation Breakthrough Collaborative (ODBC) in the United States, represent fairly well-funded efforts to increase donation rates at below-average hospitals by spreading "best practice" procurement methods. The basic idea is to increase the donor recruitment and conversion performances of all hospitals up to the levels exhibited by the most efficient hospitals. The plausibility of this approach arises from the very large observed differences in donor yields across hospitals. For example, in the United States, so-called conversion rates—the rates at which potential brain-dead donors within target age groups are recruited as actual organ donors—vary among even the largest hospitals. Some large U.S. critical care facilities exhibited conversion rates below 10 percent in 2002, while typical hospitals managed rates of between 40 and 60 percent. Some large hospitals have even obtained conversion levels above 70 percent. Thus, the system-wide average rate of conversion, perhaps 50 percent for the United States and less for many European countries, masks important variation among hospitals (see Beard, Kaserman, and Saba, 2005).

In Europe and elsewhere, many commentators look to the "Spanish model" to provide guidance for reforming organ procurement practices.[6] In 2009, Spain achieved conversion rates of over 80 percent (Rodriguez-Arias, Wright, and Paredes, 2010). Extensive review of the Spanish model has identified a number of factors thought to promote these higher conversion rates, including trained donation officers, donor officer compensation partially tied to success, and so on. The Spanish experience is reviewed in Chapters 3 and 5. We reiterate here, however, that Spanish organ officials are able to provide compensation to donor families, and the significance of this aspect of the Spanish model is uncertain. Many authors have commented on the basic incentive problems with most regional or national systems of public organ procurement. Indeed, the existence of large variations in donor conversion rates provides evidence of the weakness of most systems' incentives. It is not our purpose here to review those critiques, but two conclusions appear warranted. First, reforms such the ODBC in the United States can almost certainly increase conversion rates and save lives by expanding transplantation. Second, such reforms are unlikely to provide enough additional organs to stabilize waiting lists except under particular conditions and in selected countries. We now try to substantiate the latter point.

The ODBC was initiated in the United States in the fall of 2003 and has a multistage implementation cycle. As a consequence, it is perhaps too early to determine its long-run effectiveness. However, Howard and colleagues (2007) provide a "difference in differences" analysis of 95 hospitals that participated in the first phase of the program. These hospitals received best practices instruction and other material support to increase donor conversion rates. Evidence suggests that the ODBC has produced increases in measured donation rates among participating hospitals. Howard and his colleagues find increases in conversion rates of around 8 percentage points, a significant effect.

Although initial results for the ODBC are encouraging, it is difficult to predict what ultimate effect the OBDC might have on the U.S. organ shortage. There are several reasons for this pessimism. First, the ODBC is directed toward deceased donors, and changes in deceased-donor transplants are documented to reduce living donation in the United States (Beard et al., 2012). Second, the extent of the shortage is a reflection of the aggregate performance of the entire procurement system, not just hospitals that participate in the ODBC program. Will we observe significant improvements in aggregate transplantation statistics due to the ODBC?

Further, the ODBC is a complex bundle of numerous initiatives and changes in practices, and the contributions of the various components of the initiative are largely unknown. For example, the collaborative program will accept donors up to age 70 (as will Spain). However, standard U.S. practice as late as 2006 was to classify donors over age 60 as expanded criteria donors (OPTN, 2006). This sort of adjustment, which is inevitable in a system characterized by chronic shortages, highlights a fundamental problem in all intertemporal evaluations of donor system performance: donor classifications, medical standards, drug availability, waiting lists, and other critical descriptions of the system are always at least partially endogenous, and, therefore, they evolve on their own in response to shortage conditions. It appears, though, that the ODBC has been able to increase donation performance over all classes of donors.

All initiatives that focus on cadaveric donors are, by definition, limited by the potential supply of suitable deceased persons. The question of whether the availability of qualifying cadavers is sufficient to stabilize waiting lists or to reduce them over some reasonable period of time has been considered in the literature.[7] Precise conclusions are somewhat difficult because of several complications, including potential responses of the waiting lists to changes in organ supply; ambiguity regarding the actual supplies of deceased standard criteria donors in various countries; substitution between deceased-donor and living-donor organs, especially for kidneys; changes in the utilization of expanded criteria donors and DCD donors, which may be accompanied by changes in the efficacy of immunosuppressive drugs over time; and forecasts of future growth in the transplant-eligible population. We treat most of these factors only briefly here because they receive fuller evaluation elsewhere in this book.

The notion that waiting lists may respond to changes in organ supply is not controversial, although the practical dimensions of this effect are quite unclear. Reynolds and Barney (1988) assume such effects are to be expected. This possibility is discussed by Howard (2007), and it frequently arises in discussions with transplant surgeons and other medical experts. Kaserman (2006) notes that this assumption appears at least partially motivated by the observation, true of all countries, that the number of patients on dialysis treatment far exceeds the number on transplant active waiting lists. However, Kaserman also reports that many of these dialysis patients are not suitable for transplantation, and indeed some refuse to be registered on waiting lists. The problem with all calculations of this kind is that the criteria used to place patients on waiting lists vary over time. Even the simpler question—how many patients, given current technology and regardless of cost, would medically benefit from a transplant of some specified quality?—has not been answered to our knowledge.

Nevertheless, Kaserman (2006) gives a detailed analysis of the possibilities for deceased-donor organs in the United States to cover the various organ shortages, defined in several ways based on additions to the waiting lists. For example, one could consistently define the shortage as the net addition to the waiting list over some period of time. Defined in this way, the shortage of kidneys in the United States, for example, is only about 8 percent of the total waiting list in recent years. One may object that such a measure is extremely conservative because it ignores deaths on the waiting list and makes no adjustment for living donors. To allow for such effects, Kaserman develops two additional shortage measures: adding a portion (one-half was used) of deaths and living-donor transplants to the change in the waiting list and having the final measure simply add all deaths and living donations. Kaserman suggests that such an approach will result in the measures bracketing the "true" value, which depends on unobservable magnitudes such as waiting list deaths that are not attributable to transplantation delay. Denoting these measures as S1, S2, and S3, Kaserman's figures for shortages of kidneys, hearts, and livers in the United States for 2001 are presented in Table 6.1.

We note immediately that the degree of shortage varies widely both by the definition applied and by the organ concerned. As mentioned before,

Table 6.1 Alternative measures of the organ shortage, 2001

Shortage measure	Kidneys	Hearts	Livers
S1	3,548	−9	1,940
S2	7,373	318	3,200
S3	11,917	645	4,460

SOURCE OF DATA: Kaserman (2006).

kidneys represent the most severe case of organ shortages, and most proposals that would successfully address the problem of kidneys would solve the problem for other organs using cadaveric donors. Each deceased donor provides, on average, about one and one-half kidneys for transplant but at most one heart.

Given these requirements, the critical issue becomes the potential supply of qualified deceased donors. Several authors have provided estimates for this supply, at least for the United States. Sheehy and colleagues (2003) provide estimates of 10,500 to 13,800 per year, using data on hospital deaths for the period 1997–1999. These estimates are generally consistent with those of other researchers (e.g., Evans, Orlans, and Ascher, 1992; Gortmaker et al., 1996; Guadagnoli, Christiansen, and Beasley, 2003). Most commentators appear to believe the annual supply of potential standard criteria donors for the United States lies somewhere between approximately 10,000 and 15,000, a figure that is not growing much, if at all. Miranda, Lucas, and Matesanz (1997) provide a discussion of potential donor supply in the international context. In most industrialized countries, it appears that plausible organ donors constitute perhaps 1 percent of all hospital deaths.

Using a median figure of 12,150 potential standard criteria donors for the United States, Kaserman found that 100 percent utilization of these donors would generally stabilize or allow reduction in active waiting lists for kidneys, hearts, and livers, at least when the S2 definition of the shortage is applied. However, the margins are very tight indeed, and relatively small changes in the assumptions applied can overturn this finding. Prospects are brighter, however, for other countries, most of which have far lower numbers of dialysis patients. Many nations have dialysis rates about one-third to one-half the U.S. rate. Spain, for example, exhibited about 4.9 kidney grafts per 100,000 citizens in 2003, a fairly high rate, but it had only about 49 patients per 100,000 on dialysis. The result has been stabilization, and even declines, in the waiting list for kidney grafts in Spain. It is precisely relationships of this sort that suggest that improvements in donor conversion rates may be a more credible approach to the organ shortage in Europe and elsewhere than in the United States. Indeed, recent experience among Eurotransplant member states, which suggests some stabilization in the waiting lists for kidneys, bolsters this view.

Another approach, based on a somewhat different concept of efficiency measurement, was offered for the United States by Beard, Kaserman, and Saba (2005), in which U.S. OPOs' donation performances were analyzed using the frontier (composed error regression) technique. In this methodology, the donor yield (per hospital death) for each OPO was analyzed in a regression context, in which unexplained variations in success are modeled as arising from two distinct sources: a two-sided random factor and a one-sided "efficiency" shock. Such efficiency shocks always work to reduce yields. This modeling approach has the advantage of allowing one to speak of "eliminating" inefficiencies among firms without assuming that efficiency implies 100 percent yields from potential donors: fully efficient performance just means performance close to that of the most efficient actors. Demographic and regional factors, including race, income, education, age, and transplant educational spending variables specific to each OPO collection area are utilized as explanatory variables to control for documented or potential effects such variables have on donation outcomes.

The study found that OPO inefficiency is a statistically significant factor in explaining donor rate differences. However, even if such inefficiency were to be somehow eliminated, the numbers of donor organs, although substantially increased, would still fall somewhat short of the amounts necessary to stabilize the kidney waiting list. The authors explain as follows:

> Assuming an optimistic 1.5 successful kidney transplants per donor, the complete and costless (and miraculous) elimination of this estimated inefficiency will fail to eliminate these shortages. . . . Thus, while eliminating inefficiency helps, it will only cause the [U.S.] waiting list to grow more slowly. (p. 23)

Untried reforms in the organ procurement system are many. For example, one could attempt to increase competition among procurement organizations by tying compensation to their success in harvesting organs. This is a practice in the "Spanish model." Rodriguez-Arias and colleagues (2010) note, "Spanish professionals are paid by their hospital an incentive bonus for organ donations they undertake." In a similar vein, one could modify the protocols used to distribute available organs by allowing patients at hospitals with good donor histories to receive preferences. This provides an incentive to the transplant center and its affiliated hospitals, but it also would presumably enlist patients in this process. Hospitals with good recovery rates would be favored by patients, while poor performers would presumably see their caseloads decrease. Likewise, transplant center compensation could be reduced as a registered patient waits longer for transplantation, thus encouraging more expeditious transplantation.

It is hubris, however, to believe that such efforts will always result in only the anticipated effects. The patterns of incentives and constraints are so complicated that, in many cases, it is difficult to realistically foresee all the ramifications of even relatively innocuous initiatives. For example, reforms that introduce further nonmedical criteria into waiting list priority will probably lead to some highly publicized disasters in individual cases. Similarly, payments to hospitals tied to patient time on the waiting list could encourage poorer matches to be accepted. The list of potential problems is lengthy.

An important issue in organ procurement organizational reform concerns the potential benefits, or costs, of supranational organizations such as Scandiatransplant and Eurotransplant. In contrast to the U.S. model, which utilizes 58 regional OPOs with some autonomy, and the national systems of many countries such as the Japan Organ Transplant Network, such supranational organizations provide opportunities to rationalize the distribution of organs for medical benefit. Thus far, relatively little can be said about this question. The performances of the various members of Eurotransplant, for example, vary widely. For example, Germany, the largest Eurotransplant nation, has exhibited relatively poor organ procurement performance, despite its very high level of public spending and highly skilled medical workforce. Austria, with similar demographics, has performed quite well and has "exported" a (relatively small) number of organs to other members. (The difference between German and Austrian procurement performance may be partially explained by the countries' different consent rules: informed consent in Germany versus presumed consent in Austria.) Eurotransplant has managed to stabilize its kidney waiting lists, although it is unclear whether the organization itself has contributed to this result. In any event, the potential role of such international mechanisms deserves careful review.[8]

The Use of Nonstandard Donors

Programs that seek to increase postmortem donation rates are limited by the absolute numbers of patients who die under circumstances consistent with donation. Traditionally, this has meant that the patient needed to suffer brain death in a hospital environment, and this in turn means that traffic accidents, strokes, and suicides have provided most standard criteria organ donors. There is some dispute about the numbers of such potential donors, and this question has been the subject of extended study. However, no one believes that anything short of a very high rate of organ harvesting from brain-dead donors will stabilize the U.S. waiting lists, at least for kidneys. Thus, the issue of increasing the number of potential donors is relevant to many of the reforms discussed here.[9]

An obvious and potentially extremely important technique for increasing the availability of organs for transplantation is to allow donation from an expanded pool of deceased patients. In particular, while previous transplant practices focused primarily on "standard criteria donors," the definition of this category has become more flexible, and we have witnessed a steady if unspectacular weakening of the standards in the United States and elsewhere. For example, as of 2007, a standard criteria donor (SCD) can be 70 years old, whereas donation over the age of 55 was once discouraged. Some relaxation of requirements is to be expected, given improvements in immunosuppressive drug therapy and postoperative care. The severe shortage of kidneys for transplantation, however, has also encouraged surgeons and patients to accept organs from previously shunned sources.

The growing use of both extended criteria donors (ECDs) and donors after cardiac death (DCDs) (previously termed "non-heart-beating" donors, or NHDs) is well documented and has been observed throughout the world. In the United States, the years 1996–2005 saw an increase in standard criteria kidney grafts of 33 percent, while ECD grafts rose by 70 percent and DCD transplants performed increased by around 700 percent (from 55 to 437) in the same period (OPTN, 2010). The utilization of these substandard sources is actually even greater than these figures suggest, because on average fewer kidneys are obtained from such marginal donors. For example, the average SCD provided 1.68 kidneys for transplantation in the United States in 2005 (figures for Eurotransplant and others are similar), while the typical ECD provided only 0.90 grafts in the same year (UNOS, 2006). For the Eurotransplant countries, we see a similar increase. In 2002, 70 NHB donors were used to support transplantation, and the total increased to 155 by 2006 (an increase of 121 percent). In the United Kingdom, DCD donors provided about 19 percent of all solid organ transplants in 2006 and represent a substantial portion of the growth in deceased-donor transplantation (U.K. Transplant Center, 2006). By 2009, DCD donors represented 36 percent of all organ donors in the United Kingdom (336 of 931) (U.K. Transplant Center, 2010). Donors are growing older, more obese, and less likely to have died from trauma, a pattern repeated in many countries.

Asia represents an important and exceptional case for the use of ECDs and especially DCD/NHB donors because of the long-standing reluctance of many people to accept the concept of brain death. In Japan, for example, passage of the Organ Transplant Law in October 1997 was expected to promote the use of transplants from brain-dead donors, a procedure that was formerly quite rare and legally suspect. However, no transplants under the law were carried out for a year and a half, with the first graft being performed in February 1999. Japan places fairly stringent requirements on the use of brain-dead donors, who must have organ donor cards, must have family consent, and must die in a designated hospital. The slow acceptance of such procedures partially stems from a famous heart transplant case in Sapporo in 1968, in which a surgeon was accused of murder. Japanese parliamentarian Tomoko Abe consistently introduced bills in the Japanese Diet seeking to have organ removal from brain-dead persons declared homicide (see Abe in Potts, Byrne, and Nilges, 2000). Data summarized by Kim Dongjin (2003) for South Korea indicate that passage of the Organ Transplant Law in 1999 failed to promote brain-dead donor grafts and that the number of brain-dead donors was actually decreasing. Thus, the use of live donors and nonstandard donors is a long-standing practice in many Asian nations. For different reasons (as discussed in Chapter 3), Iran also relies primarily, though not completely, on living donors.

Nonstandard deceased-donor organs have one large advantage and two large disadvantages. The advantage, of course, is that such organs are available in relatively abundant supply when the requirement of continuing heart function is dropped. If cardiac arrest victims can be used as organ donors, then the potential supply of donor kidneys, livers, and so on becomes many times larger. The Institute of Medicine of the United States estimated in 2006 that as many as 44,000 kidneys could be obtained from NHB donors. The problems, though, have thus far limited the beneficial exploitation of these resources. First, a considerable and difficult medical realignment would be required, particularly in emergency medicine. Potential donors who are heart attack victims often die under conditions that present enormous challenges to transplantation, and an expensive effort would be required to create and maintain a system for harvesting such organs in a timely manner. Second, studies indicate that recipients of organs from substandard donors have poorer medical prospects.

Sung and colleagues (2005) document significantly higher incidences of delayed graft functioning for patients receiving ECD kidney transplants, despite efforts to reduce "cold ischemic time" (CIT), a measure of the delay in transplantation. Graft and patient survival rates for ECD and NHD transplants are uniformly lower than for SCDs, although the gaps have been narrowing. However, the differences remain significant: one- three-, and five-year survival rates for SCD patients were 96 percent, 90 percent, and 83 percent, respectively (in 2004), while ECD recipients had corresponding rates of 90 percent, 81 percent, and 69 percent (OPTN, 2006). These figures must be digested cautiously, however, because the patients selected for ECD grafts are not identical to those selected for more standard criteria organs. However, it is certain that, taking the likely characteristics of ECD and DCD organs into account, one expects grafts performed using such organs to be less medically satisfactory in most cases.

It is possible that medical breakthroughs that would allow for a more liberal use of organs obtained from heart attack victims without meaningful penalty to the recipients could "resolve" the organ shortage. The greatest challenge is likely to be creation and funding of a system that allows for the efficient collection of such organs. Emergency room medicine would have to be fundamentally changed so potential donors would be very quickly identified and tested. Some form of "pretesting," through an organ donation registry, might reduce the time requirements, but clearly the problem will be a challenging one. It is a testament to the enormous difficulty such an approach encounters that, despite the shortages, usage of such donors remains limited, irrespective of whether or not the concept of brain death is accepted.

Paired Exchange and Donation to the Waiting List

Both paired organ exchange (also called crossover donation) and donations to the waiting list are able to exploit the willingness of a donor to make a living organ donation to a near partner, while overcoming an existing tissue mismatch between donor and recipient.

As explained in Chapter 3, living donation reflects, to some extent, the failure of the current organ procurement system. In the United States and many other countries, those in need of kidney transplants (and, to a lesser extent, liver transplants) are encouraged to provide their own living donors. This is not easy, of course, for two reasons. First, living donation involves some medical risks, although they are relatively small, and most people are not willing to undergo surgery, hospitalization, loss of income, and loss of ability to perform everyday tasks. Matas (2008a) discusses the medical risks in detail and concludes, "The overall mental and physical health of donors is comparable to that of the general population" (p. 18), meaning that donation entails no significant reduction in life expectancy or other long-term health indicator. Second, and more importantly, organs must match in the medical sense for the transplant to be successful. Generally speaking, tissue compatibility testing is based on blood type and tissue typing. So-called "histocompatibility" refers to the donor and recipient sharing enough alleles, which indicate genetic compatibility. The poorer the donor–recipient genetic match, the greater the chance of rejection and graft failure, and the higher the dosages of drugs necessary to prevent rejection episodes. As a result of this scientific reality, many individuals who need transplants are only able to recruit a willing donor who is unable to provide a compatible graft.

Paired exchange programs seek to utilize such willing donors by creating matches between internally incompatible donor–recipient pairs. In this manner, the willingness of the donors is not lost, and the pool of organs for transplant is extended. Problems of organizing and implementing such systems have been studied extensively by Harvard economist Alvin Roth, the leading expert in this area, who has derived many results for matching algorithms. Roth, Sönmez, and Ünver (2004a, 2004b, 2005a, 2005b, 2007) provide a detailed and highly technical analysis of the potential efficiency gains and performance of various matching systems for organ donation. It is clear that, given the medical parameters of the kidney matching problem, it is theoretically possible to obtain significant increases in grafts performed using living donors in this way. Even if exchanges are limited to just two donor–recipient pairs, substantial improvements are feasible using mechanisms that provide patients and physicians with strong incentives to truthfully participate in the matching protocols.

A major practical problem with the use of living potential donors is that such individuals, if testing proved them incompatible with the patient who recruited them, often can disappear from the system, their willingness to donate being frustrated by parochial circumstances. The implementation of a large-scale database that included medical particulars on such individuals could be used to arrange and support a great number of pairwise exchanges. Professor Roth estimates that as many as 2,000 additional kidney grafts from living donors could be performed in the United States annually if such a mechanism were implemented.[10] While results of that magnitude will not eliminate lengthening waiting lists, they are nevertheless highly desirable.

However, the practical preconditions for a paired organ exchange are considerable. These include the information required to form a reasonable group of pairs and the necessary medical facilities to perform the transplants. Every recipient must be assured that the donor of the other pair does is not behaving in an opportunistic way—in other words, that he or she is genuinely willing to make the donation. This means, in practice, that two pairs of individuals will simultaneously need four operating rooms. However, these preconditions do not seem to pose insurmountable problems.

In September 2004, the Renal Transplant Oversight Committee of New England approved the implementation of a pairwise exchange system for New England hospitals. Legal barriers to the use of such exchanges in the United States were effectively eliminated by a U.S. Department of Justice ruling on March 28, 2007, although it seemed unlikely that such a system would be successfully challenged anyway. Proponents of the system, including the prominent U.S. transplant surgeon Francis Delmonico, who has historically been an effective and dogged critic of compensation for donation, often point to the desirable incentive properties such systems offer to surgeons and patients and note that a general increase in the quality of matches will benefit everybody.

Interestingly, the paired exchange idea has found strong support among those most critical of compensation for organ donation. This may strike some observers as odd, since a patient who has a willing but incompatible donor is not much different from a patient who has the funds to buy an organ under a market system. Additionally, live donors do not benefit from the operation, and in fact, a very small number die from it. Thus, the issue of encouraging further live donation given incomplete use of cadaver organs may be problematic on ethical grounds. Regardless, the paired exchange concept is currently being used, although the number of transplants performed under these systems remains relatively small. In the United States, OPTN reports only 51 renal grafts from donor exchanges for the year 2006. The New England Program for Kidney Exchange (NEPKE), the lead actor in the U.S. effort, reported having facilitated 83 transplants as of December 2010. Efforts to expand the scope of this program in the United States are ongoing.

The liberal stance of the United States toward paired exchange of organs is now shared by many countries. In Europe these include Austria, Denmark, the Netherlands, Spain, Sweden, and Switzerland. In the United Kingdom, 32 kidney transplants arose from paired exchanges in 2009. In the Americas, Canada also belongs to the group. All have lifted previous restrictions to living donations, specifically to paired exchange programs. An important exception, however, is Germany, where crossover donation is forbidden on the grounds that it may entail a hidden "organ deal." Moreover, German legal scholars see a specific problem in a paired exchange of organs. As Thomas Gutmann (2006), a German law professor and specialist in organ transplant law, critically reports, "The problem rests in the perceived 'inalienable right' of a designated donor not to donate—that is, in the right for opportunistic behavior—even after the donor from the other pair has fulfilled the contractual duty to provide the organ" (p. 32). From a legal perspective, it is this problem that makes simultaneous organ transplants necessary.

Besides organizing paired exchanges of organs, it is also possible to use motivated donors in a less complicated way: by permitting a donation to the waiting list. The usual lack of an appropriate blood and tissue match between two partners can be overcome by such a procedure. In return for the donation, the intended recipient is prioritized on the waiting list. Such an approach would exhaust all existing willingness to donate an organ to a near partner, and it would shorten the waiting list. Thus, it would also benefit all other organ patients listed. However, the donor–recipient relationship would then become opaque, contrary to what is prescribed by the current rules for living donation. Moreover, the defenders of the current rules argue that a donation to the waiting list may implicitly entail an "organ deal." Thus, a living organ donation to the waiting list is permitted in most countries—but not in favor of a specific beneficiary. An exception, again, is Germany, where a donation to the waiting list—even without intended benefits to a specific person—is forbidden. Such a donation, so the German Enquète Commission on "Ethics and Law of Modern Medicine" (Parliament Proceedings, March 2005) claims, would lead to a fundamental change in the aims of the German transplant law that postulates subsidiarity of living donation. Such a principal change is regarded as unjustified, given "a low additional procurement of organs."

Donation to the waiting list in exchange for a preferential allocation of a postmortem organ to the intended beneficiary poses, however, one problem that Gutmann (2006) has pointed out: such a donation may exert a distributional effect on patients on the waiting list. In a majority of cases of incompatible donor–recipient pairs, the recipient is blood type O^-, while the donor is not. Blood type O^- is not only rare, but it has a unique feature: a patient who is blood type O^- needs a donor who is blood type O^-, but a donor who is blood type O^- is a "universal donor" (i.e., can donate to individuals with any blood type). (By contrast, a patient with blood type AB^+ (which is as rare as O^-) can receive donations from individuals with any blood type.) The additional organ donation as such takes pressure from the waiting list and benefits all patients listed. But the waiting blood type O^- patients, being in need of a donation from a type O^- donor, may be disadvantaged when the intended beneficiary of the donation to the waiting list is highly prioritized for quickly getting a blood type O^- organ.

Reducing the Need for Organs

By far the most appealing means of reducing the shortage of organs for transplant is reducing the demand for those organs. Economists refer to this as "demand side management." Because many (but by no means all) organ failures requiring transplantation are associated with other conditions that can be treated or prevented, it is theoretically possible to greatly reduce the number of patients needing donor organs. For example, renal failure is caused primarily by diabetes and untreated hypertension. In both cases, lifestyle changes and improved medical care can reduce the severity of the condition, delay its onset, or completely prevent its occurrence in the first place. While some causes of kidney failure, such as genetic abnormalities or cystic disease, cannot be avoided by behavior, diabetes and hypertension account for about 70 percent of all cases of kidney failure. One can make similar arguments, with varying degrees of plausibility, for the other solid organs.

The difficulty, of course, is that the lifestyle and public health factors that lead to diabetes or hypertension are of overarching significance themselves, and their impact dwarfs that of the organ shortage. The World Health Organization (2004) provides data on causes of death in member states, and leading the list are ischemic heart disease (12.4 percent), cerebrovascular disease (9.2 percent), lower respiratory disease (6.9 percent), and obstructive pulmonary disease (4.5 percent). Blockage of arteries leading to the heart and ruptures of blood vessels in the brain are common consequences of poor diet, untreated diabetes, or obesity. Thus, the conditions that most often lead to organ failure and transplant demand are often the same conditions that lead to death.

Are Piecemeal Reforms a Realistic Option?

It is clear that there are reform programs that offer the prospects for meaningful improvements in organ collection and transplantation. Especially attractive, if only due to their demonstrated feasibility, are best practice systems such as the ODBC and paired exchange programs. The Spanish model, although it does involve many elements found in best practice programs such as the ODBC, cannot be classified as a reform of the current system, since it involves an element of donor money compensation. For those societies for which any sort of compensation beyond the most nominal kind is infeasible, the issue arises as to whether, and to what degree, other sorts of reforms can achieve similar improvements. The introduction of the "presumed consent" rule, currently in force in only half of all OECD countries, could contribute to reducing the organ shortage by providing a "signal" in the sense of Abadie and Gay (2006) to potential donors and their families and by making it easier for the medical staff to get consent for donation. However, legal and even constitutional issues seem to interfere in many countries. People in all countries must accept expropriation of incomes and assets by way of taxation—without the possibility to "opt out." But when it comes to the procurement of organs after death, legal systems in some countries provide an ultimate protection, even in opposition to the will of the deceased.

The effectiveness of donor clubs is a question of size. In the United States, the private club LifeSharers is too small (and perhaps too young) to achieve visible results, but it is legally tolerated. Unfortunately, there are no similar, let alone larger, clubs in other countries. Most effective would be a state-run club for willing postmortem organ donors—with preferential access to organs for the members. But this approach presupposes that the ubiquitous medical intervention rule "health alone counts" is replaced by the rule "health and individual behavior count." The latter rule could constitute a step toward alleviating the organ shortage but also a step toward reducing medical professionals' definitional authority over health issues.

Due to fear of "buying an organ," monetary compensation to living donors is practically nonexistent in most countries. Loss of income during the transplant procedure, including preparation costs such as travel, boarding, and lodging, and, perhaps more importantly in individual cases, additional health and income earning risks, are usually not well compensated by public systems. Compensation by the beneficiary is likewise forbidden by law. Even preferential treatment, in case the donor later develops an organ failure, is prohibited in many countries, at least officially.

Paired exchange programs are viable and in limited use in some countries. But this mechanism is rejected in many countries on the grounds that a hidden "organ deal" could be involved. Similarly, a donation by a living donor to the waiting list with preferential treatment of the intended beneficiary (and with indirect benefits to all patients registered on the list) is permitted only in some countries. In others, the instrument is forbidden due to the risk there might be a "hidden organ deal."

Conclusion

Numerous reforms to the current system for obtaining donor organs have been proposed, and a subset of these have been implemented. Despite the demonstrated effects of several important innovations, severe shortages persist in many countries, so it is likely that no single reform will, by itself, resolve the problem, if by "resolution" one means at least stabilization of the waiting lists. The "presumed consent" rules, which assume that potential donors consent to donation unless they have specified otherwise when competent to do so, have been shown to be associated with measureable increases in cadaveric donation, although the magnitude of this effect remains under study. Many European countries lacking a common law tradition have implemented such rules. Nonetheless, it is widely conceded that physicians almost always ask permission of surviving family members before removing organs.

The fundamental problem is not that legal reforms or procurement reforms, such as the Organ Donation Breakthrough Collaborative in the United States and similar efforts in Europe, do not work. Rather, they improve matters by reducing the shortage. However, there is a danger that modest success with modest proposals will delay the implementation of reforms that can actually *eliminate* the problem. Opponents of compensation for organ donation often refer to a "slippery slope," which they fear society will pass down if payment is used to influence donor behavior. One can make the same argument, of course, about the nonmarket reforms reviewed in this chapter: by entertaining more and more innovations within the current paradigm, we find ourselves ever more willing to implement further schemes that, whatever their merits, are unable to eliminate the death toll the shortage creates.

Among the reforms evaluated here, the ODBC and the use of paired exchange systems appear to be the most promising. However, it seems unlikely that either is capable of stabilizing waiting lists for kidneys in the United States, although best practice implementation in Europe (at least in the Eurotransplant countries) does appear to go some distance in that goal. In any event, we should not, as Voltaire said, make "the perfect the enemy of the good," and innovations with demonstrated promise should be embraced immediately.

Two countries have, to an important degree, "solved" the kidney shortage problem, although the natures of their problems (and their solutions) differ. Spain has achieved very high rates of donation through a combination of means—the Spanish model that involves an element of compensation, although in no sense can this be considered the sole explanation for its achievement. Iran, also, is a "success story," at least historically, and Iranian transplantation relies heavily on compensated living donation. These two countries are so different and face public health challenges of such variable character that one can identify only two primary points on which they converge: success in increasing kidney transplantation rates and some degree of compensation to donors. Although this hardly can constitute proof in any strict sense, the suggestion is plain: successful reforms should carefully consider and use targeted rewards for donors in addition to other measures familiar from the Spanish experience and the ODBC.

In our view, the introduction of more radical reforms, including money compensation for postmortem and live donors, is imperative. Not only is there strong reason to believe that such a course will greatly increase the number of organs available for transplant, thereby saving thousands of lives, but a policy of donor compensation, if done correctly, will also save a great deal of money that could then be used to good effect elsewhere. Also, increased availability of cadaveric organ donors will decrease our current reliance on living donors. Thus, we feel it is important to implement credible trials using meaningful donor compensation. The final, and ultimate, barrier to this program is neither economic nor technological, nor even political, but ethical. It is to this ethical barrier that we now turn.

7

An Assessment of the Moral Basis of Alternative Organ Donation Rules

I have set before you life and death, blessing and curse;
therefore choose life, that you and your descendants may live.
Deuteronomy 30:19

Introduction

Abiding by organ donation rules, including prohibition against or permission to sell or buy human organs, requires ethicists to consider medical (including related economic) issues and requires medical professionals and economists to analyze the moral aspects of transplantation. Moral philosophers, theologians, leaders of global health institutions, and economists may disagree not only on how the acquisition and distribution of organs should be regulated but also on the proper means to address the question. This chapter, which was written by an economist, takes the standpoint that the moral virtues of public policies have to be assessed in light of the consequences of those policies. Thus, a consequentialist rather than a deontological standpoint is taken here.[1] Moreover, it seems important not to limit the discussion to the provocative "organ market" solution but to subject different institutional settings, including the ruling "altruistic" solution, to the same criteria. Thus, we not only evaluate the ethical arguments pertaining to the sale of human organs, but we apply exactly the same scrutiny to the existing zero-compensation procurement apparatus and to some intermediate alternatives.

A Glance at the Literature

The overwhelming majority of systematic analyses of the deficiencies of both the current organ donation system and the proposals to rectify it stem from legal scholars and economists, as well as from philosophers and ethicists. Scholars of medicine, theologians, and sociologists also have contributed to this literature, but less so. And all of them have considered moral arguments in assessing the current system and possible alternatives to it. Law scholars who are relevant in this debate include Jesse Dukeminier Jr. (1970), Timothy M. Hartmann (1979), Richard M. Boyce (1983), Lloyd R. Cohen (1989), Christian Williams (1994), Robert M. Veatch (2004), Michael H. Shapiro (2005), Steve P. Calandrillo (2005), Michele Goodwin (2006), David I. Flamholz (2006), Thomas Gutmann (2006), and Eugene Volokh (2007).

Economists entered the debate somewhat later, but since then they have been involved intensively. The most important contributors include Martin Brams (1977), Richard Schwindt and Aidan R. Vining (1986), James R. Rinehart (1988), Henry Hansmann (1989), Leon R. Kass (1992), Peter Oberender (1995), Friedrich Breyer (2002), Christian Aumann and Wulf Gaertner (2004), Charles B. Blankart (2005), David H. Howard (2005), and Gary Becker and Julio Elias (2008). The late David L. Kaserman (1947–2008) may be the economist with the largest academic publication record in organ donation matters. Moreover, he stimulated a number of other economists to work on this subject, including Andy H. Barnett, Dwayne Barney, Roger D. Blair, R. Larry Reynolds, and two of the present authors.

Academic philosophers and ethicists joined the field rather late, with the exception of S. Rottenberg (1971). Significant contributors include Gerald Dworkin (1993), Janet Radcliffe Richards (1996), Leonardo D. de Castro (2003), Charles A. Erin and John Harris (2003), Stephen Wilkinson (2003), Julian Savulescu (2003), Mark J. Cherry (2005), Hartmut Kliemt (2005), James Stacey Taylor (2005), Abdallah Daar (2006), and Gert van Dijk and Medard T. Hilhorst (2007). For a sociological analysis of the issue, see the works of Renee Fox and Judith Swazey (1992), Nancy Scheper-Hughes (2000), and Kieran Healy (2006).[2]

All of these writers consider the validity of the moral arguments that have been put forward to defend the current system, and they use moral arguments to assess alternatives. Some of them propose minor changes in the current system of organ procurement, and others argue in favor of more radical changes. While basing their analyses on widely shared moral convictions, they critically scrutinize the logic, plausibility, and evidence inherent in the arguments provided by the defenders of the present rules. The analyses of the academic philosophers stand out by revealing, often mercilessly, what is valid and what is shallow in the arguments put forward, as well as by applying old philosophical beliefs (e.g., by Aquinas, Locke, or Kant) to today's organ shortage problems (see, for example, Cherry (2005) or Taylor (2005)).

Serious academic defense of the current system, again based on moral and philosophical arguments, is conspicuous in its rareness. However, P. Singer (1973), Charles Fried (1978), Arthur Caplan (1984), M. Radin (1987), M. Broyer (1991), G. M. Abuna (1991), J. B. Dossetor and V. Maneckavel (1992), and William E. Stempsey (2000) have all addressed this topic.

The majority of medical practitioners and transplant surgeons were and are the strongest supporters of the current system. Francis Delmonico and Arthur Caplan are prominent in this regard. By contrast, medical scholars and practitioners who argue in favor of profound reforms include, for example, Arthur Matas (2008a, b) and Sally Satel (2008).

The arguments, both pro and con, on moral, logical, and empirical grounds have been exchanged, repeated, refined, and subjected to critical scrutiny over many decades. They are so well known now that none can be considered any author's "private property." Thus, we treat most of these arguments as public property—which nevertheless means that our discussion is based to a very large extent on the works of other scholars.

Organ Donation Rules and Assessment Criteria

We consider three institutional settings: the current system in most industrialized countries, the current system with a number of modifications, and a system that permits outright compensation to organ donors for their willingness to donate. These regulatory frameworks are scrutinized with respect to their effects on six criteria: reducing avoidable death and suffering; respecting individual self-determination; avoiding insulting the moral feelings of fellow citizens; being fair to all; doing no harm; and avoiding a "slippery slope." All of these factors are understood here as representing widely shared values. One can plausibly suggest that an overwhelming majority of citizens—of the industrialized countries and even of the whole world—would subscribe to the values these criteria represent, although people might add other values and might attach quite different positive weights to each.

Before we describe the three regulatory frameworks and the evaluation of their moral qualities, some comments about the evaluation criteria are in order. *Reducing avoidable death and suffering* is obviously a goal of moral relevance and substance. A failure to prevent avoidable deaths, so as to tacitly accept them, demands the strongest sort of defense from those arguing for the continuation of the present system. *Individual self-determination* is also a value shared by most people in the world, although its perceived and tolerated limits—toward the family, clan, society, and public authorities—may be defined quite differently.

Avoiding insulting the moral feelings of fellow citizens plays an important role in the discussion and seems to be a major reason why many of those who define the rules of organ procurement resist compensation proposals. It should be mentioned here that the notions they put forth in that respect—for example, commodification of the human body, damage to human dignity, or simply repugnance—all imply costs inflicted on persons not directly concerned with organ donation, either as a donor or as a recipient of an organ.

Being fair, again, is obviously a moral idea. A fairer world, *ceteris paribus*, is not only a better but a morally superior world. However, fairness is a distributional and, thus, a difficult moral category. It is not just fairness between patients who need an organ, but also between current and future patients, between recipients and donors of organs, between cadaveric and living donors, and between those who do and do not care about donation laws that is at stake here. We consider fairness to be a set of societal rules that people would plausibly subscribe to as long as they can hide behind a "veil of ignorance"—in other words, as long as they do not know about their later concrete situation (income status, health status, etc.).

Doing no harm is one of the fundamental principles of the Hippocratic Oath. Doing harm, at its highest level, is causing avoidable deaths and injuries. But harm can also be inflicted on those who are on dialysis, which can be eliminated by organ transplantation. Harm, even if relatively small, is also done to living donors. And this can also be regarded as "unavoidable," given the organ need of patients, but not if the potential of cadaveric donors is not exhausted.

Finally, *avoiding a "slippery slope"* can be regarded as a relevant moral virtue here, specifically when the slope is perceived to lead into a moral abyss—for example, the person who first sells a kidney, then an eye, and finally himself into bonded servitude. However, we shall see that other regulatory systems, too, have their own moral slippery slopes.

The Current System of Organ Donation

Despite several differences among countries, we can sensibly speak about the current system of organ donation that prevails at least in rich Western countries. International institutions such as the World Health Organization or the International Society of Nephrology, together with the World Transplantation Society in their Declaration of Istanbul (2008), try to establish the basic rules of that system on a global scale. In practice, four main rules define the current system. First, no one is forced to donate an organ—for example, a kidney. Second, if a person is prepared to provide an organ, it must be a true donation—that is, an altruistic act or an act of solidarity. Buying and selling (living or post-mortem) organs or compensating the donor financially is forbidden. Third, in practice, the decision of the bereaved—and not that of the deceased—takes priority in allowing any postmortem donation. Fourth, the decision of which patients get an organ is based solely on medical considerations. This implies equal treatment of patients in two important respects: rich and poor patients have the same chance of getting an organ, and patients who need an organ *and* have previously declared their willingness to donate an organ do not get preference over patients who have refused to be donors.

This system has three important practical consequences. First, the current widespread shortage of organs leads to the deaths of thousands of those on waiting lists and years of suffering on dialysis. Second, living donations have become routine, although the potential supply of cadaveric organs is, in most countries, not exhausted. Third, the black market for human organs—mainly kidneys from living donors—subjects both donors and recipients to avoidable health risks and exploitation.

Before we consider the moral virtues or deficiencies of both these rules and their consequences, it seems fair to ask whether the rules are really to blame for the negative results. A proponent of the existing system may argue that it is not the system as such but, for example, the lack of funds for more awareness campaigns to inform the public about organ donation that is causing death and suffering. Evidence shows that awareness campaigns, which have been used for at least 30 years, have had very little effect. While some reforms and innovations have resulted in measurable improvements (see Chapter 6), few believe that the current procurement systems are adequate. (However, one can point to Spain as an example of the potentially large returns to highly focused and competent cadaveric procurement efforts. Spanish procurement officials, however, can use monetary incentives to reward donors.) Thus, it seems we must conclude that the primary constraint on the current system of organ procurement is not woefully inadequate funding but rather the nature of the system itself. The first of the rules governing our current system, the *rule of no force in donating*, is fully consistent with individual self-determination because it protects the individual against state power exercised in the name of social well-being. However, in a way, this rule may also be just as responsible for the undersupply of organs that could be mitigated by, for example, postulating a public property status for organs of deceased persons. Such a postulate, however, is usually thought to harm the principle of self-determination.[3]

The *rule of altruistic donation* is, without doubt, the main factor responsible for the persistent shortage of organs, for deaths on the waiting list, and for the failure to exhaust the full potential of postmortem donations, as well as for the black market in organs. Moreover, disallowing voluntary contracts for organ provision undermines individual self-determination. This may be regarded as a restriction of minor significance when only the potential seller of the organ is considered. After all, he or she does it "only for the money." Of perhaps greater moral significance—and less often mentioned in the literature—is the legal barrier placed before a terribly sick end-stage renal disease patient who wishes to restore his or her health by obtaining a kidney. What such a patient is denied is nothing less than the right to pursue good health and happiness. One can even say that his or her right of self-defense is denied (Volokh, 2007). Insisting on altruistic—that is, financially unrewarded—donation is not only unfair to the patient in need of a kidney, but it also causes postmortem donation rates to be below their medical potential, since all useful organs are not collected, and leads to an unnecessarily high number of living (altruistic or materially motivated) donations. Finally, this rule has given rise to a (decidedly nonhypothetical) slippery slope: the black market for kidneys (see Chapter 3). Thus, the assessment of the moral virtues of the no-compensation rule leads us to a rather negative preliminary result.

The proponents of the current system are, of course, aware of the morally problematic implications of their position. Thus, they require moral arguments that justify the negative consequences caused by the rules and that permit them to evade the question of their personal responsibility. Before we consider these arguments, we must ask whether the moral deficiencies (and the ineffectiveness) of the current system can be improved by certain modifications that fall short of "paying for organs."

The Current System with Possible Modifications

The core of the current system, the altruistic donation rule, may perhaps be accommodated by the introduction of new or changed elements. Such reforms may not only make the current system more effective, but they may also improve it from a moral point of view. We consider eight possible reforms:

1. A change in the role of the bereaved
2. A change in (a part of) the organ distribution rule
3. Legally authorized public ownership of postmortem organs
4. An enforced decision for or against donation
5. Organizing a "club" solution
6. Permission of and support for "crossover" donations
7. Full compensation of living donors for the costs and risks they incur
8. An attempt to seriously address obesity as one of the main causes of organ (kidney) failure

Limiting the Strong Position of the Bereaved

In most countries, the deceased's family has power over most transplant decisions. Their consent for explantation of organs is, in practice, sought after by the medical staff irrespective of whether the consent of the deceased is legally "assumed" or "presumed" (but with the possibility to "opt out"), whether the family must be "informed," or whether the family's consent must be "required." In some cases, the family successfully overruled (i.e., nullified) the deceased's written declaration in favor of donating his or her organs. The family's suggestion that the deceased had changed his or her mind shortly before death often seems to be sufficient reason for the medical staff to no longer pursue an explantation of organs. Let us consider an example. A wealthy woman stated in her will that half of her fortune should go to her church and the other half should go to her family members. After her death, do you think any competent lawyer who was probating her will would accept the family's statement that just before her death, she told them she wanted the church to get only one-third and the family to get two-thirds? In organ donation, however, the family makes the final decision. The overwhelming role of the deceased's family may thus amount to a violation of the principle of self-determination.

In most cases, however, no one knows what the deceased's wishes were or even whether he or she had made a decision at all. In such cases, it seems to be straightforward and fair to transfer the power of self-determination to the next of kin and to let the family make the decision. A "no" decision—as so often happens—increases the shortage of organs, but, on the other hand, it protects the family from any further attempts by the medical staff to get permission for "harvesting" the organs. Thus, such a policy shows respect for the feelings of the deceased's family. Limiting the family's decision power to only those cases in which the will of the deceased is not documented would increase the availability of organs and respect the right of the deceased's self-determination.

The German law scholar Thomas Gutmann (2006), in his critique of the current German Transplantation Law of 1997, looks at the problem from a constitutional point of view: "An opting-out solution, after explicit information and with effective documentation of the decision to opt out, seems to be constitutionally less problematic than a secondary own decision right of the deceased's family" (p. 162).

Change of Organ Access Rules for the Benefit of the Willing Donor

The distribution rule of access to organs based solely on medical grounds is plausible at first sight and widely shared, specifically with respect to the fact that income and wealth are not factors. However, there are two complications. The first is that the organ allocation principles applied in many countries are *not* of a purely medical nature, and the second is that common allocation rules can be considered unfair in at least one important respect.

The Fiction of Medical Allocation Criteria   In his preceding statement, Gutmann argues that the allocation of organs according to so-called "medical criteria"— as prescribed in many transplantation laws, including the German law—is fiction. He discusses the following allocation criteria that both Germany and Eurotransplant use:

- Time spent on the waiting list (or under dialysis) increases the chances of getting an organ. Under medical criteria, this should count negatively.
- Preference is given to persons who are highly immunized or have, due to other reasons, less chance of getting a compatible organ. This may be legally and ethically justified, but it is inconsistent with best medical practice.

- In Eurotransplant, preferences are given to patients from countries that are net suppliers of organs, such as Austria. Again, this cannot be justified on medical grounds.

None of these criteria can be justified on medical grounds, but it cannot be said that they are not justifiable. Any justification, however, should be based on ethical and legal grounds. Gutmann says the following:

> It cannot be disputed *that* normative principles determine organ allocation, . . . only *which* competing principles should be applied and *who* in *which procedure* has to decide about the relative weight of the principles. . . . The German legislature attempted to play down this insight by making organ allocation a medical decision. . . . The legislature has refused to take up the responsibility to determine the criteria according to which chances to live are distributed to seriously sick patients and has, instead, created a network of stakeholders which makes it difficult to see who, in effect, decides about organ allocation. (p. 116; italics in original)

This critique seems to apply to many other countries as well.

According to Gutmann, the criteria justified by the German constitution are those of individual need and urgency. However, this means that long-term transplant success (i.e., medical validity) cannot be determined. The consequence is that "allocation models which aim to maximize the utility of the collective of organ patients are fundamentally called into question" (p. 133). Thus, the utilitarian approach to the organ shortage problems is ruled out—but without an explicit constitutional base.

Unfair Treatment of Willing Postmortem Organ Donors   The equal access rule implies that the alcoholic who has damaged his liver, the smoker who did harm to her lungs, or the murderer who needs a kidney are all treated the same as people who do not drink alcohol, smoke, or commit murder. However, the *practice* of organ allocation seems to deviate from this rule in some countries. Instead of pursuing further the general moral problems of equal treatment in such cases, we consider a specific example: the fairness consequences of equal treatment of unequal donor card signatories.

In all countries, only a minority of persons have signed any type of organ donor card (or registered in other ways for donation) indicating their wishes regarding postmortem donation. Most of that minority express a willingness to donate postmortem, but some express an unwillingness to do so. The vast majority, however, have not signed such a card and have probably not made a decision about this question. Typically, all persons in these three categories—affirmation, disapproval, or no decision—are treated equally when the need for an organ arises.

Using accepted moral rules, we should not have any problem with an individual position that says, "I do not want to donate an organ after death" or "I do not want to receive an organ during my lifetime." However, and luckily for the "nondonor," he or she will not be forced to abide by the latter. For the established organ allocation rules, it is irrelevant whether the patient who needs an organ has or has not declined postmortem donation. This strange form of "equal treatment" can be compared to an insurance policy in which everybody is entitled to the benefits of the insurance, but no one has to pay the premiums. Thus, abolishing the equal treatment rule for nondonors would enhance the system's fairness and would contribute to reducing the organ shortage.[4]

Public Ownership of Postmortem Organs

Public ownership of cadaveric organs has been proposed repeatedly in the literature (e.g., Dukeminier, 1970; Spital and Erin, 2002; Giordano, 2005; and Kreis, 2008). The law scholar Christian Williams (1994) provides moral and legal arguments in favor of public ownership of deceased organs but eventually supports the somewhat softer solution of "presumed consent." Public ownership of deceased organs (or "conscription") would relieve the medical staff of disagreements with the bereaved and would allow society to more fully exhaust the potential of postmortem organs. This increase in deceased-donor organs would reduce the present organ shortage and, in some countries, even eliminate it, at least for the time being. These positive effects are of moral relevance because avoidable deaths would thereby be reduced, and "doing harm" to living donors could perhaps be curtailed. On the other hand, such "confiscation" could be regarded as a drastic blow to the principle of self-determination and could be termed state-enforced expropriation of body parts. However, citizens willingly accept many forms of expropriation—for example, paying taxes.[5]

In any case, fairness would require that society make some exceptions to a confiscation policy. Deeply felt religious reasons against organ donation, for example, could be respected by permitting those who qualify to opt out. In this case, however, there would presumably be no right to receive an organ should it ever be needed. Thus, in practice, the public ownership rule would amount to a rigorous presumed-consent solution with a secured right to opt out.[6]

Enforced Decision about Postmortem Donation

Previously, we mentioned the unfairness of one part of the current distributional rule—namely, that patients are placed on the waiting list irrespective of their former (and perhaps even current) willingness to become an organ donor after death. An exclusion of the outspoken nondonors from the waiting list would not only be possible—if they are outspoken—but undoubtedly would also increase the fairness of the system. However, a much larger problem arises with those who have either never made a decision about the issue or have not told anyone what they want, which is the case with the majority of people. A solution to this problem may be a publicly enforced individual decision for or against organ donation, often called "mandated choice."[7]

Such a choice—even if it stands alone and has no further consequences—may increase postmortem donations simply through enhanced public awareness about the issue of the organ shortage. But, compared to a "club" solution, it will be a relatively weak improvement in the situation. However, if an individual choice concerning the willingness of postmortem donation is not only made but also documented in a public registry, hospitals could find out donor status without having to consult the family at all.

Although mandated choice enhances fairness and contributes to lowering the organ shortage—even if not combined with any consequences of the decision—such a policy change meets stiff opposition in many countries. For example, in 2001 the Swiss parliament rejected a mandated choice solution on the grounds that this "would put force on an individual to consider his or her own death because the use of the opting-out right is only possible after having acquired relevant information and thought about the problem" (quoted in Gutmann, 2006, p. 161).

In December 2011, the German parliament followed similar reasoning and decided against a mandated choice solution. A consensus could only be reached about a "declaration" solution, where health care insurers must ask their enrollees about postmortem organ donation. The insured may answer "yes," "no," or "don't know," and he or she has the right not to reply at all. The respondent's answer, however, will have no impact if he or she should ever need an organ.

Obviously, Gutmann's arguments did not convince the German parliamentarians. Gutmann suggests that any liberal constitutional state regularly demands "minimal solidarity duties" from its citizens, even when the citizens meet as strangers. As an example, he refers to the German Criminal Code that stipulates that nonassistance to a person in danger (*unterlassene Hilfeleistung*) is punishable.

Using this rule, he concludes that it must also be acceptable for the citizen to "examine whether he or she can or will be an organ donor or not" (p. 160): "A 'right simply to be left alone' and not to be confronted with the suffering of others or one's own death is not in line with even minimal solidarity duties to other citizens" (p. 160). Gutmann further argues that such an extremely egocentric rule would be self-contradictory: "If one denies the government the right to motivate the citizens *with arguments* to make use of their right for self-determination in matters of their own body, then that would also deny the concept of the citizen as a morally responsible person—which is, however, the basis of democratic rule" (p. 161; author's italics).

Organizing a "Club" Solution

Citizens who decided "pro postmortem donation" would effectively become members of a "club," similar to the private donation club that already exists in the United States (LifeSharers). An individual would be a registered postmortem donor, irrespective of what his or her next of kin might say. If the member ever needs an organ, he or she would receive the same treatment as other club members but would get preferential access to the waiting list vis-à-vis non-members. If the individual chooses not to participate in the club, he or she will not be required to donate an organ and will either not receive an organ if the need ever arises or will be placed lower on the waiting list.[8]

When making a decision like this, most people will probably rationalize that the chances are slim that they will ever need an organ or donate an organ after death, but if the benefit is better access to an organ, then it is a good idea to join the club. It is true, however, that many people believe that signing a donor acknowledgment might lead to premature termination of care. Nevertheless, it seems highly likely that many persons would sign the club membership, that the availability of cadaveric organs would increase, and that the fairness of organ distribution would be improved. Thus, this mechanism seems to contribute to an improvement in the "moral balance" of the current system.

Two questions, however, must be addressed. First, is the state permitted to enforce such club membership decisions? Second, what happens if an individual changes his or her mind? The public enforcement of an individual decision either to join or not to join the organ donation club does, indeed, narrow the range of individual self-determination—namely, by removing the possibility of making no decision at all. But most citizens will admit that this restriction is a minor one (at least compared to paying taxes) and that it enhances fairness. To limit the restriction on self-determination to a minimum, the state might say that making the decision is only an offer and not an obligation to decide right now—or to decide at all. But with respect to fairness to other citizens, a non-decision will be treated, for the time being, as a contra-decision.

It can be expected, however, that some people will change their minds in their lifetimes, and that possibility can be troubling. In particular, the economic phenomenon of "adverse selection" is likely to occur. Charles Blankart (2005) suggests a method where citizens are free not only to have and keep their opinions, but also to change their minds—and bear the consequences. Consider this hypothetical case: Norman joined the club when a decision was mandatory. For a time, then, Norman belonged to the group of potential donors and potential receivers of organs. A few years later, Norman decides to leave the club, which is his right whether or not he received an organ while he was a member. (We know Norman was never a donor because he is still alive.) As long as Norman is not a member of the club, he will be neither a donor nor a recipient. But what happens if, a year later, Norman decides to rejoin the club? Maybe he has been having kidney problems and expects he may require a transplant at some point. But the club, in the interest of its members, should avoid attracting primarily "bad risks"—that is, individuals who are more likely to become recipients than donors. To overcome this problem of "adverse selection," as it is called in insurance markets, the club could introduce a waiting period during which the new (and old) member would only be a potential donor, not a recipient. The longer the period of time the person was not a club member, the longer the waiting time will be. And the sooner the club member decides to be a donor, the shorter the waiting time will be.

A similar waiting period would apply for somebody who chose not to join the club when initially invited, but later decided to join. Thus, the freedom to change one's mind is respected, but to be fair to club members, such a decision should have some stipulations.

Crossover Donation and Donation to the Waiting List

Willing living organ donors often are blood and tissue incompatible with the intended beneficiary. A solution to this problem can be found by connecting two (or more) donor–recipient pairs and organizing "crossover" donations. Such procedures are already performed in some countries, such as the United States, the United Kingdom, and the Netherlands (e.g., in Rotterdam). In other countries, such as Germany, it is forbidden because the law stipulates that a *personal* relationship must exist between the (living) donor and the recipient. Moreover, it is argued that a crossover exchange, implicitly, might entail a hidden "organ deal." The principles of fairness and self-defense, however, speak in favor of lifting the ban on crossover donations and even supporting such donations by publicly run donor registers.

A living organ donation to the waiting list in exchange for a preferential allocation of a postmortem organ to a (tissue- or blood-incompatible) relative in need of an organ is similarly forbidden in most countries. (To our knowledge, it is practiced only in some U.S. states.) Again, there can be no personal relationship between the donor and the direct recipient (only between the donor and the intended but indirect recipient), and an organ deal also might be involved.

Moreover, it is sometimes argued that donation to the waiting list is "cutting in line." This argument is faulty, however, because an additional organ is brought into the pool.[9] On the other hand, the argument points to a relevant distributional effect if the donor supplies an organ of a ubiquitous blood group, while the intended recipient needs and receives an organ from a rare blood group.[10] In this plausible case, those patients on the waiting list who need such a rare organ would be at a disadvantage because their waiting time would increase. However, failing to give (at least some) priority to the intended beneficiary would also be unfair because the consequence of a lower number of available organs is disadvantageous to other patients on the list. A solution may be found in carefully defining the priority the intended beneficiary receives in such cases.

Full Cost Compensation to Living Donors

In some countries—for example, Germany—the no-compensation rule is enforced very strictly. A living donor not only gets no compensation for his or her willingness to donate an organ, but the donor is not even compensated for the actual costs and risks he or she incurs before, during, and after the transplant operation. Such costs include loss of income and travel expenses, but also subsequent health treatment expenditures caused by the operation. In some countries, this type of compensation is provided, but it is kept confidential so as not to raise suspicions about an "organ deal."

This stance even falls short of the organ donation rules stipulated by the Declaration of Istanbul (2008). On the one hand, the Declaration condemns organ "trafficking" (using fraud, coercion, abduction, deception, and so forth against the donor) and "transplant commercialism" (all forms of paying for organs). But on the other hand, the Declaration is very outspoken and detailed in demanding "comprehensive reimbursement of the actual, documented costs of donating an organ," including foregone income of the donor.

Gutmann (2006) explains this reluctance toward cost compensation of (living) organ donors with the very narrow definition of *altruism*—as used, for example, by the influential Enquète Commission of the German Parliament on "Ethics and Law of Modern Medicine" in 2005. In it, altruism is defined as "a disinterested, self-forgetful activity without self-interest." Gutmann, however, argues that within a constitution of law and freedom (*freiheitlicher Rechtsstaat*), a citizen is permitted to pursue selfish intentions such as satisfying psychic needs or needs of the soul, heightening one's self-confidence, or acting as an example to others. According to Gutmann, to qualify as "altruistic," an organ donation must only be devoid of pure commercial motives—for example, any intention of self-enrichment. This, in turn, means that full compensation of the actual costs and risks the donor has incurred should be considered as being above suspicion of commercial motives or self-enrichment.

However, the simple provision of full compensation for actually incurred costs and risks would probably have a rather limited effect on donation rates. If the health system does not provide such compensation, the organ patient could do it, at least when he or she was financially able. But publicly providing this type of minimum compensation is a requirement of fairness to the donor. Moreover, failing to do so makes it impossible for some people with low incomes to donate at all.

Fight against Obesity

Obesity (together with hypertension) is one of the main causes of kidney failure. We typically observe smaller organ shortages in countries with less obese populations. To take obesity seriously from a public policy point of view, we must regard it the same as smoking—namely, as an individual and public health risk—and run similar public awareness campaigns. The positive effects on the availability of organs and on deaths on the waiting list could be significant and morally relevant. These benefits, though, would only occur in the distant future.

A Modified Altruistic System—a Realistic Option?

These reforms to the current system, if implemented correctly, would probably significantly increase (postmortem) donation rates, although even very high levels of deceased donation are unlikely to stabilize the waiting lists in most countries. Is it realistic, though, to expect the arguments for reform to prevail in the "real world" in which such decisions are made? Many eloquent defenders of the current system fight not only for retaining the ban on donor compensation but also for preserving the allocation rule: "Individual behavior should not play any role in organ allocation." If this rule is strictly applied, willing donors will not receive preference on the waiting lists, and being an explicit nondonor will not incur any negative consequences. One of the most powerful "modifications" short of donor compensation—the club solution— would be impossible.

However, it seems likely that a shortage of kidneys, for example, would persist in many countries, even if virtually *all* of these reforms were implemented. Just as no one suggests the current system is optimized and cannot be improved, no one should claim that because improvement is possible within the current system, we should not evaluate more fundamental changes. In the next section we assess the arguments usually raised against what we believe is the most important and useful fundamental reform: donor compensation.

The Arguments against Permitting Organ Donor Compensation

As discussed in previous chapters, it is highly probable that payments for the willingness to donate a postmortem or a living organ would act to relieve the shortage of human organs for transplantation. In some years' time, shortage-caused deaths on waiting lists and unnecessary suffering on dialysis could be largely eliminated. Black markets would no longer be needed with their dire health risks, financial consequences for both donors and recipients, and unfair effects on poor patients. The potential for postmortem donation could be more fully exhausted, which would moderate living donations and the (small) harm done to living donors. Nevertheless, opponents of donor compensation, even if convinced that it would end the shortage, defend the current rules and oppose compensating the organ donor, using a number of recurrent arguments that we will now consider.

Allocation Rules Would Change

A common charge leveled against compensating donors is that with compensation, the way organs are allocated to patients would change in immoral ways. Income and wealth of the recipients, for example, would influence the allocation of organs. This complaint, however, conflates the use of compensation to help obtain organs and the methods used to allocate them among patients. There is no reason why income should influence the allocation of organs if compensation is allowed. It is, ironically, the current system, with its severe shortages and long waiting lists, in which income and wealth play an important role in allocating the organs—namely, via the black market. In a well-designed compensation system, there would be no black markets, and the allocation of organs would become a purely public affair. The notion of a strict and publicly maintained system of organ distribution is an element of all realistic reform proposals that include donor compensation. Compensating donors is different from using the price mechanism to allocate organs.

Hurting Human Dignity

While donor compensation need not lead to any changes in organ allocation principles, the question of human dignity under compensation requires serious consideration. The most common claim is that financially compensating a willing organ donor is tantamount to buying the organ in question, and that is considered inconsistent with the human dignity of the contractual partners and, therefore, should be forbidden. Does this claim have merit? Obviously, we should not conclude that merely donating, receiving, or transplanting organs per se undermines human dignity. Janet Radcliffe Richards (1998) cited the confusion of some claimants who intend to argue against paid donation but end up arguing, in effect, against all organ donations. Some people may indeed feel uneasy about organ donation in general and may not want to receive or donate an organ. The point is that it is *paid*, in contrast to *unpaid*, donations that are said to cause harm to human dignity.

The central concept motivating the distinction between unpaid and paid donations is the "commodification" of human body parts. A paid donation is said to commodify human organs—that is, it converts organs into articles of trade, deprives the organs of spiritual value, reduces the human body to a set of spare parts, and ultimately destroys human dignity. Most proponents of these arguments feel the only solution is to ban the buying and selling of organs. Let us first address the first part of this argument.

The belief that human organs should not be commodified is undoubtedly an acceptable individual conviction. (Whether this conviction should be forced on other people is another matter; we address this later.) Many people share a similar conviction in other respects—for example, that sex should not be commodified (by prostitution) or that motherhood should not be commodified (by paid surrogate motherhood). But apart from the question of who makes the rules, we should also examine legally tolerated cases of commodification.

The commodification of blood and sperm is a fact of life in most countries in the world. Surrogate motherhood is accepted in many countries, and in some, even paid surrogate motherhood is permitted. Organs are, in most countries, "protected" from commodification, but the services of the medical staff and the goods (commodities) used in transplantation are not. Under more narrow inspection it becomes clear that even a human organ, after having been donated altruistically, becomes a commodity in the resulting transplantation procedure. The difference between the zero price the (postmortem or living) donor receives and the (hypothetical) market value of the organ increases the value of all the other transplant activities by this amount. In other words, the unpaid value of the organ is capitalized in the incomes of the individuals and institutions involved in the transplant process—except for the donor.

Human organs can, indeed, be considered of higher significance than even the most skilled medical care, and our awe at their function is understandable. However, similar regard is often accorded to the healing services of the physician who saves a child's life. To the parents, at least, the physician performed a miracle. We consider the child's restored health as a great and unearned gift, and we feel deep respect and gratitude toward the doctor, but nevertheless, we consider it reasonable to pay the doctor for her services. It is not our gratitude that makes us believe the physician deserves payment, however, but the contract we have with her. Our thankfulness may only serve to make us accept the bill less grudgingly. Moreover, we know why we have to pay the physician: because otherwise there wouldn't be enough doctors available.

It is widely felt that certain areas of life should be exempt from commerce. However, where should we draw the line, and with what justification? The decisive difference between an acceptable and an unacceptable commodification of human body parts (from living donors) is often claimed to lie in whether the organ is regenerative (blood and sperm) or not (kidneys). But such a line is inconsequential. It would *permit*, for example, the commodification of parts of the liver and the lung because these organs have some capacity to regenerate. Moreover, for cadaveric donation, this dividing line is of no relevance.

We feel that the attempt to protect some areas of life from the forces of an impersonal market has validity and deserves our respect and, perhaps, even our support. However, we recognize that the current dividing line—probably every conceivable dividing line—is not without arbitrariness and cannot be expected to command any general agreement.

But suppose we accept the human dignity issue just for the sake of argument. Why, then, must paid donation be forbidden? Why not let the people involved decide—as we do with unpaid donation—how they want to preserve their dignity given the other aims they might pursue with the contract (e.g., earning money to pay for a life-saving operation for a child)? It has been argued that the persons involved in a paid donation must be protected from "themselves." But this argument not only presupposes that there *is* an undermining of human dignity but also that *either* this negative effect is so overwhelming that it overrules any other consideration regardless of its importance *or* that the people involved are incapable of weighing their personal dignity against other possible consequences. Of course, children and incapacitated adults are not able to effectively weigh such factors, but they would be excluded from the potential donor pool.

Stirring Repugnance

In the preceding section, it was the persons involved in a paid donation who had to be protected, so the argument went, against the consequences of their own actions. Now, when we consider the issue of "repugnance," it is the persons who are not involved who need "protection." This is a somewhat different matter.[11]

Undoubtedly, certain voluntary commercial contracts can make even individuals who have no involvement with them uncomfortable—for example, prostitution, surrogate motherhood, or artificial insemination. These uninvolved but concerned persons may also be quite sure they would never engage in buying or selling an organ or in organ transplantation. So what should an individual do if he feels this way, and what should society do for these individuals? The individual could do several things. First, he or she could try to simply ignore these activities. Another way is to develop a feeling of moral superiority. In this case, the individual can even profit, in some sense, from the unworthy acts of other people. The individual could fight for legal prohibition of such contracts or work toward a society where such contracts are undesirable. Many people would agree that this last solution is morally superior to the others, whereas trying to outlaw such contracts suggests an unreasonable desire to deprive these activities from those who want them. It accepts, in practice, the black market, and it tolerates the continuing existence of the underlying motives for repugnant contracts. Practical experience suggests that prohibitions of privately advantageous contracts do not usually eliminate such transactions but only reduce their numbers, move them "underground," and make monitoring the transactions far more difficult. The result is fewer, though less safe and effective, transactions.

How can a government protect citizens from what they consider repulsive contracts? Of course, the first solution is prohibition—which is what most governments do with respect to the selling and buying of organs. Better solutions, however, would have been making sure unpaid living donors got adequate postdonation health care and health insurance, that paid donors were not defrauded by black markets, or that donors got compensated for time off by their employers. In other words, governments can reduce the force of these objections by taking responsibility for the welfare of the donors. Indeed, the repugnance some people feel for compensating organ donors seems to be derived not so much from the idea of compensation as from the tragic results of black markets, which are the direct result of shortages.

Now let us turn again to the question of whether the acceptance of the virtues of keeping organs out of a market implies that selling and buying organs, be it from postmortem or living sources, must be prohibited. A prohibition basically rests on the proposition that the feelings of those who have no involvement in the activities in question are more important than the rights of self-defense and self-determination of those who are involved (sometimes fatally).[12] However, it is difficult to see how such a proposition can be defended on moral grounds. Most people would agree that the right of a person to defend his or her life should carry more weight than others' feelings of repugnance.

Exposing Donors to Risks

Most people agree that the wishes of deceased persons who indicated they did not want to donate their organs should be honored. The same deference, however, is not extended to willing living organ donors. In the current system, black market donors are, in many cases, badly exploited, but kidney recipients suffer from dire circumstances as well. Curiously, however, it is not the existing black market but the nonexisting permitted market for organs that defenders claim causes the suffering and exploitation of donors.

A widely used argument is that donors must be protected against donation decisions that are not in their best interests. Donors might act prematurely by not properly weighing the immediate additional income against the long-term consequences for health and working capacity, a failure perhaps due to insufficient information. They may be betrayed by organ brokers or hospital staff as well and later regret a decision that, unfortunately, cannot be reversed. To protect potential donors against these risks—so the argument goes—paying financial rewards to them must be prohibited.

In the existing black market, donors are often badly informed, may make premature decisions, and may be betrayed by brokers and clinics. None of these problems would arise in a legal (and well-supervised) setting with donor compensation. Thus, critics appear to confuse the dire circumstances in the existing black market with what could and would occur in a realistic, legally supervised system with compensation. A regulated market could require and provide safeguards for donors with respect to compensation and postdonation health care. Moreover, such arguments are of a paternalistic nature, they treat the potential donors as minors, and they do not respect their right for self-determination.

Exploitation of Donors

Another argument that is more serious, at least at first glance, is that a market for organs could lead to exploitation. Emergency situations that befall unfortunate potential donors could be used in exploitative ways by organ buyers.[13] This could be avoided by banning financial compensation. Except in extremely serious circumstances, few people would consider selling an organ while alive. However, when an individual needs to pay a child's college tuition, has been unable to find employment for years, or requires expensive surgery, selling an organ might seem to be an attractive way make some money. The implication of the exploitation and prohibition thesis, however, is that preventing people in such emergency situations from donating is good for them. So again, those who are not burdened with such financial situations believe they should be able to set the rules for those who are.

Another argument that is often used by proponents of the current system is that an organ contract is not really voluntary, at least for the seller, and therefore should be forbidden. They believe such a contract is involuntary because the seller is in an emergency situation and the amount of money offered is hard for the seller to resist. Let us look at the latter argument.

Often an employee will get a job offer from her company's competitor that pays a much higher salary. If the employee accepts the offer, is this an involuntary act because the salary made it too hard to resist? What if a Filipino who makes the equivalent of U.S.$1,000 per year was offered U.S.$4,000 for a kidney? Would that transaction still be considered involuntary?

An outside observer would most likely consider the sale of an organ voluntary if the seller had carefully considered the conditions and consequences, had done a lot of research on organ donation, and had discussed it with his family. Neither the observer nor the potential seller, however, would feel the high amount of money offered made the sale less voluntary. Rather, both might reasonably conclude that the sole effect of a higher price for the kidney is it makes the option more attractive in comparison to other options.

However, involuntary organ contracts, as most people understand the concept, are indeed possible. Consider the situation where an Indian peasant farmer is heavily indebted to his landlord. Both know that, realistically, the debt can never be paid. One possible solution is bonded labor, which might be a satisfactory solution to the landlord but is an extremely undesirable prospect for the farmer and his family. Suppose the landlord suggests to the farmer that bonded labor will not be necessary if he sells one of his kidneys. Now the farmer has even *fewer* options than before. When the only option was bonded labor, the farmer could try to buy some time, and the landlord might die or the tenancy laws might change. Now the only option is to sell a kidney, so it is an involuntary contract.

Hence, it is indeed conceivable that the option of selling a kidney leads to a contract that may be regarded as "involuntary" for one side. But in this case, the problem is not the powerful lure of the money offered but a change in the distribution of options available to the relevant participants. Moreover, it is rather strange to consider a financial incentive for doing something that will lead to an involuntary action. Usually, we look at it the other way around: it is fewer options and lower selling prices that reduce the freedom to act. Taylor and Simmerling (2008) even suggest, "Indeed, perhaps it is exploitative not to compensate the donor" (p. 57).

The implication of the protect-the-donor stance has been concisely summarized by Savulescu (2003): "It is double injustice to say to a poor person: 'You can't have what most other people have and we are not going to let you do what you want to have those things'" (p. 139). On balance, the most common arguments against donor compensation reviewed to this point appear weak. These arguments either mischaracterize the nature and workings of any plausible public system of donor compensation or they implicitly assume that people lack the capacity to make reasonable decisions about donation. Further, in many respects none of these arguments against donor compensation apply to deceased donors. However, the prospect of donors receiving compensation is also criticized from a quite different perspective, which is popularly termed the "slippery slope" argument.

The Slippery Slope

The "slippery slope" theory argues that compensating organ donors is not morally deficient, but it could *lead to* increasingly morally deficient situations elsewhere. Without any restrictions on market-based human interactions, the world would become less humane for all of us. We already lost the fight against the commodification of blood, sex, and surrogate motherhood. Although the current restrictions against commodifying organs may indeed be inconsequential and arbitrary, it is the last, best hope for enduring success before human values are totally degraded. We are on a slippery slope toward dehumanization, and we are almost at the bottom. If we stand firm and defend this last front, we can prevent altruistic acts from being superseded by commercial transactions such as the sale of eyes, limbs, and children. Thus, the slippery slope theory argues that it is incumbent upon all of us to prohibit organ sales.

Now let us offer some rebuttals to this argument. First, it is highly unlikely that all altruistic acts will vanish. The legalization of prostitution, for example, has not resulted in a decline in ordinary sexual relationships. Similarly, if it becomes legal to sell a kidney, altruistic donations would still occur, especially among family and friends. Moreover, complementary effects are likewise possible. A living donation may be offered out of a genuine desire to help others, and payment can be made as a gesture of gratitude for a life-saving act. This is similar to paying priests. Most priests study theology for reasons other than financial compensation, but they still require an income to practice their ministry. Most likely, we see no reason to be grateful to the car dealer who sells us a car, but we still pay them. Thus, a truly human interaction is not precluded by a contractual relation. Both may exist side by side and may even reinforce each other.

Is a slippery slope slippery—and is it a slope? If so, this would mean that once the prohibition on donor compensation was lifted, it would become increasingly difficult to erect or maintain other barriers against some of the conjectured consequences (e.g., the selling of eyes, etc.). However, this scenario is not very plausible, since the current organ donor compensation ban was initiated decades ago and has endured despite hundreds of thousands of deaths due to the shortages.

If the slippery slope is actually a slope, then it is important to examine the potential horrors at the bottom. Even if eyes, arms, or children were donated altruistically, people would still be horrified. Thus, the very nature of the act in question, rather than the compensation involved, clearly plays a large role in our feelings. With few exceptions, many opponents of compensation actually support transplantation. Most people consider it appropriate to pay someone who has done something praiseworthy, such as saving someone's life. Given these facts, it is difficult to see how the introduction of compensation for donors will trigger any radical change in social mores. However, it must be acknowledged that a policy of social acceptance for any sort of privately negotiated contract is problematic, and one can surely imagine circumstances in which private agreements produce results that are ethically abhorrent.

Is prohibition the solution to this problem? This issue has two parts. First, the prohibition of a market for goods that people desperately want or need leads, unavoidably, to the establishment of a black market. As real-life experience has shown, there is no realistic way to completely avoid this.[14] As we have seen, black markets are worse—for both participants and the nonparticipants alike—than legal (and regulated) markets. The black market is, in fact, the slippery slope of the altruistic system. Second, when revulsion over certain horrific organ contracts is widespread (as the proponents of a prohibition maintain), then there is no real need for prohibition. Few people would even consider such contracts because of moral convictions, the lack of need for such contracts, or both.

An Intermediate Balance

Let us try to find a middle ground in these arguments. The dire moral consequences of the current system can hardly be ignored. Moreover, the arguments put forward for defending the status quo and attacking a more liberal system appear to be implausible, illogical, or, at best, unconvincing on moral grounds. The slippery slope argument must be taken seriously, but the risks it represents seem so unlikely that they cannot be determinative in organ procurement policy. We already have black markets; compensation in a well-designed and effective system (in Spain); and outright payments (in Iran). If there is a slippery slope, we should be close to the bottom by now. All of these considerations lead us to assume the existence of a fundamental motive for opposing compensation.

Reasons to Defend the Current System

The arguments for opposing a more liberal donation system that we have seen to this point cannot be easily defended on moral grounds. Nevertheless, many opponents of reform stick to their position for different reasons. The influential U.S. transplant surgeon Francis Delmonico (2004b) declared that paying for organs would threaten "the nobility of the medical profession." This position, however, has no moral qualities but reveals an egoistic motivation. Arguments used to defend the current system, such as "commodification of body parts," "preserving human dignity," and so forth can be regarded to serve a purpose.

Broyer (1991) presents another reason for this steadfastness, which is widely shared within and outside the medical profession but rarely discussed openly. He claims that paid living donation would be "a visible and intolerable symptom of the exploitation of the poor by the rich" (p. 199). Janet Radcliffe

Richards (1996) reached the same conclusion. To summarize, she believes that people in rich countries will not be able to tolerate the practical consequences of paying for organs: kidney sellers from poor countries queuing up in front of our hospitals. It will be a repugnant view of obvious exploitation that will convulse us. We shall not be able to bear it. Thus, it is understandable when society protects itself against such experiences by prohibiting compensation.

This view, as expressed so openly by Broyer, has no moral qualities but is an egoistic position. However, it is usually combined with the assertion that a prohibition of compensation is also necessary to protect the sellers from poor countries against exploitation. This argument adds a benevolent quality to an egoistic stance. Moreover, the image of the world's poorest selling their body parts, which is a devastating critique of the many injustices in the world, motivates many of the most eloquent defenders of the donor compensation ban.

Is this image of the poor selling body parts realistic, and if so, how should it be assessed from a moral point of view? If a country permits everyone, even those from other countries, to sell organs, this scenario could very well become real. Also, most likely the world's poor would sell their kidneys to buyers in affluent countries. But will only rich people in those countries receive the kidneys? Probably not. Just because people are permitted to sell organs, it does not mean anyone can buy them. Most likely, the public health system will be the only legal buyer. This idea is included in every realistic reform proposal, including the proposal of the current authors, which is examined in Chapter 8. Moreover, the distribution rule may (and would) remain largely unchanged, with no role for income or wealth of the patient.

However, giving everyone, including foreigners, the option to sell their organs is not necessary. Some proposals exclude foreigners and restrict the permission to sell kidneys to nationals. These proposals expect that "local" sellers will be less desperate and that the average citizen will not be disturbed at the sight of sellers lining up in front of hospitals. Moreover, there is another advantage to the "home-grown" solution. The typical national donor need not be among the poorest. With respect to organ donation, the poorest have the disadvantage of obesity and sickness being relatively widespread in their group. Thus, a large percentage of compensated organ donors are expected to come from middle-income groups. The point is that the society concerned, through its public institutions, will establish the criteria under which a living donor could be compensated for an organ.

The prohibition of donor compensation has either the intended effect or the unintended pleasant side effect of sparing us from the unfairness in the world when it comes to organ donation. The prohibition allows us to sleep at night and not to quarrel too much with our consciences regarding our complicity in the situation. And the claim that it is only being done to protect the world's poor makes us feel even better. Only the deaths on waiting lists and the black market cause us concern. But this dire situation is, regrettably, the price that must be paid—by others, not by us—for our support of the principles of human dignity and altruism.

Janet Radcliffe Richards (1996) presents an ingenious counterpoint to the argument against compensation: If it is true that the sale of organs is a "visible and intolerable symptom of the exploitation of the poor by the rich," then "that is a reason for allowing it to continue. If we are forced to suffer the intolerable symptoms, we shall less easily forget the disease" (p. 410).

It is best to conclude with a quotation from the unfortunately prophetic Jesse Dukeminier Jr.: "Society must ultimately face the fact that . . . a hard choice must now be made. It must decide whether to advance the policy of preserving life or to stand paralyzed by its taboos" (p. 866).

Conclusion

Professional academic critiques of the ruling altruistic organ donation system have a long history. Besides criticizing the system's (lack of) effectiveness in preserving human life, arguments on moral grounds have been put forward to justify a more liberal system that does not forbid compensation to organ donors for their willingness to donate. The contributions of academic philosophers, as well as of some ethicists, legal scholars, medical professionals, and economists, have highlighted the flaws in the moral arguments provided to defend the current system and to inhibit real change.

We just examined the moral grounds of three organ donation systems: the "altruistic" system in its current usual form; an altruistic system with some modifications, which, however, do not encompass compensating donors; and a system in which donors are compensated financially for their willingness to donate. We argued that the current system is weak on *moral* grounds because it accepts avoidable death and suffering, limits individual self-determination and actions of self-defense, and treats organ patients unfairly by allocating organs to patients who have previously declined to be potential organ donors.

We then argue that some of these moral deficiencies could be corrected by certain reforms within the altruistic setting. One important step would be to define "altruism" less narrowly than it currently is. If an altruistic donation rule is unavoidable, it should exclude only those living donors who donate for commercial motives or self-enrichment. Moreover, we find that the donation principle of altruism is not the only hindrance to realizing important reform steps and improving the system's moral balance. The organ allocation rule that grants equal access to organs, if need be, to willing postmortem donors as well as to nondonors is a second pillar of the system. If this rule is not lifted, one of the most effective and fairness-enhancing reforms—the club solution—is not possible.

We believe, however, that an end to avoidable death and suffering can only be achieved by a more decisive reform step that permits compensating donors for their donation, on top of the costs and risks they incur. The common counterarguments (loss of human dignity by commodification of human body parts, repugnance felt by persons not concerned, need for donor protection against exploitation, and the danger of the "slippery slope") are discussed. We accept only the latter argument to a certain degree, but we find that all of them lack force, specifically with respect to the usual conclusion: compensating donors for their willingness to donate must be forbidden. We regard this largely as a non sequitur. Moreover, we consider the existing black market as the slippery slope of the current system.

Taking all of these arguments together, we are convinced that a system that permits adequate compensation to living and postmortem organ donors is not only more effective but also morally superior.[15]

The next chapter develops a specific version of Dukeminier's "hard choice." The reform we propose tries to advance the policy of preserving life, while respecting important social taboos and taking more seriously widely shared moral convictions.

Compensation for Organ Donation and a Proposal for a Public Monopsony for Organ Acquisition

Introduction

While inefficiencies in most countries' procurement systems would allow some improvement in performance without introducing economic incentives for donation, we argue that such incentives are an indispensable part of any reform effort capable of eventually eliminating the waiting lists and ending avoidable deaths. Even with such incentives, eliminating the lists is going to take years. However, for many reasons, introducing economic incentives for donation, for both deceased and living donors, is likely to fundamentally eliminate the organ shortage problem. The introduction of such incentives is itself a significant problem in economic institutional design, however, and while many such systems can be imagined, we propose a particular sort of approach that offers conceptual and practical advantages.

It is our hope that this chapter will stimulate serious debate and, as soon as possible, action in the introduction of economic incentives. We recognize the high degree of resistance such a change is likely to encounter, but we hope that some of the suggestions made here will mitigate those complaints sufficiently so that something effective can be brought forward.

Proposals for Material Incentives to Donating Organs

Several important questions about donor incentives have been posed in the literature, and these must be addressed. What sort of "market" should be introduced, and how should it be organized and/or regulated? How would property rights be allocated, and how would that allocation affect system performance? Would both living and cadaver donors receive compensation, and would such compensation vary? What does the performance of other markets for body parts, such as whole cadavers, eggs, semen, tissue, and blood and blood products, tell us about the likely workings of an organ market? What would be the financial consequences of such a compensation-based system, and what prices might prevail? How would such a system guard against abuses of donors or prevent the allocation of organs by criteria that are ethically dubious?

Conceptual Problems with a "Market for Organs"

It is important to emphasize, with Barnett and Kaserman (2002), that one should distinguish between a "market," as that term is ordinarily used, and proposals that merely involve economic compensation. For the economic layman, "market" often seems to imply a generally chaotic "free for all," in which anything and everything is for sale to the highest bidder. This image, which has been steadily reinforced by the very negative picture presented by unregulated organ markets in poor countries, may be partially to blame for the unwillingness of many physicians to support compensation proposals. Yet, in the proper meaning of the term, focusing on its institutional framework and legal constraints, we have a market now. The difficulty is that the market we have is regulated in the most extreme fashion imaginable: reciprocal trade is illegal, and violators face public sanctions. These rules limit the ability of those who need the organs (demand side) to induce those who have them (supply side) to actually provide the organs.

These considerations lead us immediately to the problem of what is being supplied and what is being demanded. Clearly, organs are inputs to transplants, so their demand is derived—that is, arises from—and depends on the demand for something else. Further, transplants are desired by people who, by and large, do not pay for them: in almost all countries, the greater part of all solid organ transplants are financed by public money. In countries with national insurance funds, dialysis, pre- and postoperative care, transplantation costs, organ procurement costs, and drug therapy are all publicly financed. Even in the United States, where there is no system of universal health care payment, the End Stage Renal Disease (ESRD) program and allied programs pay these costs in most cases (private payers are involved in at most 10 percent of transplants).[1] Third-party payment is by no means rare in the medical industries, but it does raise the conventional problems of moral hazard and inefficiency.

Furthermore, it is not really realistic to say that a particular ESRD or cirrhosis patient "demands" a transplant in the economic sense. Rather, in concert with, and under the advice of, his or her physician, the patient agrees to be placed on the waiting list or to seek a living donor among family or friends. Indeed, some physicians who are skeptical of compensation for donation suggest that any increase in organ supply will be matched or exceeded by an increase in demand as physicians put more patients on the waiting lists. This conjecture suggests that they view the "demand" as being largely, or totally, under the physicians' control.

In most cases, earlier discussions of organ markets, or of organ compensation systems generally, have skirted these complexities, and the approximate one-to-one relationship between a suitable organ and an organ transplant has made these simplifications less than fatal. For example, Becker and Elias (2008) describe the "demand for transplants" and reasonably portray this demand as conventionally downward sloping in price on the grounds that "in most nations, the cost of transplant surgery is mainly borne either by governments or by private health insurance companies. Their willingness to qualify individuals for this expensive surgery increases as its costs decline. This is the main reason why effective demand . . . increases as costs fall" (p. 8). Other researchers, such as Barnett and Kaserman (2002) and Wellington and Whitmire (2007), define the quantity demanded of transplants (of kidneys) as being equal to the number of current transplants, plus the appropriate change in the waiting list, controlling for removals for death or sickness. In this case, demand is inelastic—that is, it is not dependent on price, at least over relevant intervals of costs.

As mentioned earlier, most analyses of the shortage take as their starting point the supply and demand model, which has the virtue of illustrating the shortage directly as the distance between demand and supply at a price of zero (for the organ). In this framework, the solution to the shortage is to allow the prices paid for organs to rise to a level that would equate supply and demand. This is, indeed, a sensible view. However, this conceptualization masks at least two important factors that may materially affect any attempt to implement a compensation scheme.

First, it is difficult to envision what an adjustment process would look like when one accepts essentially universal third-party fixed payments. Unless patients themselves, or agents acting for them, were to somehow enter into a bidding process, it is not clear how the price adjustment is supposed to occur. If we were to compensate organ donors, then for reasons discussed following and elsewhere, we should expect to obtain more organs than currently are. However, would we necessarily obtain the number of organs that would "clear the market" in the sense suggested by the competitive analysis? Even if a public funding authority took it upon itself to adjust prices to achieve some reasonable and explicit target, such as reducing the end-of-year waiting list by 10 percent, only experience is likely to allow them to come close to that goal. Thus, although the supply–demand analogy is a very useful one, it does not by itself suggest a clear means for implementing a compensation system by a third-party authority.

Second, circumstances are even murkier when the variety of possible payment mechanisms for organ donation is considered. For example, the influential essay by Hansmann (1989) proposes a rather special system related to that of Schwindt and Vining (1986), which utilizes a "futures market" based on annual (one-year) contracts, in which health insurers would pay for obtaining the agreement of the potential donor to allow for organ removal should circumstances allow it. In these cases, obviously, supply and demand would refer to these future contracts, rather than the organs themselves, and the prices involved would be prices of these contingent claims. We discuss this more later in this chapter.

The Becker and Elias Model

Perhaps the most important previous "market" model is that of Becker and Elias (2008), and it is useful here to review it briefly, if only in broad outline. Becker and Elias specify the relevant demand as representing the demand for renal transplants, of which a kidney is an indispensable input. Currently, compensation to suppliers is regulated at a zero level, resulting in a shortage. Using recent and fairly reasonable data on the cost of a U.S. kidney transplant and attendant care ($160,000), they illustrate the shortage as equal to the difference between the quantity supplied and the quantity demanded at a zero kidney price. In Figure 8.1, Q_0 represents the quantity of kidneys available for "free," and Q_2 equals the quantity demanded at this price. The curious appearance of the supply curve reflects an assumption regarding the supply of living-donor kidneys described below. The shortage is the difference $(Q_2 - Q_0)$. Demand is downward sloping for reasons discussed previously. In order to specify the effect of allowing donor compensation on the supply of kidneys for transplant, Becker and Elias argue, as have others, that (1) the number of deceased donor kidneys is probably insufficient to meet the demand in the United States so that compensated living donors will be necessary, and (2) the number of potential living donors is very large, so one may take the supply of living-donor

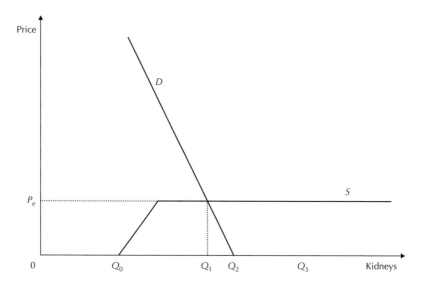

Figure 8.1   The organ market and the shortage, including living donors (after Becker and Elias)

kidneys to be infinitely elastic at some price P_e per kidney. In other words, living donors will be the "marginal" suppliers, so their supply price will determine the market clearing price. Using a risk–compensation calculation, Becker and Elias propose about $15,000 as a reasonable estimate of the supply price of a living-donor kidney in the United States. In terms of Figure 8.1, then, P_e can be taken to be this "market clearing" price for a kidney, and Q_1 the resulting market quantity.

We address the specific method used to obtain the kidney donor compensation rate of $15,000 later in this chapter. Here we want to discuss two limitations of this approach: the use of a representative consumer type model and the lack of an explicit relationship between the market clearing price and the waiting list. The representative consumer type calculation places a value on the risk a donor undergoes in making a donation (on average) and certain other considerations, such as quality of life after donation. The assumption of a nearly unbounded supply of living-donor kidneys that are medically acceptable at a price of $15,000 may eventually be borne out, but such a calculation, based on an expected utility model for a representative consumer, can at best only estimate the price an "average" potential supplier might require, though only a fraction of people will be close to this average. Thus, many persons would surely require far higher prices, while likewise some might be willing to sell for less. Although living donors may well constitute the "marginal" supplier, it is quite unlikely that the marginal living supplier would be, in any sense, "average." The maximum number of feasible transplants in a year that would be medically reasonable greatly exceeds the one-year shortage as measured by adjusted changes in the waiting list. Yet, even if one assumed the United States began performing 40,000 renal grafts a year after introduction of compensation, the implied number of compensated living donors is still minuscule compared to the potential supply of living-donor kidneys. If one accepted living donors from abroad, the supply would be larger still. (The Becker/Elias calculations, by using U.S.-level income data, implicitly rule out such international supply.)

More importantly, though, the Becker/Elias approach, by utilizing the supply–demand framework and identifying the shortage in the conventional manner, may well understate the numbers of transplants a compensation policy should allow. Clearly, it is fair to say that stabilization of the waiting lists, with appropriate allowance for deaths and other sorts of removals, can be denoted an "elimination of the shortage," and we accept this nomenclature. It is also apparent that no policy short of a great medical breakthrough would allow for the elimination of the waiting list in any period as short as one year. Moreover, the Becker/Elias assumption that those transplant components other than the organs are available in infinitely elastic supply is a proposition that seems unlikely to be literally true. At some point, the costs of transplants and organs become a consideration despite the high costs of dialysis, and economists have long observed that while increases in quantity can lower unit costs, the greater the time allowed for a plan to be fulfilled, the lower the total costs can be.

Spot versus Future Markets

In the case of a cadaveric organ, it is possible either to buy the right for organ removal from the individual prior to his or her death or to buy the organ from the bereaved. Generally, the body of a deceased person is the property of his or her family or estate, although even the common law is sometimes unclear on this question, since numerous prohibitions on the use of a cadaver are also recognized. Compensating the bereaved for the right to remove organs for transplantation purposes is only possible after death. Here, organ explantation and compensation would be effectuated by a "spot market."

Buying the right to remove an organ postmortem from a living person, however, is possible in two ways. In the first, the donor makes an agreement that organs may be removed postmortem on the condition that he or she dies in specific circumstances suitable for organ donation. Upon this promise, the

(potential) future donor is immediately compensated. Due to the low probability that the specified circumstances will occur, the compensation will also
be low.[2]

The second case differs from the first in one important way. The compensation is paid only after death if the circumstances suitable for organ transplant
actually occur. Here, high levels of compensation are possible, but it must go to
the donor's estate.

Convincing the bereaved to donate the organs of a deceased family member has proven to be difficult for medical staff, even when a valid donor card
exists.[3] Meaningful compensation to the bereaved could provide a considerable
number of organs that remain in the deceased and, thus, are wasted. Offering
compensation in exchange for a promise of organ donation may be assumed
to lead to similar results. Immediate compensation will be low, but it will also
be guaranteed and acquired by the (still living potential) donor, whereas future
compensation, necessarily of a potential nature, would only be acquired by
the bereaved. The Spanish model approach relies completely on compensation
postmortem, and we suspect this is the most efficient mechanism.[4]

Postmortem versus Living-Donor Organs

Although compensation holds the promise of greatly expanded organ supply,
the way compensation will be used will differ substantially among organs, primarily (but not solely) due to the necessity of obtaining hearts, pancreas, almost
all lungs, and most livers from deceased donors. While liver transplants from
living donors are possible, and are actually common in Japan, the burden on the
donor is much greater than in the case of kidneys, and such transplants represent only about 4 percent of liver grafts in the United States (OPTN, 2011).[5]
Fortunately, cadaver donor numbers may be adequate to provide for substantial
increases in transplant rates for livers in many countries, including the United
States. In contrast, the supply of cadavers, even if they were literally confiscated
in every feasible case, is almost certain to be inadequate to stabilize adjusted
waiting lists for kidneys, at least in the near future. (For various estimates of
the numbers of potential cadaver donors in the United States, see Evans et al.,
1990, 1992; Sheehy et al., 2003; and Delmonico et al., 2005.) Thus, as Breyer
and colleagues (2006) and other researchers have suggested, it may well be
necessary to have active living-donor programs in most industrialized nations.
In less wealthy countries, cadaver utilization is even less palatable due to the
lack of trauma centers equipped to perform the necessary removals. Thus, in
the case of kidneys, aggressive expansion of transplants will ordinarily require

compensating living, unrelated donors. (Related living donors will no doubt persist under any system.)

Donor Reaction to Compensation

Historically, many of the most influential objections to compensation/market reforms have focused on the effects of the introduction of explicit economic incentives on donor behavior. In particular, if one could credibly argue that compensation would reduce the numbers of organs obtained or would degrade their average quality, any reform of that sort would face a serious hurdle, to say the least. However, all arguments in favor of economic incentives for donors assume that the numbers of organs obtained would thereby increase and that their quality would not be degraded in any serious manner. The related problem of the proper use of living versus cadaveric donors, when such choices are feasible, is also relevant here, as many of the critics of compensation systems make arguments that have quite different implications for these two organ sources.

The Issue of Strictly Altruistic Donors

The claim that the introduction of compensation would dissuade many altruistic persons from making donations must be addressed, and such conjectures are closely tied to ethical arguments against compensation. The essential claim arises from the belief that altruistic behavior can be undermined, or "crowded out," by the introduction of monetary incentives. This point of view is strengthened by research showing that, in some cases, monetary incentives can lead to a reduced supply of the desired article or behavior. However, from the social perspective, the primary question is, will compensation lead to an increase in the net number of organs for transplantation (at a reasonable cost)?

The criticisms of compensation systems briefly mentioned earlier may also be illustrated using Figure 8.1. The claim that legally institutionalized compensation would undermine altruistic donation implies that the supply curve with altruistic quantity Q_0 would move to the left. However, there also are the nonaltruistic donors who react positively to price incentives. What may be the net effect on total supply? We explore this question by using a simplified version of the analysis provided by Barnett, Beard, and Kaserman (1993) and refer to Figures 8.2 to 8.4.

We consider two groups of potential donors. Members of group A donate their *maximum* amount of organs, during some relevant time period, at a price of zero. With rising prices *paid to others*, members of A donate increasingly

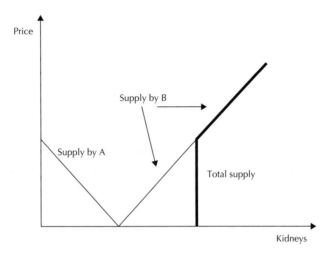

Figure 8.2 Total organ supply—groups A and B exhibiting equal (absolute) supply elasticities

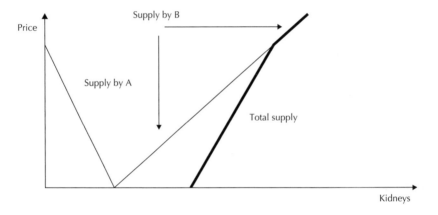

Figure 8.3 Total organ supply—group A's supply elasticity is (absolutely) smaller than group B's

less. Group A, by donating less the more others are paid, may be called the "repugnance group." In contrast, members of group B donate their *minimum* amount at a price of zero but increase their donations with rising prices paid to members of B. Group B may be called the "egoistic group." Group A exhibits a negative and group B a positive price elasticity of supply.

We consider three constellations of price elasticities of supply: group A's elasticity may be equal to, smaller than, or larger than that of group B (in

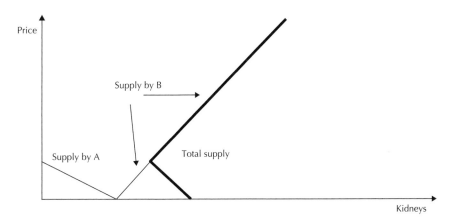

Figure 8.4   Total organ supply—group A's elasticity is (absolutely) larger than group B's

absolute value). The amount of group A's (negative) price elasticity of supply is an indication of the degree of its repugnance to price incentives offered to others. For illustrative simplicity, we only consider the case where the maximum supply quantity of group A equals the minimum quantity of group B. However, other assumptions in this respect do not change the results.

When the organ supply elasticities of A and B are equal (Figure 8.2.), total supply is at first constant—that is, it does not react to an increasing price. Beyond a certain price threshold, however, total supply increases with rising prices. When group A's supply elasticity is smaller than group B's (Figure 8.3), total supply increases over the whole price range with rising prices. When group A's supply elasticity is larger than group B's (Figure 8.4), total supply at first decreases with rising prices. Beyond a certain price threshold, however, total supply increases with rising prices.

The simple diagrammatic presentation suggests the following:

- When the price elasticity of supply of group A (those disgusted by price incentives) is smaller than that of group B (those stimulated by price incentives), the total supply of organs increases with increasing prices over the whole range.
- When, by contrast, the price elasticity of supply of group A is larger than that of group B, the total supply of organs at first decreases, then increases with increasing prices. However, there is a price above which total supply starts to increase. A constant or even decreasing total supply is only possible in a "low" price range.

- Thus, the introduction of too low or too slowly rising financial incentives may initially have no positive net effect on donation, and could in fact reduce it.[6] However, the eventual occurrence of a positive net effect with rising prices is rather plausible.
- The development of total supply (by groups A and B) under the influence of increasing prices is principally independent of the group size—that is, independent of the relative amounts of the maximum and minimum quantities supplied at zero price.
- A significant (and preliminary) decrease, after the introduction of financial compensation, is only possible when group A is large compared to group B.

Thus, it is an empirical question which situation—Figure 8.2, 8.3, or 8.4—is most relevant and at what price threshold total supply will begin to rise.

A significant percentage of organs obtained worldwide for transplantation (some estimates place it at 10 percent—see Brown and Glenn, 2007) are paid for, although often in illegal or legally dubious circumstances. Such payments themselves may damage the altruistic system, a phenomenon we call "dirty altruism." However, it is clear that, despite the shortcomings of the current procurement apparatus, thousands of people continue to make donations under more or less altruistic circumstances. This implies, of course, that these donors are not dissuaded from donation because others sell organs, albeit illegally. Regardless of how the procurement system is ultimately constituted, it is clear that we will observe both altruistic donation, especially among family members needing kidneys, and sales.

Finally, there is limited evidence on willingness to sell cadaveric organs. Surveys conducted by Barnett and Kaserman (2002) and Wellington and Whitmire (2007) provide some information. However, this evidence does not really address the issue of whether or not compensation and altruism can successfully coexist, except to the extent that the survey instruments did include an opportunity for respondents to express unwillingness to sell their organs. Unfortunately, the design of the instruments does not allow the researcher to reliably distinguish between unwillingness to sell at any price and a willingness to donate at a price of zero. However, large numbers of participants express their willingness to accept compensation now for the removal of their organs upon their deaths, a sort of option market experiment. If these percentages are in any way indicative, then there are sufficient numbers of persons willing to sell cadaveric organs such that the loss of altruistic suppliers (except those living donors donating to family members) would not cause total donations to fall.

Rodrigue and colleagues' (2006) survey-based analysis presents evidence on the attitudes of family members of potential deceased donors in the United States. A total of 561 people, of whom 348 consented to donation and 213 did not, were queried on their attitudes toward compensation, presumed consent, and "donor consent" rules (also termed "primary donor" policies, in which the expressed consent of the deceased toward donation is implemented regardless of the views of the next of kin). Particular interest attaches to differences, if any, between the feelings of donors and nondonors regarding payments for donation. In the great majority of cases, people state that the offer of compensation would not have affected their decisions, although those who did not donate are statistically more likely to change their choice (and donate) in response to such offers than are those who donated. Unfortunately, it is difficult to generalize these results due to the construction of the sample used and the highly hypothetical nature of the questions asked. However, the results suggest both that financial incentives are effective and that the degree of aversion to compensation may differ between donor and nondonor groups. We have several examples of actual donor compensation that, if inconclusive, certainly provide no evidence that would suggest paid donation for solid organs is dysfunctional. These examples include Iran, Spain, sales of whole cadavers in the United States, black or gray market sales, and data from public surveys.

Iran, which is discussed in Chapter 3, relies primarily on compensated living donation by strangers, with substantial public oversight by religious officials. There is relatively little evidence on altruistic donation in Iran, although there clearly is some. However, the Iranians made substantial progress in reducing, even eliminating, the waiting list for kidney grafts, so it is difficult to claim the Iranian experience is any sort of indictment of living-donor compensation. Donors receive around U.S.$1,000, health insurance benefits, and other forms of compensation.[7]

The Spanish system (also discussed in Chapter 3), in which families can receive financial assistance—described variously as a funeral allowance or the like—is not transparent: the existence of these awards is not publicized, and procurement officials, who are highly trained and regarded as competent, use their judgment in the process. In this case, though, we have the undeniable evidence of Spain's success, of which the compensation function is a part. Whatever role economic incentives play in Spain's system, and we believe it is meaningful, it is at least obvious that such incentives have not undermined their efforts. The dire predictions of some critics regarding the effects of introducing compensation have *not* occurred in Spain. Rates of living-donor transplants, which are not compensated, have been increasing.

In the United States, while compensation ("valuable consideration," as the NOTA describes it) for organ donation is a criminal offense, it is perfectly legal to compensate families (or deceased's estates) for whole-body donation. (This practice is discussed in Chapter 6.) As a result of payments to families or estates (couched again as "funeral assistance"), there is a surplus of cadavers, and this surplus has occasionally led to scandals in which bodies were treated without due respect. Since entire bodies are available for a few thousand dollars, it seems unlikely cadaveric organ costs would be very high, at least in the United States.

Existing Disincentives to Donors

As pointed out by Matas (2007), the coexistence of altruistic actions and rewards for merit is quite normal: most people regard the actions of police officers, firefighters, and emergency medical technicians as often involving essential elements of altruism. Yet, it seems quite unlikely that the common practice of making awards for heroism to such persons discourages, on net, heroic action. Similarly, many people might well wish to make an altruistic donation of an organ to a family member or close friend but feel unable to do so because of the financial distress it would cause. Lost wages due to hospitalization, travel and other costs, a potential inability to obtain health insurance in some countries, and other penalties currently fall on altruistic donors, and not only do these donors receive no compensation, but they actually suffer as a result of their noble acts. As discussed in Chapter 6, in the United States, compensation to living donors for lost wages, travel, and so on, while legal, is quite limited. As Gutmann (2006) has argued, full compensation for actual costs should not be taken to represent a violation of the altruistic requirement, since this rule cannot be taken to imply donors must literally suffer.[8]

These disincentives even apply to cadaveric donation, at least in the United States: Reilly and colleagues (1997) found as much as $30,000 in additional patient hospital charges attributable at least indirectly to actions taken to facilitate organ removal from brain-dead donors.[9] Altruistic activities, including, for example, charitable giving, are not unresponsive to economic incentives, and most societies reward such gifts by tax reductions or other benefits. Clearly, there is a perceived benefit in giving social recognition and approval to laudable acts, and compensation for donation can obviously be presented in precisely that light. If it improved donation rates to label compensation as an award to recognize noble behavior, no one could reasonably object.

The "Taint" of Compensation

A number of researchers have questioned whether the potential "taint" of compensation is even relevant for many important subgroups of donors. For example, Goodwin (2006) laments the very low rate of donation among African Americans in the United States[10] and argues that this unfortunate circumstance is a result of a lack of autonomy many feel within the U.S. health care system. Due to a number of racist-inspired medical crimes committed against American blacks (such as the infamous Tuskegee syphilis trials), many potential donors feel their interaction with health care providers affords them neither dignity nor control. This can be changed, however, by the introduction of a compensation system, since in such a case the donor's status is reinforced by actual money payments. Persons who receive meaningful compensation have more status, Goodwin argues, than those who do not.

From the theoretical perspective, Byrne and Thompson's (2001) model provides a cautionary note regarding the risk monetary incentives could pose for cadaveric donations that are determined by the decedent's family. Byrne and Thompson view the registration decision of the decedent as a signaling device in the economic sense. In any system in which the organ officials refer to the potential donor's family, the introduction of a money payment for registering as a donor causes this signal to be degraded: if society compensates registrants, then after death, surviving family might suppose the deceased registered merely for the money and did not really wish to donate organs. This, in turn, can produce a negative effect on donation under certain circumstances. Byrne and Thompson suggest that persons be required to explicitly register as donors *or nondonors*, thereby allowing the construction of rewards for donor registration that, in their words, "would exclude perverse supply responses and ensure that there exist prices at which cadaveric organ supply rises significantly" (p. 82).

Lessons from Markets for Other Body Parts

Behind many arguments that compensation will degrade either the number of donors or the quality of organs lies the idea that the sale of body parts is inherently different from the sale of other things, especially when one considers nonregenerative tissues. These concerns appear related to the Kantian notion that persons are not means but ends, and they must be treated as such. (We address ethical issues in Chapter 7, and the interested reader should see Cherry

(2005) for a careful analysis.) It is important, however, to point out that the United States and other countries already have markets that deal in body parts or products, and by and large, these markets work along conventional lines. Because these markets provide potentially useful insight into how a compensation system might look, we review them briefly here.

Perhaps the most influential critique of economic incentives in markets for body products is Titmuss (1970), who combined the claim that paying for blood products in the United States led to serious contamination of the blood supply, with moral arguments in opposition to compensation. Both Titmuss's practical arguments and his moral reasoning have solicited considerable commentary and criticism, not least from Nobel laureate Kenneth Arrow (1972), who found Titmuss's claims quite unconvincing. Later evidence and analyses by Schwartz (1999), Callero (1991), Goodwin (2006), and especially Hippen and Satel (2008) have pointed out serious shortcomings in Titmuss's study. For instance, blood contamination problems should be attributed to the lack of effective screening during the period reviewed by Titmuss, not the fact that compensation was paid. Whenever money is offered for something, there is always an incentive to obtain that money by unscrupulous means. However, this incentive is not usually so large that one willingly foregoes the compensation mechanism to avoid it. Further, as Goodwin (2006) notes, the source of some blood contamination in the United States was homosexual men who unknowingly transmitted the HIV virus while making voluntary donations under altruistic motivation. Such donors were, demographically speaking, exactly the sort Titmuss claims are lost under paid donation systems: high-income, educated individuals acting out of public spiritedness. The problem, which would not apply to organ donation under current technology, was a lack of effective, quick screening for diseases, not the presence of donors Titmuss might not approve of.

In the United States, whole blood is obtained almost exclusively through altruistic donation, and pleas for donation due to critical shortages are a regular part of public life, particularly during the summer months when college students have returned home. This altruistic system allowed widespread contamination by HIV, attempted to cover it up, and precipitated an international scandal. In contrast, blood plasma suppliers in the United States are compensated, and this function is largely handled by private firms. One consequence has been widespread exporting of plasma products from the United States to Europe—and no U.S. shortages.

A recent experimental study of blood donation by Mellström and Johannesson (2008) examined the effects of modest compensation (around U.S.\$7 at the time) on blood donation by Swedish men and women. They found that while male subjects were largely unaffected by compensation, women responded negatively to the small payments offered but that this effect could be overcome by alternatively making the payment to a charity of the donor's choice. This result is consistent with the famous findings of Gneezy and Rustichini (2000) concerning the effects of small fines for late arrivals by parents picking up their children at Israeli day care centers. Imposing small fines led to more tardiness, since evidently parents felt that their obligation to be on time was undermined by the payments they made for lateness. However, Gneezy and Rustichini's work does not offer any particular indictment of compensating organ donors, except perhaps the observation that very trivial levels of compensation, offered, for example, to grieving families, might well be worse than no compensation at all. Meaningful compensation, presented as recognition by society of a laudable act, is quite another matter.

Other body parts markets have also been seen to function "normally." For example, sales of eggs and semen and the use of women's' uteruses by compensated arrangement (i.e., surrogate motherhood), which have allowed many thousands of infertile couples to have children, amount to a multibillion-dollar industry in the United States (Goodwin, 2006). Prices for these services vary in a manner consistent with the degree of intrusion each represents, although payouts are not astronomical. For example, egg donors are paid between \$5,000 and \$15,000 dollars, and egg removal requires surgery, hormone treatments for several weeks, and recovery time. Semen donors receive very small compensation even if they are desirable sources (e.g., healthy medical school students). Recent news accounts also establish that egg donation rates respond strongly to economic conditions. One may object, of course, that the examples of eggs, sperm, blood, and so on are inapt because these are materials that the body generates or has in abundance. In contrast, kidneys, liver lobes, and so on are quite limited and will be missed. While accurate, this complaint cannot be said to apply to compensation for deceased donor organs and therefore cannot be taken as a criticism of that practice.

The history of blood donation and surrogate motherhood in the European Union differs from that of the United States in several important respects, and these differences reflect the gap between European and U.S. attitudes toward commercialization in health care. However, it is inaccurate to claim that the

European community has adopted a uniform approach: various countries differ widely in their attitudes and practices, and the gap between the strict legal requirements and observed practices can be quite wide.

Some European institutions, such as the German Red Cross (DRK), subscribe to the ethical guidelines of the International Society for Blood Transfusion (ISBT). In general, blood donations are expected to be voluntary and unpaid. Vouchers or small awards for reimbursement of travel costs and incidental expenses, in addition to the provision of refreshments, are permitted. Blood procurement institutions are expected to be nonprofit, and the donor–recipient relationship must be anonymous (contrary to living organ donation). As a consequence, Germany has faced some problems in blood supply and has seen fairly widespread small-scale entry of alternative, private blood procurement organizations, such as Haema. The DRK has, of course, strongly protested against entry (i.e., competition) in blood procurement, and although the DRK has influential political allies, community procurers and university hospitals have actively expanded their blood activities in the last decade. While DRK pays donors nothing, Haema currently pays 15 euros, and university clinics pay as much as 25 euros for blood, with even higher payments for specialty donations such as thrombocytes. For the most part, such payments have been tolerated as within the scope of the "allowances" permitted by regulation.

More controversial than blood procurement, the practice of surrogate motherhood has induced some countries to institute total bans rather than just prohibit payments. In Germany, the Embryo Law of 1991 (Embryonenschutzgesetz) prohibits surrogate motherhood, placement of children through surrogate arrangements, and the offering of surrogate services. Similar bans are formalized in France, Norway, Sweden, Austria, and Switzerland. In contrast, Belgium, Greece, the United Kingdom, the Netherlands, Spain, and Italy have either ambiguous laws or no specific laws banning surrogate motherhood as a medical procedure, although some countries, such as Britain, proscribe any payment to a surrogate mother. In addition, the legal status of surrogate parenthood is quite unclear; it appears that in many of these countries the courts are unwilling to enforce private contracts involving surrogate mothers. However, persons who are desperate enough to attempt to navigate the legal and social minefield of surrogate adoption have pushed the boundaries in this area, and surrogate motherhood activities are at least tolerated in many places lacking a clear prohibition.

On balance, a fair-minded reading of the evidence suggests that compensation for donors, if done correctly and sensibly, would increase, probably substantially, the number of organs available for transplant. In the cases of both deceased donors (and their families) and living donors, available evidence confirms the observation that people respond to incentives.

The Issue of Organ Quality

There remains the issue of organ quality under compensation, but here again, Titmuss's (1970) assertions lack force (Strauss et al., 1994; Hippen and Satel, 2008). In fact, there are good reasons to suspect that moving to a system of incentives may very well increase average qualities. To see this, we need only note that the increase in organ availability with compensation would almost surely allow stricter criteria by procurement officials. Indeed, one of the hallmarks of the growing shortages is the use of organs of increasingly poorer quality, as documented in Chapter 3. The increasing use of expanded criteria and non-heart-beating donor organs is sensible in these times of severe shortages, but it need not be in an environment with a greatly expanded organ supply. In response to the claim that persons who are willing to sell organs may be disreputable, one need only point out that today's testing and screening protocols are very advanced, and inferior organs will be detected. In the case of compensated living donors, one could impose a six-month period of testing and evaluation prior to organ removal. Matas (2006) provides a detailed discussion of desirable screening techniques under a compensated donor system. The issue of organ quality is also relevant for a public monopsony buying organs and is examined later in this chapter.

Will Supply Drive Demand?

Some medical practitioners and others oppose compensation on the grounds that it would boost *demand* for organs and would therefore never reduce the waiting lists (see, for example, Scheper-Hughes, 2000). They suspect that their colleagues (and themselves as well) would loosen the admission criteria for the waiting list in line with a growing availability of organs. Three objections can be raised here. First, this suggestion implicitly admits that compensation might be a powerful instrument to increase organ supply. Second, admission criteria are defined, at least in principle, by medical authorities, not by individual physicians. However, physicians indeed have some leeway to interpret the rules. But it is unrealistic to assume that the rules will be loosened solely due to an increasing availability of organs. Third, even if demand increases, what is wrong with that? An increased supply of organs will in any case reduce unnecessary death and suffering of patients, especially if these persons would not have been placed on the waiting list before. Patient welfare, not waiting list statistics, should be the criteria for measuring progress.

Prices of Organs

It is important to distinguish among organ prices that might arise in some hypothetical competitive market, organ prices that would be socially optimal under some reasonable criteria, and prices that have actually been observed in a variety of circumstances, most of which do not remotely resemble a well-designed compensation system. Complicating matters, one may obtain price estimates by a variety of means, including surveys, market models, and ordinary observation of transactions. In the case of models, assumptions on the structure of the market will materially affect predicted prices. For example, under single-buyer proposals, the mandate and resources given to the procurement organization will materially affect prices. Prices may refer to deceased donor organs, living-donor organs, or both. Finally, prices may reflect spot transactions, futures market type transactions, and so on, and many commentators (e.g., Matas, 2006) propose combining money prices with other benefits such as insurance coverage and cost reimbursement, leading to complex nonlinear prices and bundling.

Thus, it is entirely inadequate to speak of the likely "price of a kidney," for example, without substantial qualifications. In this section, our goal is extremely modest: we wish to arrive at some reasonable "guesses" at the order of magnitude of the prices organs might receive under plausible conditions. Thus, we will tie our review of organ price predictions made by other researchers with brief explanations of the methodology they employ and the degree to which that methodology is potentially realistic. Although estimates of organ prices exhibit substantial variation, we think it quite plausible that cadaveric organ prices will be very low (compared to transplant or dialysis costs). Prices for kidneys from living donors are difficult to estimate, but the benefits of renal grafts are so large that even very high prices would still support socially beneficial transplantation.

Hypothetical Market Prices

We begin by considering hypothetical competitive market prices for organs under legal trade. Three studies have considered this problem: Becker and Elias (2007), Wellington and Whitmire (2006), and Barnett and Kaserman (2002). The first assumes an infinitely elastic supply of living-donor kidneys at a price calculated from consideration of the risk imposed by donation for a representative seller. Barnett and Kaserman (2002), and later Wellington and Whitmire (2006), use survey data, combined with observed donation levels for cadaveric kidneys under zero compensation rules to construct a hypothetical supply curve. This curve is then interposed over a completely inelastic demand for transplants obtained from analysis of changes in the waiting list. The underlying assumption is that potential suppliers will sell "once and for all" options on their kidneys should they die under medically acceptable conditions.

Thus, the latter studies obtain option market prices for cadaveric organs for which one pays the seller now, while Becker and Elias obtain spot prices for living-donor kidneys, and these prices may also apply to deceased-donor kidneys, with these latter suppliers receiving payments in excess of the minimums they would accept. Depending on how the futures option contracts are structured, one expects to see prices that vary from modest to very low due to the minimal probability of any person becoming a donor under standard conditions. Howard and Byrne (2007) calculate these probabilities and find that they are quite small: the lifetime probability that someone age 18 will become an organ donor is somewhere under 0.003. (Despite these low probabilities, the authors demonstrate that the social value of additional registrants to organ donor lists is significant—between several hundred and several thousand U.S. dollars—due to the very large social value of a kidney transplant.) Thus, if one envisioned payments made now for (presumably binding) future donations should the circumstance arise, it is apparent that the social benefit calculus will allow these payments to be nontrivial, though not enormous by any means. The payments donors would actually require may be lower still. Spot sales of living-donor organs are clearly quite a different matter.

Becker and Elias (2008) follow a different course. Unlike the preceding studies, they argue that equilibrium prices for kidneys will be determined by an infinitely elastic supply from living donors, of whom there are very many in comparison with patients needing grafts. Thus, renal transplantation is viewed as a constant cost industry, and long-run equilibrium prices will equal (minimum) long-run average costs. By assuming constant returns in transplantation, one need only estimate the long-run supply price of the kidney input. This is done using an expected utility model to estimate the willingness of the donor to accept living kidney removal. Donor costs arise from (1) a very slight increase in risk of death due to the surgery; (2) a small risk of nonfatal injury, reducing life enjoyment; and (3) lost wages and other costs of hospitalization and inconvenience. One calculates the payment that would make a representative individual indifferent between selling a kidney or not. This approach is widely used in labor and insurance economics to evaluate compensating differentials for risky jobs and the like. One obtains different values (and thus predicted prices) for a kidney by imposing different assumptions on foregone earnings, value of life, the impact of nonfatal injury, and so on. Given fairly reasonable inputs, Becker and Elias suggest a market clearing price of about $15,000.

One must remember, however, that with free entry by suppliers (even within a country), the lowest-cost sellers determine prices. One problem with many analyses of the supply curve for organs arises from the inevitable use of "average" or "representative" values for model parameters. The price one would have to pay an "average" person to sell a kidney is largely irrelevant if the number of kidneys to be purchased is such that "average" sellers are not involved. Thus, if one were to buy 20,000 kidneys in a year, one would presumably have to pay only the amount equal to what the 20,000th least-cost seller will accept. Among millions of potential sellers, that individual may have a reservation price well below the average.

Survey Evidence

Rather informal survey evidence using college students led Barnett and Kaserman (2002) to predict low prices for options on cadaver organs: "Hence, these preliminary data suggest that, had market-clearing supply prices been used for organ procurement [in the United States] in 1997, the market-clearing supply price for donors would have been less than $1,000" (p. 144). They infer this by noting that, according to survey results at that time, an increase in prices paid from $0 to $1,000 would increase the number of surveyed potential donors agreeing to sell by 117 percent, which, given their procurement target, would clear the market.

Wellington and Whitmire (2006) base their analyses on the Barnett and Kaserman methodology, but they use a somewhat larger sample that they suggest is more representative. Their survey instrument is nearly identical. Again, the number of organs needed to meet a transplant target, based on waiting list changes with and without replacement of current living donors by cadavers, implies a completely inelastic demand. The implied elasticity of supply obtained by Wellington and Whitmire, however, is lower than Barnett and Kaserman's, leading to radically different estimates of the option prices: in 1996, the price necessary to produce equilibrium without replacing live donors was $135,242 (in the United States), while in 2003, equilibrating the market with living-donor replacement would cost $1.2 *trillion* per donor. These values, for options on cadaveric organs, defy comprehension and are the result of perfectly inelastic demand (infinite marginal benefit) and very inelastic supply. Unfortunately, the survey instrument used to solicit values is truncated at a maximum willingness to accept value equal to $10,000, so one should interpret their findings primarily as suggesting that prices might be "high." They conclude, "Given our findings, a competitive market for organs does not appear to be realistic" (p. 142). Certainly, competitive markets for goods with infinite marginal valuations and very inelastic supplies are not realistic.

While the Becker and Elias estimate is derived for living-donor kidneys, one would certainly expect that deceased-donor organs should sell for less, unless one were somehow required to obtain so many that purchases from extremely resistant sellers were necessary. Thus, one could look at the Becker and Elias numbers as providing strong support for the much lower cadaveric prices of Barnett and Kaserman. However, both the latter analysis and that of Wellington and Whitmire (2007) impose an infinite marginal benefit condition on the analysis, and that assumption is what causes the latter's estimates to become so large. Becker and Elias have downward-sloping demand for transplants, although their analysis does not shed light on what elasticity that demand might have.

Price Observations from Illegal Markets for Body Parts

Evidence on organ prices obtained from simple observation must be regarded as suspect, since the observed market institutions are seldom wholly legal and transparent. Journalists Susan Brown and David Glenn (2007) provide a summary of various observations on prices collected from numerous, disparate sources. They report, for example, living-donor kidney sales in Brazil producing prices ranging from about U.S.$2,000 to U.S.$10,000 before the "racket was shut down in 2003." Similarly, they note that the Iranian authorities pay about U.S.$1,300 (plus other valuable consideration) in their compensated program. In 2004, the World Health Organization (WHO) released a bulletin suggesting that international sales by vulnerable persons would support a living-donor kidney price of as little as U.S.$1,000. Nancy Scheper-Hughes (2000), a harsh critic of organ sales, reports on sales of organs from executed prisoners in China for about U.S.$30,000, although this apparently includes the transplant surgery and other care. Saudi Arabia began implementation of a program in 2006 that would have paid living kidney donors the equivalent of U.S.$13,330, plus health insurance benefits, but dropped the effort under a storm of criticism from outside medical authorities. Somewhat ironically, the Saudi effort was partially motivated by a desire to reduce travel by Saudi nationals abroad, where scandals involving kidney purchases in Pakistan and India had occurred in the past. (Indian sales have been discussed at length by critics of compensation.[11])

Numerous reports of black market sales of living-donor kidneys are available, often at prices of U.S.$10,000 to U.S.$20,000, not including surgical and ancillary costs. Middlemen of various stripes are often alleged to receive the bulk of these payments, leaving donors with relatively small proceeds. Except in the Iranian and Saudi case (the latter not being implemented), all of these examples involve illegal or wholly unregulated trade (or are pure speculation).

Price Evidence from Legal Markets for Body Parts

We now turn to evidence from legal, regulated markets for human tissue and other body products. The variation in prices observed among such easily obtained, nonvital materials as sperm, blood plasma, and hair (typically less than $200 in the United States) and eggs ($5,000 to $30,000), which must be surgically removed after a course of hormone treatments, suggests that donor inconvenience and suffering play a dominant role in determining costs. In the case of kidneys, the most likely live donor organ to be sold, donors undergo a low-risk but quite intrusive surgical procedure, and require weeks of recovery and follow-up examination for infections and so on. Further, some donors report difficulty in obtaining health insurance after donation, and many activities and jobs prohibit those with a single kidney from participation. The importance of these factors will undoubtedly vary widely across countries: nations with universal health funds will find it easier to attract donors than the United States, given the health insurance handicap. However, it is clear that living-donor kidneys obtained from sources in wealthier nations may be relatively expensive.

In-Kind Compensation

It is relevant to remark that most compensation proposals of which we are aware, including the extended proposal by Matas (2006), typically envision living-donor compensation that includes benefits, such as health insurance, in addition to a cash payment. No doubt such an idea will be necessary in the United States, where no national insurance fund exists, but in-kind compensation also will appeal to many persons who harbor suspicions of monetary incentives. From the economic point of view, in-kind compensation is ordinarily inferior to cash compensation sufficient to purchase the same bundle of goods. However, by translating some of the compensation into medical insurance, one might conceivably assuage a conscience bothered by the surgery the physician performs on the donor. Governments, which tend to be shortsighted in the extreme, may embrace the idea of giving compensation whose costs only come due in the future. Our sense is that no compensation reform will succeed without significant support from physicians, who will remain intimately involved in the transplantation decision. If the provision of insurance benefits assists in recruiting their support, it is well worth examining.

Some donors, also, may respond more effectively to compensation that combines money with other benefits and forms of recognition, since the motivations of persons to respond combine what Frey (1997) calls "extrinsic" and "intrinsic" components. Economics ordinarily focuses almost exclusively on extrinsic sorts of motivations (i.e., money rewards or penalties), while feelings of solidarity or moral obligation, called "intrinsic" factors, clearly play a role in organ donation. The practical significance of this circumstance arises because actions that affect extrinsic motivations can simultaneously undermine their intrinsic counterparts. Frey (1993) provides examples of economic relationships in which motivational "crowding out" appears to be significant.

Importance of Deceased Donor Organs

Finally, the importance of deceased donor organs in any reform effort should be apparent. It is likely, Wellington and Whitmire notwithstanding, that cadaveric source organs will be far cheaper than those provided by living donors, even when living donation is highly feasible. The opportunity cost of a cadaveric organ is perhaps zero. One need not worry about violating the rights of cadavers, nor do they need insurance coverage or other ongoing support. Moral objections to compensation for cadaveric donation appear weak. Cadavers are, and will remain, the only source for organs such as hearts and lungs. For some organs, deceased donor supplies may be sufficient to support expanded transplantation going forward. The difficulty, though, is that one cannot obtain the actual donor's permission postmortem: it must either be done premortem or dispensed with altogether. To obtain permission before death, one must rely on a futures type mechanism, and such a system may be costly or unwieldy. On the other hand, obtaining permission from the family is a source of great frustration for many in the transplantation field, and a reduction in family involvement is the frequently cited wish of many physicians and a bedrock principle of "primary donor" proposals. It is perhaps in this area that direct and immediate financial compensation can have its greatest effect with the least possible controversy. By offering a grant for funeral assistance, the procurement officer is given another means of encouraging donation. The situation in Spain provides evidence in this regard.

A Model for Donor Compensation Using a Public Monopsony

Although several authors have debated and examined hypothetical markets for human organs, we feel it is unrealistic to expect any country to implement a true competitive mechanism. Rather, the ethical dimension of the organ procurement problem, combined with the many powerful interest groups involved, suggests that a rather more bureaucratic approach is far more likely to be feasible. To that end, we describe in this section our proposal, which relies on the establishment of a public monopsony organ procurement authority. We are especially interested in evaluating the behavior of such an organization under the requirements of social welfare maximization. This sort of framework is similar to Goodwin's (2008) proposal, but it has not previously been formally analyzed. Our framework here is quite simplified, but it retains those elements necessary to resolve questions such as the relationship between living-donor and deceased-donor organ prices or the roles of explantation costs in optimal organ procurement.

Outline of the Model

If an unregulated competitive market for organs is unlikely, an unregulated private monopoly market is only slightly less improbable. Thus, we focus here on a publicly owned, welfare maximizing authority, which we envision as the sole legal purchaser of organs for transplantation. This authority will set compensation levels for both living- and deceased-donor organs, which must be obtained through voluntary supply by the legitimate owners. For simplicity, we ignore the dynamic nature of the problem, although we will say more about this complication later. Finally, we frame our discussion and analysis in terms of kidneys, although most of the basic principles will apply to other organs as well. Kidneys, however, are, and will likely remain, the primary organ of interest in discussions of reform.

We consider simple characterizations of the optimal behavior of a welfare-maximizing public monopsony organ procurement agency. Such an agency may potentially obtain organs—we will say kidneys—from two sources: deceased donors (denoted by the letter D) and living donors (denoted by the letter L). Transplants require organs on a one-to-one basis. Although some organs of both sorts may be obtained at no cost, quantities in excess of these limits require payments from the authority to the suppliers—that is, the donors. As is usually done, we take these payments, at the margin, to represent real costs from the social point of view. Further, we assume the compensation paid to donors occurs in a spot market, with deceased donor awards going to the donor's family.

Because we wish only to characterize the set of plausible solutions in a simple, intuitive manner, we assume that costs and benefits of transplants, from the social perspective, may be well approximated by piecewise linear functions. Strictly speaking, this implies that the underlying problem has a quadratic form. However, since our interest does not extend to pathological circumstances such as multiple solutions, this simplification is adequate to the current purpose.

We may introduce the following notation:

Q_L = quantity of living-donor kidneys

Q_D = quantity of deceased-donor kidneys

P_i (i = L, D) = compensation per kidney of type i paid by the authority

T_i (i = L, D) = social cost for a transplant using a kidney of type i

The "Organ Procurement Authority" (OPA) chooses quantities of both types of organs to maximize the net social benefits of transplants, written $B(Q_L, Q_D) - C(Q_L, Q_D)$. Following our earlier simplification, we assume that the marginal costs and benefits may be written as piecewise linear functions of organ quantities. In particular, we have for the marginal benefits:

$$MB_L = A - Q_L - Q_D \qquad (8.1)$$
$$MB_D = \theta(A - Q_L - Q_D) \qquad (8.2)$$

where the parameters A and θ have given, known values. In particular, the value of A is our simple measure of the value of a transplant when very few are being done, and an increase or decrease in A shifts the marginal benefit curve upward or downward uniformly at every quantity. Thus, changes in A have a very simple interpretation. Likewise, θ is a measure of the difference in the social benefit of a transplant performed using a deceased-donor organ as opposed to a living-donor organ. Thus, from the medical perspective, we have the condition $0 < \theta < 1$, indicating the diminished performance of cadaver-donor organ with respect to patient survival, delayed onset of graph function, required medication, and so on. Thus, any change in θ shifts the social marginal benefit of deceased-donor organs in the same direction.

It is important to recognize the hidden assumptions embodied in equations (8.1) and (8.2). Linearity aside, the representation given here implicitly assumes that if any type of organ is obtained, it will be transplanted into an appropriate recipient in social priority order. The problems of tissue typing and compatibility are largely ignored. Although matching of organs to recipients is a crucial function of the public transplant authorities, the mechanics of this process will be ignored in our model. This is almost surely too strong, even given the very large shortages currently observed. Some donor organs are more socially valuable than others because of genetic differentiation and heterogeneity of patients on the transplant waiting list. It is probable that optimal pricing policies will, in fact, pay "bonuses" for certain types of hard-to-obtain or otherwise highly desirable organs. Our interest here is limited to the much simpler question of the determinants of price differences when qualities and costs differ. In that sense, having two classes of organs is sufficient.

Further, we have the marginal benefits of transplants declining in the usual manner. This presumably occurs because of differences in the health status and tenure of wait-listed patients. Socially, it is quite plausible that there may be widespread support for giving priority, encompassed here by the marginal benefit, to patients who have waited a long time for a transplant, although medically such patients benefit less (often far less) than patients who have dialyzed only for a short time or have not used dialysis at all.

Thus, we view living-donor and deceased-donor organs as strong but imperfect substitutes, the degree of their inherent substitutability given by θ. Of course, in choosing how many organs to procure, the OPA will also take into account supply prices and transplant costs, and these may differ substantially. Further, some supplies of both sorts are expected to be available to the OPA "for free."

From the cost side, the OPA incurs, or takes account of, two types of costs: payments to organ suppliers (if necessary) and all other costs of the transplant therapy, which should be understood in a very broad sense. Transplantation as a treatment for, say, ESRD involves multiyear drug regimens, continuous monitoring and adjustment of immunosuppressive therapy, and so on. In the case of living donors, though, these transplant costs must be understood to include costs incurred by society with respect to the donor. While the assignment of costs into categories is somewhat arbitrary, living donors are likely to require some forms of nonprice compensation, such as an insurance benefit or medical monitoring, which should be taken to be part of the transplantation costs to society. Thus, we do *not* assume that the levels of compensation P_i are merely money payments to organ providers.

Thus, we define the marginal social costs of transplants as the sum of compensation to the seller and the costs of transplantation:

$$MC_L = P_L + T_L \tag{8.3}$$

$$MC_D = P_D + T_D \qquad (8.4)$$

The prices paid to donors may, however, be zero in those cases in which the authority uses less of one type of organ than donors offer willingly at a price of zero. This phenomenon causes the analysis here to differ from the conventional cases in which all input prices are positive. Although some quantities of organs are expected to be offered at no cost, these quantities will be less than the optimal quantities in many cases.

To capture this complication in the easiest feasible manner, we suppose that the supply curves are piecewise linear functions and that the supply decisions are not interdependent. Thus, we take the supply prices to be

$$P_L = 0 \text{ if } Q_L < L$$
$$P_L = k(Q_L - L) \text{ if } Q_L \geq L \qquad (8.5)$$
$$P_D = 0 \text{ if } Q_D < D$$
$$P_D = r(Q_D - D) \text{ if } Q_D \geq D \qquad (8.6)$$

so the given constants L and D represent the zero price supply quantities of living and deceased donor organs, respectively, and the given positive parameters k and r represent the responsiveness of supply prices to quantities obtained, respectively. Thus, the responsiveness of the quantity supplied of living-donor organs is inversely related to k, and similarly for Q_D and r.

We restrict our attention to those cases in which the OPA will pay for at least some organs from some vendors. This is reasonable given the evidently profound shortage arising currently under the zero price regimes.

Equating marginal benefits and costs yields a system of piecewise linear optimality conditions that are displayed in Figure 8.5, which is drawn assuming that the optimal policy of the OPA will be to purchase both types of organs. We investigate the cases in which only one type is paid for below. However, the optimality conditions have the following generic properties for all admissible values of the parameters. First, both optimality curves are convex, with the indicated slopes for their various segments. Second, the condition for optimal utilization of living-donor organs is flatter than that for deceased–donor organs for every value of Q_D for which both curves are defined. These facts imply that any optimal solution must be unique.

We note next that, generally speaking, there are three possible solutions, depending on where the curves cross, and these solutions will correspond to the cases where (1) only living-donor organs are paid for, (2) both types are

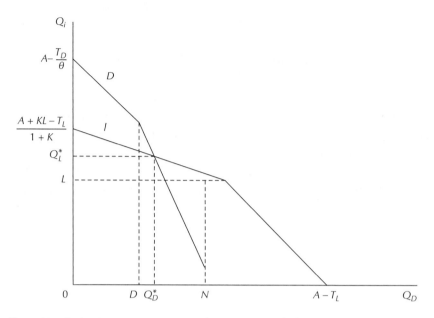

Figure 8.5   Optimal organ procurement with positive prices for both sources (living and cadaveric)

paid for, and (3) only deceased donor organs are paid for by the OPA. Because of the large number of degrees of freedom in this system, it is relatively easy to generate parameter values that produce each of these solutions in turn. We begin our analysis with what appears to us to be the most plausible case: that in which both types of organs are purchased from vendors.

In the case of both types of organs being purchased, considerable algebra leads to the following expressions for the optimal quantities of organs:

$$Q_L^* = L + [r(z + (T_D/r)) + k(r + \theta(-T_L/k))]*[rk + r + k\theta]^{-1} \qquad (8.7)$$

$$Q_D^* = D + [\theta k(z + (T_L/k)) + r(1 + k)(-T_D/r)]*[rk + r + k\theta]^{-1} \qquad (8.8)$$

where we have introduced the variable $z = A - L - D$, which has the convenient interpretation of being a measure of the marginal benefit of another best-quality organ at the point where free organs have been exhausted. Thus, $z > 0$ is true in the region where both organs receive positive compensation. The right sides of the equations are strictly positive in the region of interest, and these expressions allow us to derive a variety of comparative static results for optimal organ procurement. First, though, it is readily apparent that the prices associated with the optimal quantities will generally differ except by chance. How they will differ, however—that is, which type of organ will have the higher price—is harder to say. Intuition strongly implies that living-donor organs bought for transplantation into strangers will be relatively costly compared to deceased-donor organs.

Comparative statics results for the effects of changes in parameter values on optimal quantities and prices are straightforward, given the reduced forms in (8.7) and (8.8). In the case of living-donor organs, increases in the marginal benefit A, or the free supply L, increase optimal organ quantity, but at a less than one-to-one rate. Increases in deceased-donor free supply D reduce optimal living-donor organ use, again less than one-to-one. Increases in the social marginal cost of a deceased donor transplant increases the use of living-donor organs, and the contrary effect is observed in the case of living-donor transplant costs. All of these results are relatively intuitive. Parallel results are obtained for optimal deceased-donor organ use. These results are shown in Tables 8.1 and 8.2. Given independent supplies for organs of both types, the price responses to parameter changes are straightforward as well.

Note that an increase in the free supply quantity of an organ—say, $\Delta L > 0$—will increase the number of the same type of organs used, but the price paid for them will fall because of a net substitution toward the free organs, and price depends solely on the number of organs used beyond the free supply quantity. In addition, the quality level of the deceased-donor organs determines the degree to which they are good substitutes for living-donor organs, with the expected price effects at the optimal choices of the OPA.

We turn next to a review of the cases in which only one type of organ is bought, with the other being accepted only at levels low enough for the

Table 8.1 Comparative statics results for optimal quantities

Quantity change	Parameter					
	ΔA	ΔD	ΔL	ΔT_D	ΔT_L	$\Delta \theta$
ΔQ_L	+	−	+	+	−	−
ΔQ_D	+	+	−	−	+	+

SOURCE: Authors.

Table 8.2 Comparative statics results for optimal prices

Price change	Parameter					
	ΔA	ΔD	ΔL	ΔT_D	ΔT_L	$\Delta \theta$
ΔP_L	+	−	−	+	−	−
ΔP_D	+	−	−	−	+	+

SOURCE: Authors.

free supply to satisfy the need. An examination of Figure 8.5 provides some insight into how these outcomes may occur. Consider first the case in which no deceased-donor organs are purchased. In this case, the intersection of the optimality conditions occurs on the northwest portion of the figure, which requires that $(A + kL - T_L)/(1 + k)$ be sufficiently close to, but less than, $(A - T_D/\theta)$. This can occur in a variety of ways, the simplest being a sufficiently large value for L. In other words, the optimal plan will involve paying only living donors if the supply of free living donors is "large." Alternatively, if the quality of deceased-donor organs, given by θ, is sufficiently low, or the social cost of deceased-donor transplantation T_D is sufficiently high, cadaveric donors will not be compensated in the optimal plan. Finally, if the free supply of cadaver donors is very small, it is inevitable that society will want to pay for deceased-donor organs.

The other case of asymmetric payments, in which deceased donors are compensated, while living donors are not, is also plausible, although here one must point to the absolute upper bound in potential deceased donors of medical usefulness. It is quite likely that in some countries (especially the United States), even very high utilization of deceased-donor organs will not be sufficient, and living donors will be needed. We represent this in Figure 8.5 by introducing an upper bound on Q_D and disregarding all points to the right of it. Calling this constraint point N, we may obtain an additionally constrained solution if $N < (\theta A + rD - T_D)/(\theta + r)$. The more severe this potential limit, the less likely it is that society will not pay living donors. So, ignoring this complication, we see that a solution without compensation to living donors is more likely when $(\theta A + rD - T_D)/(\theta + r)$ is close to, but does not exceed, $(A - T_L)$. Again, there are a variety of ways this can occur. Low cadaveric organ transplant costs, high numbers of free deceased donor organs, and lower marginal social values for transplants all make this result more likely. High living-donor transplant costs can also cause this to happen. However, it seems implausible to us that this sort of solution is likely to occur in most circumstances, for several reasons. First, in many countries, the cadaveric organ supply is almost nil due to a lack of medical facilities for maintaining respiration and heartbeat in brain-dead patients. The example of Iran is relevant to this case. This translates here into a very small value for D and a very large value for r. Second, we expect very large social values for transplants, particularly in the beginning, which translates into a very large value for A. Since $\theta < 1$, this makes it increasingly unlikely that the optimal choice will involve no compensation for living donors. Finally, although we have witnessed global increases in reliance on living donors, this growth must to some degree reflect the dire circumstances of the shortage. While highly motivated to donate to a loved one, most family members are not, from the cost (rather than benefit) perspective, the "low-cost" donors one would expect to see provide many of the organs under a compensated regime.

The analysis presented here ignores the role of time and the problem an OPA would have in optimally "working through" the waiting list. This is intentional. As is clear from the simplest model, the problem of optimal organ procurement with compensation will involve numerous parameters of largely unknown magnitude, and these are likely to vary across countries. Thus, one can obtain a variety of plausible solutions. Adding the problem of dynamic reduction of the waiting list would require further parameters relating to discounting, dynamic evolution of the patient population, and heterogeneity among patients on the waiting list. This complexity, in turn, will produce even further classes of solutions, all dependent on the values of parameters that are unlikely to be known well or at all. Each national OPA is likely to be required to develop its own model that reflects its own unique circumstances.

In summary, the analysis of this section suggests the following broad, relevant conclusions. First, optimal compensation systems will involve positive, though different, compensation levels for living versus deceased donors when the shortage is severe. As the waiting lists are reduced, one can easily imagine a suspension of compensation for one type of donor (probably the living donor), while the other sort continues to receive payment. Increases in the "free" supply quantities of different types of donor organs increase the total use of those organs, but at a less than one-to-one rate. Higher levels of compensation are offered for organs of greater value, but transplant-associated costs suppress the optimal payment. All these conclusions are fairly intuitive.

The social welfare maximizing monopsony model presented here is overly simple, and many important issues in organ procurement reform are purposively ignored. However, we believe that this kind of approach is far more useful and far more practical than are discussions based on competitive supply-and-demand models. Our discussions that follow will, when appropriate, refer to this regulated monopsony framework, which we view as the best feasible template for reform in most countries.

Questions of Institutional Design

As the previous discussion suggests, we imagine a publicly funded organization, probably developed from existing OPOs in most countries, that can make compensation available to both cadaveric and, where appropriate, living donors. Payments would be transparent and available to all who qualify. Prices would be set, initially by trial and error, in an effort to reduce waiting list sizes at reasonable rates. Explicit cost-benefit analysis can be used to assist in price setting and recruitment goals. An outside board composed of physicians, laypeople, policy analysts, and representatives of patient organizations would oversee the compensation program. Although initial operations will be somewhat experimental, it must be remembered that even a poorly managed compensation system is likely to increase organ procurement success when compensation levels are not set too low.

It is unlikely that these new procurement agencies will have to deal with the difficult decision of how to utilize substandard organs for any great length of time, since compensation will increase availability and, thus, choice. It is likely that direct payments on a spot basis—to the donor himself in the case of living kidney donation and to the family in the case of deceased donors—will be the most effective and the easiest to implement quickly. Offering insurance benefits to living donors should be studied carefully and may be desirable in gaining acceptance for the compensation model. Evaluation of cadaver donors would not differ greatly from current protocols.

Another possibility, previously not discussed to our knowledge, would dispense with "efficient" price setting for donor compensation and instead implement prices that satisfy certain normative (ethical) standards. The idea here, as with insurance provision, is to gain wider acceptance of compensation among the health care community. For example, since a donation will lead to possible potentially large savings to public insurance funds, one could compensate donors with a "share" of these gains, thus setting the level of compensation to reflect a "fair share" of the gain realized by the donation. Of course, unless the fair share is small, this mechanism is likely to lead to higher compensation than the pure economic mechanism. One plausible consequence of such high levels of compensation would be an "excess" number of willing donors: since the rate of compensation would not be calculated based on the supply response, there is no reason to suspect any balance between the numbers of organs offered and the benefits their use would create.

In the case of living kidney donors, several important criteria must be applied to ensure public interest. First, donors would be screened for some months prior to the organ removal to eliminate disease risk. Such screenings would also probably involve psychological assessment of donor motives and allow for a "cooling-off" period. Individuals who recently suffered traumatic life events, such as the death of a spouse, divorce, loss of employment, and so on, could be asked to wait for later reevaluation. Lifelong follow-up would be implemented on all donors to constantly reassess the health risks of donation for persons in various health states, although current medical evidence suggests such risks are very low (Matas, 2008; quoted in Satel, 2008).

For many reasons, the best approach for the introduction of compensation mechanisms in many countries will involve trials. Goodwin (2008), in the context of the United States, proposes using the U.S. states as "laboratories" for this purpose and offers some model language to be used to modify the relevant laws to allow such experimentation. In the United States, the federal government has a long history of offering waivers to various states to conduct demonstration projects in areas such as welfare, job training, and so on.

One practical complication that accompanies the introduction of differing compensation regimes is a problem familiar to economists: when prices of any good differ among jurisdictions, an incentive for "arbitrage" is created by sellers seeking the best deal. One could imagine family members wishing that a deceased relative's organs be removed and transported to some other location where a trial offers compensation. Similarly, a living donor contemplating providing an organ to a stranger might seek out the most beneficial jurisdiction. The practical consequences of such flows are unknown, but it is not unlikely that some policy to deal with them will be necessary.

The Allocation of Organs

The institution of a compensation regime for organ procurement need have no effect whatsoever on the algorithms used to allocate organs among patients. The use of compensation to motivate behavior is here restricted solely to *obtaining* organs. We presume that the organs thus obtained will be distributed in a medically and ethically defensible manner. In all probability, the increase in the numbers of organs available under compensation will make the task of allocating them far easier, as poor matches need not be contemplated and those patients representing somewhat reduced prospects need not be removed from the active lists so readily. Probably about 30 percent of the patients on a typical kidney transplant waiting list have high panel reactive antibodies levels, indicating that they may be difficult patients to successfully transplant. Such persons suffer tremendously under the current shortages, both because of a reduced likelihood of obtaining a good kidney match and the reluctance of transplant physicians to "waste" scarce organs on patients with reduced prospects. It is such persons, in the direst condition, who will most benefit from the increase in organ availability. It is hard to regard that result as morally problematic.

Concerns of Political Acceptability and Fairness

The use of living donors raises several questions that are not, primarily, of an economic character. For example, should foreign nationals be allowed to enter a country and sell their organs if they qualify? Economists might be tempted to say "yes" based on efficiency (cost) arguments. However, viewed more broadly, it is easy to imagine that such activities might severely undermine public support for the organ procurement system (see Chapter 7). By restricting suppliers to "locals," one avoids many potential pitfalls, such as an inability to do follow-up on residents of foreign countries and difficulty in assessing motivation and past health history. As a result, we believe restricting sales to citizens of the home country, as is done in Iran, is likely to be desirable.

In addition, much criticism of compensation proposals comes from people who suggest such activities will amount to poor (i.e., "desperate") persons "selling their bodies" to perhaps rescue a rich person from the consequences of a self-indulgent or debauched lifestyle. This image has so much weight with some critics that they give no consideration to the thousands of deaths the shortages cause. More importantly, this objection raises the sociological question, who will the donors be, and how will they differ from nondonors?

As influential critics of compensation, such as Dr. Francis Delmonico in the United States, often point out, evidence from India and Iran suggests that rich people do not sell their kidneys. Rather, suppliers of organs are typically in the lower socioeconomic classes. Although the actual data presented by Ghods (2002) are somewhat ambiguous, basic economic reasoning suggests that the most willing suppliers of organs will be those with lower incomes and, economically speaking, lower opportunity costs. The same is true in many countries with respect to police officers, soldiers, high-rise construction workers, and other dangerous occupations. Having a kidney surgically removed is not a pleasant experience. Thus, it is not realistic to expect that the wealthy will become paid organ donors.

In our proposed framework, however, the public authority that is charged with screening living donors and obtaining organs for transplantation could apply any criteria to donation that was both legal and had wide public support. If a society is offended by allowing the poor to become paid organ donors, they could in principle prohibit it. Alternately, the authorities could pay higher prices for donations from wealthier people, although such a scheme sounds ridiculous on its face. However, the criteria for living donation, particularly in its sociological aspects, will undoubtedly be a topic for debate. For deceased donors, these issues may be less important.

The degree to which kidney supply will uniformly be a business of the poor, however, is by no means clear. In the case of deceased donor organs, the poor do not face any lower opportunity cost than the rich; the alternative use of the organs is to bury them. More generally, if, as Matas (2006) and many other proponents suggest, society were to treat and regard donors as heroes, then the differential between the donation participation of poorer and richer persons would be reduced as the monetary component of the reward became relatively less influential. As in the case of military service with volunteer forces (as in the United States, the United Kingdom, and Germany), it seems inevitable that those needing opportunities will be disproportionally represented, but it is not inevitable that participation need be so skewed as to undermine support for the institution itself.

On the other side of the donor demographic equation, of course, are those awaiting transplantation. Here, one can find reasons to doubt the criticisms based on donor status. In the United States, for example, the poor and minority populations are vastly overrepresented on the kidney waiting list: African Americans constituted about 34 percent of kidney transplant candidates on the waiting list in 2012, but account for only around 13 percent of the U.S. population. Transplants supported by organs obtained from disadvantaged or minority donors are likely to benefit minority patients. Prohibiting certain persons from receiving compensation for organ donation directly impacts other persons, often from the same disadvantaged populations, who are awaiting transplant therapy. Some analysts, such as Michele Goodwin (2006), have persuasively argued for introducing compensation based squarely on considerations of fairness to minority communities.

Conclusion

From the evidence provided in this chapter we conclude that material compensation to organ donors would raise (and surely not reduce) the number of organs available for transplant. A monopsonistic agency, permitted to offer compensation to donors and committed to achieving something like a social optimum, would be a workable solution that can be realized quickly because the necessary institutions already exist in most countries. The organ "price" (compensation package) is likely to be in a moderate range, especially for deceased-donor organs and especially when compared to the current cost of an organ transplant. Compared to the costs of continuous dialysis, the prices paid for organs will perhaps be negligible. Moreover, the monopsonistic organ agency would substitute for any direct interaction of donor and final beneficiary. Finally, the agency's procurement efforts could be restricted to its national boundaries. Thus, an "international trade in organs," let alone its legalization, is neither a necessary element of this proposal nor supported by us. By contrast, the increased availability of organs can contribute greatly to a reduction of the currently existing international black market in organs.

However, it is likewise important to stress that we do not really know the "organ supply function"—that is, how the availability of organs rises in response to increasing compensation to donors. This may not only differ across countries but also between organs, and not least between organs from deceased and living donors. Moreover, the necessity to use organs from living donors will greatly differ among countries. Thus, what should be initiated is a wave of pilot projects in many countries with different systems of compensation to donors. The projects must be conducted in a scientifically controlled way to permit unequivocal conclusions and, eventually, to end unnecessary suffering and death of organ patients.

We believe that the introduction of compensation, done correctly, publicly, and transparently, will save thousands of lives and billions of dollars or euros. It is unnecessary and probably undesirable to move to a competitive market in human organs: in most countries, tremendous benefits will arise merely from introducing reasonable compensation within a reformed version of the current organ procurement apparatus. In our view, providing trained teams the ability to offer financial recognition to donors, both deceased and living, will be a powerful tool that will increase organ supply immediately. We believe that all available evidence suggests that such a course will be successful and that it is necessary.

9

Conclusion

In a recent article in the online periodical *Econ Journal Watch*, author Jon Diesel asked, "Do economists reach a conclusion on organ liberalization?" Not surprisingly, the answer was, they do. He goes on to note, "It is fair to say that organ policy is one issue on which economists who are vocal take exception to status-quo restrictions. . . ." (p. 329). Similarly, a survey of professional economists studied by Whaples (2009) found that 70 percent favored the legalization of compensation for organ suppliers. In this instance, at least, the conventional wisdom that economists never agree appears to be substantially faulty.

If economists agree on Proposition X, a cynic might say, then it is likely that Proposition X is wrong. In the case at hand, however, we maintain that the economists are correct and the use of compensation, *in the appropriate manner*, is the single most useful policy response to the global shortage of organs for transplantation. This conclusion, though, is by no means merely the uncritical application of "the market" to the problem at hand. It is very unlikely that society would be able to tolerate any sort of unregulated market in which human organs are bought and sold like wheat or pork bellies. Human organs *are* different.

Yet, a human kidney, or even a human cadaver, is not a human being. In contrast, those people waiting, and too often dying, on the transplant lists *are* human beings, and it is their welfare and their dignity that must be at the center of any discussion of organ procurement reform. Most people—including, we suspect, most economists—would prefer a world in which altruistic donation of organs, particularly from deceased donors, was sufficient to satisfy all serious medical needs for them. Unfortunately, this is not the world in which we live.

Thus, we face a choice, and the choice we make will materially affect the lives of hundreds of thousands, and perhaps millions, of people all over the world. The source and nature of that choice are the subjects of this book. As economists, we believe the tools of economic analysis are useful in making this choice, and we have applied these tools in various ways. But the choice we all face in this regard is not solely of an economic character. There is a profound moral dimension involved, and, as many critics of donor compensation correctly point out, not everything can or should be the subject of a financial calculation. And ultimately, it is precisely this moral dimension that compels us to argue for the use of compensation.

It is true that there are very good reasons to believe that the introduction of donor compensation will increase organ supply, promote an expansion of transplantation, diminish the use of dialysis (in the case of kidneys), and produce large and ongoing savings to public insurance funds. These are good reasons to favor liberalization. It is likewise true that the prohibition on compensating donors legally bars seriously ill people from making voluntary arrangements to greatly improve or even save their lives, a violation of their rights of self-defense and personal autonomy. Again, these are powerful reasons to allow liberalization. Ultimately, though, it is the preservation of the lives of potential transplant patients that provides the fundamental reason to allow compensation. The deaths on (and off) the waiting lists are a relentless argument for reform.

It is ironic that several of the greatest products of human ingenuity and skill—our ability to transplant human organs, suppress the immune response, and mimic the function of the human kidney using a machine—have brought, along with their undeniable blessings, this ongoing crisis. In no sense would anyone wish that these medical advances had not been made: even with the failures in organ procurement policy, many hundreds of thousands of persons have had their lives saved or fundamentally improved by transplant therapy or dialysis. Yet, these achievements serve to some degree to sharpen our perception of the extent of the policy failures and to make those failures harder to tolerate. To make matters even worse, it is our contention—supported by the overwhelming evidence we provide in this book—that the shortage of organs for transplantation is man-made. The problem can be solved readily, using our existing understanding of the market allocation mechanism, without ethical compromise and without the need for any additional public or private resources. Indeed, even when a relatively short time frame is selected, the introduction of compensation for donation will save both lives and substantial amounts of money. Over the longer term, the benefits become steadily greater in both the human and financial senses.

It is quite difficult to think of any other public policy change for which such strong claims can credibly be made. The extraordinary mixture of success and tragedy that organ transplantation represents and the stubborn persistence of the policies we enforce in organ procurement has been made possible by the unique confluence of fundamental forces organ transplantation envelopes. Issues of what it means to be human, of religious conviction, of the perceptions of unfairness and special privilege in organ distribution, and of the tremendous financial costs of transplantation and dialysis all combine to present problems that nearly everyone can be concerned about. Further, the relative rarity of the medical need for transplant therapy allows the great majority of people to adopt moral positions for which they are unlikely to ever have to suffer martyrdom, and martyrs, of course, are in notoriously short supply.

The arguments in this book constitute our evidence for the following propositions:

1. The current ("altruistic") system of organ procurement evolved in an environment in which only transplants from living and related organ donors were medically possible, while organs from deceased and living, unrelated donors could not be transplanted. As a consequence, the prohibition on donor compensation had few initial effects.

2. Medical advances, particularly those advances involving immune response suppression, made donations from strangers or deceased persons first feasible and eventually highly successful. The insufficient provision of organs from postmortem and living donors led to quickly expanding waiting lists of transplant candidates needing suitable organs. The organ shortage became an issue of considerable medical, social, and political concern. Due to the shortage, dialysis therapy—despite high social and individual costs—became a "second best" solution for a steadily rising number of kidney patients.

3. Consequences of the growing shortages are many and include deaths of patients on waiting lists, very long waits for transplantation, reduced transplant success, large dialysis populations, and the expanded use of

both substandard and living organ donors. Substandard donors provide fewer organs of generally lower quality, resulting in diminished patient outcomes when compared to standard criteria donors.

4. The persistence of severe shortages of organs in many high-income countries has led to a growing black market, in which the worst fears of those opposed to compensation are realized in unregulated and often illegal settings.

5. Renal grafts, as a therapeutic alternative to hemodialysis, are highly cost-effective from even the most narrow financial perspectives, and society benefits enormously from any reasonable expansion of kidney transplantation activity.

6. Transplantation of most solid organs other than kidneys is far less economic, and transplants of organs such as hearts, lungs, and intestines are very unlikely to be cost-saving for insurance funds with current rates of life expectancy and medical cost.

7. The primary cause of the persistent shortage of organs for transplantation is the nearly universal prohibition on providing compensation to organ donors. Those few parallel cases in which one might validly draw comparisons—such as the organ procurement programs in Iran and Spain and the U.S. policy for whole-cadaver donation to medical schools—all strongly suggest that compensation can resolve the worst of the shortage.

8. In response to growing shortages, many countries have implemented various reforms in procurement practices, almost all of which fall short of donor compensation. Several such reforms have been shown to increase organ supplies, although in most cases gains are insufficient to reduce waiting lists.

9. The most important and successful "partial" reforms include the Organ Donation Breakthrough Collaborative (ODBC) in the United States and similar efforts in the Eurotransplant countries, pairwise exchange programs, donor "clubs," and presumed consent laws, all of which offer either documented or credible potential improvements in organ harvesting or utilization. The Spanish model, while quite successful, utilizes presumed consent and payments to donor families.

10. There is scant support worldwide for totally free, unregulated markets in human organs, and if such institutions were practically required in order for society to obtain the benefits from donor compensation, prospects for effective reforms would be small.

11. Almost all analysts who favor compensation for organ donation envision a state-sponsored and tightly regulated monopsony structure so financial incentives would be used solely to obtain organs, while organ distribution among potential recipients would continue to be based on medical and ethical criteria and would be subject to public oversight.

12. The existing organ procurement agencies in most countries could, in the first instance, be reconstituted as the sole official "buyers" of human organs, and their ongoing operations would, in many areas, be reasonably unaffected by this change. Rather, the organ procurement officials would merely add the additional tool of direct financial compensation to their current portfolio of recruitment techniques, at least in the case of deceased donors. However, the initiation of compensated living donation would require significant new structures to be put in place in many countries.

13. Simple mathematical analysis of a monopsony problem of donor recruitment, including both living and deceased donors and some measure of altruistic donation, suggests that the actual optimal policies of donation agencies will typically involve obtaining both deceased- and living-donor organs, which will receive different levels of compensation. As time passes and waiting lists shrink, suspension of most payments for living donation are likely, while financial compensation for deceased donation will continue.

14. Evidence from other markets for human body materials, such as eggs, sperm, and blood products, does not suggest any fundamental difficulty with donor compensation. The historical failures of the U.S. blood supply documented by Titmuss are not valid criticisms of donor payment.

15. The hypothetical "prices" for donor kidneys have been the subject of several types of analyses, which have led to a very wide range of price "forecasts." While this issue is made quite difficult by the different ways in which organs could be paid for (e.g., spot versus futures markets), it is our view that likely kidney prices for living donors in developed countries will be in the tens of thousands of dollars, with cadaver donor kidneys receiving (perhaps much) smaller payments. We believe that spot market organization is the most practical market form, but we do not rule out other options in appropriate cases.

16. The final barrier to donor compensation will surely be that constructed from the allegedly sturdy timbers of moral imperative.

However, the moral arguments in opposition to donor compensation are neither convincing nor, in most cases, internally consistent.
The bulk of such arguments cannot possibly apply to compensation
for cadaveric donation, and when such donation is entirely transparent
and voluntary, most remaining arguments appear weak. Moreover, the
moral weakness of the current system must be taken into consideration.

The introduction of donor compensation, within a public system of transplantation funding, is not the radical reform so many of its critics make it out
to be. However, it does represent a fundamental policy change, and the political
risks of introducing payments in a poorly managed way are immense. Should
this final reform "fail," the consequences for patients and their families, as well
as public health funds, will be severe. There is therefore the strongest possible
incentive to see that such a reform is implemented in a manner most likely to
reveal its real potential. Because many influential medical officials will not want
the donor compensation reform to succeed, it is imperative that any initial
trials be conducted by unbiased, expert investigators and that the research be
carefully overseen by public committees that include advocates for reform, experienced public health administrators, and patient representatives. Great care
must be taken to see that medical organizations dominated by ideologues not
be given the sole authority to conduct the relevant trials, since it is quite conceivable such groups might use that opportunity to sabotage the effort itself.
However, it is also apparent to us that, for the donor compensation reform to
succeed, the support of physicians is absolutely necessary. In the same spirit, any
trials or initial implementation must also be overseen by those who oppose
compensation, so no one can credibly claim that the evaluation was less than
rigorous and fair.

It is our view that donor compensation can succeed in relieving thousands
of sick people of the risks of severe illness and death and that this approach,
and this approach alone, has the potential to fulfill the enormous promise that
transplantation therapy represents.

Notes

Foreword

The author is professor of economics at the University of Konstanz and president of the German Health Economics Association, 2012–2013.

Chapter 2

1. The Indian surgeon Samhita, however, reportedly investigated skin grafts as early as 1000 BCE.

2. See Carrel (1902).

3. Corneal transplants, which we do not address in this book, form a partial exception.

4. Xenografts are commonly seen in the replacement of defective heart valves using donor material from either pigs or cattle. Attempts to use xenografts for larger organs have not been successful to date.

5. Nonstandard criteria donors typically provide fewer organs that are suitable for transplantation. For example, U.S. data for 2005 indicate that expanded criteria donors yield 0.9 kidneys each, on average, compared to 1.68 for standard criteria donors (UNOS, 2005).

6. Some larger countries, such as the United States and Germany, divide their territories into smaller regions that operate with limited autonomy in organ distribution.

7. An alternative form of treatment is peritoneal dialysis, which the patient does at home. Only about 7 percent of all dialysis patients in the United States employ this treatment modality, and its use is falling (UNOS, 2007). Additionally, for various reasons, many renal patients who could benefit from a graft are not referred to the transplant lists in the United States and elsewhere (Schold et al., 2008).

8. In the United States, approximately 15 percent of kidney grafts currently go to second or later transplants (OPTN, 2010).

9. The budget of the ESRD program, which is funded under the Medicare system, has risen from $4.7 billion in 1991 to more than $24 billion today (USRDS, 2011).

10. In general, the organs collected are allocated within the acquiring OPO's region unless there is no acceptable recipient in that region or a perfect match is located outside the region.

11. National Organ Transplant Act, 1984, Public Law 98-507.

12. "Any person who violates subsection (a) of this Section shall be fined not more than $50,000 or imprisoned not more than five years, or both" (274e, U.S. Code).

13. For a more detailed account of Dr. Jacobs's efforts, see Denise (1985).

14. See Cherry (2005, pp. 178–179).

15. See, for example, Caplan (1984) and Sells (1993).

Chapter 3

1. This latter category is sometimes termed "donation after cardiac death" (DCD) donors.

2. A more extensive and comprehensive accounting is given later in this chapter.

3. Health consequences include infections, hypertension, muscle cramps, and clotting at the access site. For the effect of dialysis on future transplant success, see Matas and Sutherland (2005). Moreover, Perez-Pena (2006) gives a good account of life on dialysis.

4. OECD data consistently show the United States with among the highest rates of diabetes and obesity. In 2007, prevalence of diabetes among persons 20 to 79 years of age was 9.2 percent in the

United States, as opposed to 6.4 percent in Australia, 4 percent in the United Kingdom, and 7.2 percent in South Korea, to mention some examples. However, some countries have even higher rates. OECD *Health Data 2006* reports a U.S. obesity rate of 30.6 percent (for 2002), the highest value of all OECD countries. See also Dor et al. (2007).

5. Uniquely, the Agency not only collects organs but also engages in genetic research aimed at producing organs.

6. Even Buddhist monks do not seem to be free from considerations of getting remuneration by selling a kidney. On January 14, 2007, the following was posted online: "I am a Buddhist monk from Sri Lanka. I like to donate my kidney, but I need some help. If you can help me to study or to get visa to USA. . . ."

7. The authors provide a model for this phenomenon.

8. This is not irrational. See Howard (2007).

9. Not only are the figures mentioned in the text impressive, but the increase is impressive as well. In January 2011, the results from the same Google search were 473,000 for "black market kidney"; 2,280,000 for "selling kidney"; and 1,930,000 for "buying kidney."

10. A third one is a book by Michele Goodwin (2006). Its title, *Black Markets: The Supply and Demand of Body Parts*, has a double meaning. It uses the term *black* to refer to both illegal markets and African Americans, but it does not provide an empirical description of the black market.

11. Francis Delmonico, a leading U.S. transplant surgeon, recently estimated the number of annually sold organs at 5,000.

12. By contrast, in countries with a national health care system, persons with new organs obtained abroad could be denied care or charged for it.

13. In 1994, the Israeli Ministry of Health allowed private reimbursement, and since 2001, public funds have been offered for transplant abroad. See Mor (2009).

Chapter 4

1. "Weakness" is in the eye of the beholder. Katz et al. (1999) regard a matching rate of 69.3 percent as good.

2. UNOS provides some data on this. Also see Brooks et al. (2006).

3. Dialysis costs totaled almost $18 billion for Medicare in 2006. Costs for transplants in that year were about $1 billion. Maintenance and care for patients with functioning grafts cost about $1.2 billion. Graft failure costs Medicare about $200 million. Patients with functioning grafts cost Medicare about $17,000 per year and per patient, versus about $70,000 per year for someone on dialysis (HCFA, 2007).

4. This phenomenon is important and is touched on in Chapter 3. See also Mange, Joffee, and Feldman (2001).

5. Sickness removals are nearly the same thing as deaths in practical terms, and including those nearly doubles the carnage among wait-listed patients.

6. The analysis assumes that this goal is attainable.

7. Personal communication.

Chapter 5

1. Of special significance in the earliest literature of the organ shortage is Jesse Dukeminier's "Supplying Organs for Transplantation," *Michigan Law Review*, vol. 68, published in 1970, in which the current shortages were predicted.

2. Roth (2007) provides an analysis of the role of "repugnance" in many areas.

3. Alternatively, one could imagine agents who obtain the organs from primary donors and then supply them to transplant centers—in which case, the price would include compensation to those agents.

4. Blood and tissue screening has improved almost beyond recognition since Titmuss's commentary. More generally, a hypothetical and very poorly managed compensation system is taken as evidence of a danger implicit in compensation as such.

5. This is not to say no controversy has arisen from such practices, which are usually illegal in Europe. For a discussion, see Harmon (2009).

6. For some insights into this business and its international aspects, see Barnett (2006).

7. Beard, Kaserman, and Saba (2005) provide some discussion of the difficulties in comparing OPO performance.

8. This complaint varies widely across different countries. In the United States, for example, funding appears far better than in the European Union, although such comparisons are very difficult because of the completely incompatible funding mechanisms used.

9. See Barnett, Beard, and Kaserman (1993), reprinted in Ekelund (1998).

10. Family noncompliance with donation requests is a profound problem. Sheehy et al. (2003) document the extent of the problem in the United States.

11. This is not true of NHB donors in general.

12. See www.ncbi.nlmonih.gov/pubmed/18701611.

13. The National Kidney Foundation of the United States, however, strongly opposes compensation. However, one would not characterize it as a patients' rights organization.

14. The prominent transplant physician Francis Delmonico remarked that donor payments would threaten "the nobility of the medical profession," a very serious charge indeed. See Delmonico (2004b).

15. See, for example, the eloquent defense of compensation in Matas (2004).

16. As noted in Chapter 4, the Milliman figures are billings, not payments, and they exceed the reimbursement levels of Medicare, the relevant U.S. health insurance fund. However, the simulation only requires relative values to make its point, and the Milliman figures are credible for this purpose. If anything, the Milliman figures perhaps understate the relative costs of rarer transplants. For example, UNOS reports first-year liver transplant costs of about U.S.$314,600 in 2008, and the corresponding Milliman figure in 2005 is U.S.$392,500. Thus, the calculations introduce a bias against a finding of insurance fund resistance to expanded cadaveric transplant activities.

17. Current debate in U.S. insurance policy is so serious that it is unlikely that larger insurance companies are particularly focused on this problem.

18. Stason (1968), p. 927, as cited by Goodwin (2008), p. 112.

Chapter 6

1. It is, however, a special form of property that is subject to myriad restrictions in use.

2. There are important variations, depending on the type of donor. See Andrés et al. (2009).

3. Caution is needed when comparing across countries. See Jansen et al. (2009). The Spanish case is very important in this regard. Rodriguez-Arias et al. (2010) report Spanish families refused deceased donation in only 16.4 percent of cases in 2009, "almost half the French rate" (p. 1101).

4. Later, Pennsylvania reprised this approach. See "Debating Organ Donor Compensation," ABC News, June 16, 2002.

5. See "China Admits Death Row Organ Use," BBC Wednesday, August 26, 2009, and Budiani-Saberi and Delmonico (2008).

6. See, for example, Leslie (1995) and Matesanz (2003).

7. There are also discussions in Becker and Elias (2008), Howard (2007), and Kaserman (2006).

8. Canada, a country with a universal health care system, is nearly unique in having no national organ transplant authority.

9. It is probable that the use of substandard organs is, within the altruistic framework, socially desirable.

10. As described in the NSF Discovery release "Kidney Exchange: A Life-Saving Application of Matching Theory," October 5, 2005.

Chapter 7

1. Holding such a position can, of course, be disputed. Recently, Pope Benedict XVI claimed that we are living in a time where "an ethical stance is replaced by a calculus of the consequences."

2. The works mentioned are usually an early one and in most cases one of a larger oeuvre. Moreover, some authors fall in more than one of the categories used to roughly characterize the field of their contributions.

3. Concerning postmortem organs, some authors take another position. See, for example, Kreis (2008), Spital and Erin (2002), and Giordano (2005).

4. As Radcliffe Richards (2008) said, "If donation is to remain optional, therefore, there is nothing in the least discriminatory in saying that access to transplantation should be limited to people who belong to the donation scheme" (p. 390). Arthur Caplan (1992) writes convincingly, "The connection between the ethics of procurement and allocation is reciprocal. Few people will feel obligated to help

those in need if they perceive inequities in the system used to designate exactly who is most in need and most deserving" (p. 157).

5. Moreover, it is disputable whether the next of kin becomes the "owner"—in the usual sense of the word—of the deceased.

6. This is what Christian Williams proposed in 1994.

7. As early as 1983, Al Gore, in a U.S. congressional hearing on the National Organ Transplant Act (NOTA), envisaged that altruistic donation may become insufficient. As one possible option, he proposed the "mandated choice." Postmortem donation "would remain completely and totally voluntary, but the choice would have to be made yes or no" (quoted in Satel (2008, p. 165)).

8. Stacey Taylor (2005, p. 12) points out that a mandated choice without consequences—namely, to become a member of a "club" or to be excluded from it—is rather useless because it does not provide an incentive to opt in favor of becoming a (postmortem) donor.

9. See Radcliffe Richards (2008, p. 384).

10. See, for example, Ross et al. (1997).

11. In this respect, Arthur Caplan (1992) refers to John Stuart Mill and says the philosopher and economist "was disturbed by the prospect that persons, expert or not, might be allowed to force their judgments of right and wrong, good and bad, on others" (p. 25).

12. As Radcliffe Richards (2004) says, "Insisting on the ban amounts to allowing the people who support it—mainly ones who are too rich to need to sell, and unlikely to die for want of a transplant—to indulge their feelings of disgust at the expense of the sick and destitute whose interests are being offered as the justification of the policy" (p. 277).

13. A detailed analytical exposition of the meaning of "exploitation" is provided by Alan Wertheimer. His article in the *Stanford Encyclopedia of Philosophy* incorporates repeatedly examples pertaining to transplantation and the buying and selling of human organs.

14. Ambagtsheer and Weimar (2011) complain that the Declaration of Istanbul has so far not led to an effective and realistic fight against transplant commercialism and organ trafficking, and they suggest ways to improve the current prohibitive approach. Their article is available on the *American Journal of Transplantation* website (www.amjtrans.com). Only ten days later, Glazier and Delmonico (2011) offered a competing view in their article "The Declaration of Istanbul Is Moving Forward by Combating Transplant Commercialism and Trafficking by Promoting Organ Donation." Thus, they reiterate an old hope.

15. Stacey Taylor (2005) even states that markets in human body parts are "morally imperative."

Chapter 8

1. The United Kingdom has gone so far as to ban all privately financed transplants, although this action is primarily a response to foreigners receiving self-financed transplants in Britain using organs donated to the NHS.

2. But see Howard and Byrne (2007) for careful calculations of the social value of potential cadaveric organ donors.

3. Abadie and Gay (2006) provide a "signaling" interpretation of donor cards. Breyer (2006) provides a discussion of the problems with family consent in Eurotransplant.

4. Barnett and Kaserman (2002) give a discussion favoring spot (as opposed to futures) market organization.

5. For living-donor liver transplants in Japan, see Todo et al. (2003).

6. This is what Gneezy and Rustichini (2000) have in mind—though in a different context—when they say, "Pay enough or don't pay at all."

7. The Iranian system has faced severe financial stresses in recent years, and the value of the compensation offered to donors has declined. See Zargooshi (2008 a, b).

8. Even the Declaration of Istanbul (2008) demands "comprehensive reimbursement" of the costs of donating an organ.

9. This evidence refers to billings; what families actually pay in the end is unknown.

10. It is lamentable because the distribution of blood groups differs among population groups. A low organ donation rate of African Americans increases the waiting time for organ patients of this group.

11. Goyal et al. (2002) provide a widely cited review of the circumstances of Indian living kidney donors.

References

Abadie, A., and S. Gay. 2006. "The Impact of Presumed Consent Legislation on Cadaveric Donation: A Cross-Country Study." *Journal of Health Economics* 25 (4): 599–620.

Abe, T. 2002. "Philosophical and Cultural Attitudes against Brain Death and Organ Transplantation in Japan." In *Beyond Brain Death*, edited by M. Potts, P. A. Byrne, and R. G. Nilges. 191–99. New York: Springer.

Abecassis, M. M. 2006. "Financial Outcomes of Transplantation—A Provider's Perspective." *American Journal of Transplantation* 6 (6): 1257–63.

Abuna, G. M., et al. 1991. "Commercialism and Rewarded Gifting: The Negative Impact of Paid Organ Donation." In *Organ Replacement Therapy: Ethics, Justice, Commerce*, edited by W. Land and J. B. Dossetor, 164–72. Berlin: Springer.

Adams, A. F., A. H. Barnett, and D. L. Kaserman. 1999. "Markets for Organs: The Question of Supply." *Contemporary Economic Policy* 17 (April): 147–55.

Ambagtsheer, F., and W. Weimar. 2011. "A Criminological Perspective: Why Prohibition of Organ Trade Is Not Effective and How the Declaration of Istanbul Can Move Forward." *American Journal of Transplantation* 12 (3): 515–16.

Andrés, A., S. Vazquez, M. Cebrian et al. 2009. "Lower Rate of Family Refusal for Organ Donation in Non-Heart-Beating versus Brain-Dead Donors." *Transplantation Proceedings* 41 (6): 2304–5.

Anyanwu, A., A. McGuire et al. 2002. "An Economic Evaluation of Lung Transplantation." *Journal of Thoracic and Cardiovascular Surgery* 123: 411–20.

Anyanwu, A., C. Rogers, and A. Murday. 2001. "Assessment of Quality of Life in Lung Transplantation Using a Simple Generic Tool." *Thorax* 56: 218–22.

———. 2002. "Intrathoracic Organ Transplantation in the United Kingdom 1995–99: Results from the UK Cardiothoracic Transplant Audit." *Heart* 87 (5): 449–54.

Arrow, K. 1972. "Gifts and Exchanges." *Philosophy and Public Affairs* 1 (4): 343–62.

Ashraf, O., et al. 2005. "Attitude toward Organ Donation: A Survey in Pakistan." *Artificial Organs* 29: 899–905.

Aufderheide, D., and M. Dabrowski, eds. 2002. *Gesundheit, Ethik, Ökonomik: Wirtschaftsethische und moralökoomische Perspektiven des Gesundheitswesens* [Health, ethics, and economics: economic-ethical and moral-economic perspectives of the health system]. Berlin: Dunker & Humblot.

Aumann, C., and W. Gaertner. 2004. "Die Organknappheit: Ein Plädoyer für eine Marktlösung" [Shortage of organs: a plea for a market solution]. *Ethik in der Medizin* 16: 105–11.

Baard, E., and R. Cooney. 2001. "China's Execution, Inc." *Village Voice*, May 1.

Badovinac, K., et al. 2006. "Organ Utilization among Deceased Donors in Canada, 1993–2002." *Canadian Journal of Anaesthetics* 53: 747–52.

Bagheri, A. 2005. "Organ Transplantation Laws in Asian Countries: A Comparative Study." *Transplantation Proceedings* 37 (10): 4159–62.

Barber, K., et al. 2006. "Potential for Organ Donation in the United Kingdom: Audit of Intensive Care Units." *British Medical Journal* 332: 1124–27.

Barnett, A. 2006. "Blue-Eyed, Musical US Physicist: Sperm for Sale, a $500 Shot." *The Observer*, May 7.

Barnett, A. H., T. R. Beard, and D. L. Kaserman. 1993. "The Medical Community's Opposition to Organ Markets: Ethics or Economics?" *Review of Industrial Organization* 8: 669–78.

Barnett, A. H., R. D. Blair, and D. L. Kaserman. 1996. "A Market for Organs." *Society* 33: 8–17.

Barnett, A. H., and D. L. Kaserman. 1995. "The 'Rush to Transplant' and Organ Shortages." *Economic Inquiry* 33 (July): 506–15.

———. 2002. *The U.S. Organ Procurement System—A Prescription for Reform.* Washington, DC: American Enterprise Institute.

Barzel, Y. 1989. *Economic Analysis of Property Rights.* Cambridge: Cambridge University Press.

Beard, T. R., J. Jackson et al. 2010. "A Time-Series Analysis of US Kidney Transplantation and the Waiting List: Donor Substitution Effects and 'Dirty Altruism.'" Working Paper 2010-01, Economics Department, Auburn University, Auburn, AL.

———. 2012. "A Time-Series Analysis of U.S. Kidney Transplantation and the Waiting List: Donor Substitution Effects." *Empirical Economics* 42 (1): 261–77.

Beard, T. R., J. D. Jackson, and D. L. Kaserman. 2008. "The Failure of U.S. Organ Procurement Policy." *Regulation* 30 (4): 22–30.

Beard, T. R., and D. L. Kaserman. 2006. "On the Ethics of Paying Organ Donors: An Economics Perspective." *DePaul Law Review* 55: 827–50.

Beard, T. R., D. L. Kaserman, and R. P. Saba. 2004. "Limits to Altruism: Organ Supply and Educational Expenditures." *Contemporary Economic Policy* 22 (October): 433–41.

———. 2005. "Inefficiency in Cadaveric Organ Procurement." *Southern Economic Journal* 73 (1): 13–26.

Becker, G., and J. L. Elias. 2008. "Introducing Incentives in the Market for Live and Cadaveric Organ Donations." *Journal of Economic Perspectives* 21 (3): 3–24.

Bein, T., D. Boesebeck et al. 2005. "Hirntodbestimmung und Betreuung des Organspenders—eine Herausforderung für die Intensivmedizin" [Determination of cerebral failure and care for the organ donor—a challenge for intensive care medicine]. *Deutsches Ärzteblatt* 102: 278–83.

Bellagio Task Force. 1997. "The Bellagio Task Force Report on Transplantation, Bodily Integrity, and the International Traffic in Organs." *Transplantation Proceedings* 29 (6): 2739–45.

———. 2009. *The Bellagio Task Force Report on Transplantation, Bodily Integrity, and the International Traffic in Organs.* www.icrc.org.

Bénabou, R., and J. Tirole. 2006. "Incentives and Prosocial Behavior." *American Economic Review* 96 (5): 1652–78.

Bergstrom, T. C., R. Garrett, and D. Sheehan-Connor. 2007. "One Chance in a Million: Altruism and the Bone Marrow Registry." CESifo Working Paper Series 2090, CESifo Group, Munich.

Black, D., and T. Kneiser. 2003. "On the Measurement of Job Risk in Hedonic Wage Models." *Journal of Risk and Uncertainty* 27 (3): 205–20.

Blair, R. D., and D. L. Kaserman. 1991. "The Economics and Ethics of Alternative Cadaveric Organ Procurement Policies." *Yale Journal on Regulation* 8: 403–52.

Blankart, C. B. 2005. "Spender ohne Rechte—Das Drama der Organtransplantation" [Donors without rights—the drama of organ transplants]. *Perspektiven der Wirtschaftspolitik* 6 (2): 275–301.

Boyce, R. M. 1983. "Organ Transplantation Crisis: Should the Deficit Be Eliminated through Inter Vivos Sales?" *Akron Law Review* 17 (Fall): 283–302.

Brams, M. 1977. "Transplantable Human Organs: Should Their Sale Be Authorized by Statutes?" *American Journal of Law and Medicine* 3 (2): 183–95.

Breyer, F. 2002. "Möglichkeiten und Grenzen des Marktes im Gesundheitswesen" [Possibilities and limits of a market in health systems]. *Zeitschrift für medizinische Ethik* 48: 111–23.

Breyer, F., et al. 2006. *Organmangel. Ist der Tod auf der Warteliste unvermeidbar?* [Organ shortage. Is death on the waiting list unavoidable?]. Berlin: Springer.

Breyer, F., and H. Kliemt. 1995. "Solidargemeinschaft der Organspender: Private oder öffentliche Organisation?" [Solidary community of organ donors: private or public organization?]. In *Transplantationsmedizin: ökonomische, ethische, rechtliche und medizinische Aspekte* [Transplant medicine: economic, ethical, legal and medical aspects], edited by P. Oberender, 135–60. Baden-Baden: Nomos.

Brooks, J., et al. 2006. "Effect of Dialysis Center Profit-Status on Patient Survival: A Comparison Risk-Adjustment and Instrumental Variable Approach." *Health Services Research*, 41 (6): 2267–89.

Broyer, M. 1991. "Living Organ Donation—The Fight against Commercialism." In *Organ Replacement Therapy: Ethics, Justice, Commerce*, edited by W. Land and J. B. Dossetor, 97–99. Berlin: Springer.

Broyer, M., et al. 1987. "Kidney Transplantation in Children." *Advances in Nephrology from the Necker Hospital* 16: 307–33.

Broyer, M., et al. 1993. "Five Year Survival of Kidney Transplants in Children: Data from the European Registry." *Kidney International* 43: 22–25.

Budiani-Saberi, D., and F. Delmonico. 2008. "Organ Trafficking and Transplant Tourism: A Commentary on the Global Realities." *American Journal of Transplantation* 8 (5): 925–29.

Burgess, J., and P. Wilson. 1996. "Hospital Ownership and Technical Efficiency." *Management Science* 42 (1): 110–16.

Busko, M. 2007. "Dutch Living Donor Kidney Exchange Program Has High Success Rate." *Medscape Medical News*, January 11.

Byrne, M., and P. Thompson. 2001. "A Positive Analysis of Financial Incentives for Cadaveric Organ Donation." *Journal of Health Economics* 20 (1): 69–83.

Calandrillo, S. P. 2005. "Cash for Kidneys: Utilizing Incentives to End America's Organ Shortage." *George Mason Law Review* 13 (1): 69–133.

Callero, P. 1991. *Giving Blood: The Development of an Altruistic Identity*. Baltimore: Johns Hopkins University Press.

Campion-Vincent, V. 1997. *La legende des vols d'organes*. Paris: Les Belles Lettres. Translated by J. Simpson as *Organ Theft Legends*. Jackson: University Press of Mississippi, 2005.

———. 2002. "Organ Theft Narratives as Medical and Social Critique." *Journal of Folklore Research* 39 (1): 33–50.

Canadian Institute for Health Information. 2007. *2007 Annual Report. www.cihi.ca.*

Caplan, A. L. 1984. "Ethical and Policy Issues in the Procurement of Organs for Transplantation." *New England Journal of Medicine* 311 (15): 981–83.

———. 1992. *If I Were a Rich Man, Could I Buy a Pancreas?—And Other Essays on the Ethics of Health Care*. Bloomington: Indiana University Press.

———. 1999. *The Ethics of Organ Transplants: The Current Debate*. New York: Prometheus Books.

Carrel, A. 1902. "La technique operatoire des anastomoses vasculaires et la transplantation des viscères." *Lyon Médical* 98: 859.

Cherry, M. J. 2005. *Kidney for Sale by Owner—Human Organs, Transplantation, and the Market*. Washington, DC: Georgetown University Press.

Cho, W.-H., and Y.-S. Kim. 2003. "Landmarks in Clinical Transplantation in Korea." *Yonsi Medical Journal* 45 (6): 963–67.

Chugh, K. S., and V. Jha. 1996. "Commerce in Transplantation in Third World Countries." *Kidney International* 49: 1181–86.

Clarke, K., S. Klarenbach et al. 2006. "The Direct and Indirect Economic Costs Incurred by Living Kidney Donors—A Systematic Review." *Journal of Nephrology, Dialysis and Transplantation* 21 (7): 1952–60.

Clay, M., and W. Block. 2002. "A Free Market for Human Organs." *Journal of Social, Political and Economic Studies* 27 (Summer): 227–36.

Cohen, L. R. 1989. "Increasing the Supply of Transplant Organs: The Virtues of a Futures Market." *George Washington Law Review* 58 (1): 1–51.

———. 1998. "Increasing Supply, Improving Allocation, and Furthering Justice and Decency in Organ Acquisition and Allocation: The Many Virtues of Markets." *Graft* 122: 1–3.

Cohen, B., and C. Wight. 1999. "A European Perspective on Organ Procurement: Breaking Down the Barriers to Organ Donation." *Transplantation* 68 (7): 985–90.

Collins, A. J., et al. 2003. "Chronic Kidney Disease and Cardiovascular Disease in the Medicare Population." *Kidney International* 64: 24–31.

Commission of the European Communities. 2005. *Green Paper: Promoting Healthy Diets and Physical Activity: A European Dimension for the Prevention of Overweight, Obesity and Chronic Diseases*. Brussels: Commission of the European Communities.

Council of Europe, Steering Committee on Bioethics. 2004. *Survey on Organ Trafficking*. Strasbourg: Council of Europe.

Council of Europe/United Nations. 2009. *Trafficking in Organs, Tissues and Cells and Trafficking in Human Beings for the Purpose of the Removal of Organs*. Strasbourg: Council of Europe.

Daar, A. S. 2006. "The Case for a Regulated System of Living Kidney Sales." *Nature Clinical Practice Nephrology* 2: 600–601.

Davies, J. B., et al. 2007. "The World Distribution of Household Wealth." World Institute for Development Economic Research, United Nations University.

Davis, C. L., and F. L. Delmonico. 2005. "Living-Donor Kidney Transplantation: A Review of the Current Practices for the Live Donor." *Journal of the American Society of Nephrology* 16 (7): 2098–110.

De Castro, L. D. 2003. "Commodification and Exploitation: Arguments in Favour of Compensated Organ Donation." *Journal of Medical Ethics* 29 (3): 142–46.

Declaration of Istanbul. 2008. www.ncbi.nlmonih.gov/pubmed/18701611.

De Klerk, M., et al. 2005. "The Dutch National Living Donor Kidney Exchange Program." *American Journal of Transplantation* 5 (9): 2302–5.

Delmonico, F. L. 2004a. "Living Donor Kidney Transplantation in a Global Environment." *Kidney International, Proceedings*, 11–13.

———. 2004b. "No Payments for Organs." In *Ethical, Legal and Social Issues in Organ Transplantation*, edited by T. Gutmann, A. S. Daar, R. A. Sells, and W. Land, 294–97. Lengerich, Germany: Pabst Science.

———. 2004c. "Exchanging Kidneys—Advances in Living-Donor Transplantation." *New England Journal of Medicine* 350 (18): 1812–14.

Delmonico, F. L., et al. 2005. "Organ Donation and Utilization in the United States, 2004." *American Journal of Transplantation* 5 (4): 862–73.

———. 2008. "Transplant Tourism and Organ Trafficking, an American Perspective." In *Organ Transplantation: Ethical, Legal and Psychosocial Aspects*, edited by W. Weimar, M. A. Bos, and J. J. Busschbach. Lengerich, Germany: Pabst Science.

Delmonico, F. L., and N. Scheper-Hughes. 2002. "Why We Should Not Pay for Human Organs." *National Catholic Bioethics Quarterly* 2 (3): 381–89.

Denise, S. H. 1985. "Regulating the Sale of Human Organs." *Virginia Law Review* 61 (5): 1015–38.

Deutsche Stiftung Organtransplantation (DSO). 2002ff. *Organspende und Transplantation in Deutschland* [Organ donation and transplantation in Germany). Neu-Isenburg: Deutsche Stiftung Organtransplantation.

Dewar, D. 2010. *Essentials of Health Economics.* Sudbury, MA: Jones and Bartlett.

Diesel, J. 2011. "Do Economists Reach a Conclusion on Organ Liberalization?" *Econ Journal Watch* 7 (3): 320–36.

Dor, A., M. V. Pauly, M. A. Eichleay, and P. J. Held. 2007. "End-Stage Renal Disease and Economic Incentives: The International Study of Health-Care Organization and Financing." NBER Working Paper 13125, National Bureau of Economic Research, Cambridge, MA.

Dossetor, J. B., and V. Maneckavel. 1992. "Commercialization: The Buying and Selling of Kidneys." In *Ethical Problems in Dialysis and Transplantation*, edited by C. M. Kjellstrand and J. B. Dossetor, 61–71. Dordrecht: Kluwer.

Douzdijian, V., F. Escobar, W. Kupin et al. 1998. "Should a Living-Donor Kidney Transplant Take Priority over Simultaneous Pancreas-Kidney Transplant? A Cost-Effectiveness Analysis." *Transplantation* 66 (8): s42.

Douzdijian, V., D. Ferrara, and G. Silverstri. 1998. "Treatment Strategies for Insulin-Dependent Diabetics with ESRD: A Cost-Effectiveness Decision Analysis Model." *American Journal of Kidney Diseases* 31 (5): 794–802.

Drake, A., S. Finkelstein, and H. Sapolsky. 1982. *The American Blood Supply.* Cambridge, MA: MIT Press.

Dubner, S. J., and S. D. Levitt. 2006. "Weighing the Repugnance Factor." *Freakonomics* 9.

Dukeminier, J., Jr. 1970. "Supplying Organs for Transplantation." *Michigan Law Review* 68: 811–66.

Dworkin, G. 1993. "Markets and Morals: The Case for Organ Sales." *Mount Sinai Journal of Medicine* 60 (January): 66–69.

Egan, T. 2002. "QALYs or Quackery? The Quagmire of Quantifying the Cost of Breathing." *Journal of Thoracic and Cardiovascular Surgery* 123: 449–54.

Ekelund, R. B. 1998. *Foundations of Regulatory Economics.* 3 vols. Cheltenham, UK: Elgar.

Enckevort, P., et al. 1998. "Technology Assessment of the Dutch Lung Transplantation Program." *International Journal of Technology Assessment in Health Care* 14: 344–56.

English, B. 2009. "Recession Spurs Egg and Sperm Donations." *Boston Globe*, April 7.

Erin, C. A., and J. Harris. 1994. "A Monopsonistic Market: Or How to Buy and Sell Human Organs, Tissues and Cells Ethically." In *Life and Death under High Technology Medicine*, edited by I. Robinson, 134–53. Manchester: Manchester University Press.

———. 2003. "An Ethical Market in Human Organs." *Journal of Medical Ethics* 29 (3): 137–38.

Etzioni, A. 2003. "Organ Donation: A Communitarian Approach." *Kennedy Institute of Ethics Journal* 13: 1–18.

Eurotransplant International Foundation. 2009. *2009 Annual Report.* www.eurotransplant.org.

Evans, R. W. 1993. "Organ Transplantation and the Inevitable Debate as to What Constitutes a Basic Healthcare Benefit." *Clinical Transplantation* 11: 359–91.

Evans, R. W., et al. 1990. "The Quality of Life of Hemodialysis Recipients Treated with Recombinant Human Erythropoietin." *Journal of the American Medical Association* 263 (6): 825–30.

Evans, R. W., and D. Kitzmann. 1998. "An Economic Analysis of Kidney Transplantation." *Surgical Clinics of North America* 78 (1): 149–74.

Evans, R. W., C. E. Orlans, and N. L. Ascher. 1992. "The Potential Supply of Organ Donors: An Assessment of the Efficiency of Organ Procurement Efforts in the United States." *Journal of the American Medical Association* 267 (2): 239–46.

Evans, R., D. Manninen, and F. B. Dong. 1993. "An Economic Analysis of Pancreas Transplantation: Costs, Insurance Coverage, and Reimbursement." *Clinical Transplantation* 7 (2): 166–74.

Finkel, M. 2001. "This Little Kidney Went to Market." *New York Times Magazine*, May 27.

Finn, R. 2000. *Organ Transplants: Making the Most of Your Gift of Life.* New York: Patient Centered Guides.

Flamholz, D. I. 2006. "A Penny for Your Organs: Revising New York's Policy on Offering Financial Incentives for Organ Donation." *Journal of Law and Policy* 14: 329–75.

Ford, J., and D. L. Kaserman. 2000. "Ownership Structure and the Quality of Medical Care: Evidence from the Dialysis Industry." *Journal of Economic Behavior and Organization* 43 (3): 279–93.

Fox, R. C., and J. P. Swazey. 1974. *The Courage to Fail: A Social View of Organ Transplants and Dialysis.* Chicago: University of Chicago Press.

———. 1992. *Spare Parts: Organ Replacement in American Society.* Oxford: Oxford University Press.

Frey, B. S. 1993. "Tertium Datur: Pricing, Regulating and Intrinsic Motivation." *Kyklos* 45: 161–84.

———. 1997. *Markt und Motivation* [Market and motivation]. Munich: Vahlen.

Frey, Bruno. 1993. "Motivation as a Limit to Pricing." *Journal of Economic Psychology* 14 (4): 635–64.

Frey, B. S., and F. Oberholzer-Gee. 1997. "The Cost of Price Incentives: An Empirical Analysis of Motivation Crowding-Out." *American Economic Review* 87 (4): 746–55.

Frey, B. S., and A. Stutzer. 2002. *Happiness and Economics.* Princeton, NJ: Princeton University Press.

Fried, C. 1978. *Right and Wrong.* Cambridge, MA: Harvard University Press.

Friedlander, M. M. 2002. "The Right to Sell or Buy a Kidney: Are We Failing Our Patients?" *The Lancet* 359: 971–73.

Garcia, V. 2003. "Living Kidney Transplantation in Brazil: Unwanted Procedure of Choice in View of Cadaver Organ Shortage." *Transplantation Proceedings* 35 (3): 1182–84.

Garwood, Paul. 2007. "Dilemma over Live-Donor Transplantation." *Bulletin of the World Health Organization* 85 (1): 5–6.

Gaston, R. S., et al. 2006. "Limiting Financial Disincentives in Live Organ Donation: A Rational Solution to the Kidney Shortage." *American Journal of Transplantation* 6 (11): 2548–55.

Gaston, R. S., and J. Wadström, eds. 2005. *Living Donor Kidney Transplantation: Current Practices, Emerging Trends and Evolving Challenges.* London: Taylor and Francis.

Geertsma, A., et al. 2000. "Improving Efficiency of Lung Transplantation." Paper presented at the annual meeting of the *International Society of Technology Assessment in Health Care* 16: 996.

Ghods, A. J. 2002. "Renal Transplantation in Iran." *Journal of Nephrology, Dialysis and Transplantation* 27 (1): 222–28.

Ghods, A. J., and S. Savai. 2006. "Iranian Model of Paid and Regulated Living-Unrelated Kidney Donation." *Clinical Journal of the American Society of Nephrology* 1 (6): 1136–45.

Giordano, S. 2005. "Is the Body a Republic?" *Journal of Medical Ethics* 31 (8): 470–75.

Gjertson, D. W., and M. Cecka. 2000. "Living Unrelated Donor Kidney Transplantation." *Kidney International* 58: 491–99.

Glazier, A. K., and F. Delmonico. 2011. "The Declaration of Istanbul Is Moving Forward by Combating Transplant Commercialism and Trafficking by Promoting Organ Donation." *American Journal of Transplantation* 12 (3): 515–16.

Gneezy, U., and A. Rustichini. 2000. "Pay Enough or Don't Pay at All." *Quarterly Journal of Economics* 115 (3): 791–810.

Goette, L., and A. Stutzer. 2008. "Blood Donations and Incentives: Evidence from a Field Experiment." IZA Discussion Paper 3580, Institute for the Study of Labor, Bonn.

Golmakani, M. M., M. H. Niknam, and K. M. Hedayat. 2005. "Transplantation Ethics from the Islamic Point of View." *Medicine Science Monitor* 11: 105–9.

Goodwin, M. 2006. *Black Markets: The Supply and Demand of Body Parts.* Cambridge: Cambridge University Press.

———. 2008. "Rethinking Federal Organ Transplantation Policy: Incentives Best Implemented by State Governments." In *When Altruism Isn't Enough: The Case for Compensating Kidney Donors,* edited by S. Satel, 111–21. Washington, DC: American Enterprise Institute.

Gortmaker, S. L., et al. 1996. "Organ Donor Potential and Performance: Size and Nature of the Organ Donor Shortfall." *Critical Care Medicine* 24 (3): 432–39.

Goyal, M., et al. 2002. "Economic and Health Consequences of Selling a Kidney in India." *Journal of the American Medical Association* 288 (13): 1589–93.

Gruessner, R., and E. Benedetti, eds. 2007. *Living Organ Donor Transplantation.* New York: McGraw-Hill.

Guadagnoli, E., C. Christiansen, and C. Beasley. 2003. "Potential Organ Donor Supply and Efficiency of Organ Procurement Organizations." *Health Care Financing Review* 24 (4): 101–10.

Gubernatis, G. 1999. "Organization of Organ Donation—Concepts and Experiences in Niedersachsen/Ostwestfalen (Germany)." *Journal of Nephrology, Dialysis and Transplantation* 14 (10): 2309–14.

Gubernatis, G., and H. Kliemt. 2000. "A Superior Approach to Organ Allocation and Donation." *Transplantation* 70 (4): 699–707.

Gutmann, T. 2004. "Allocation and Transplantation of 'Marginal' Donor Organs—Ethical and Legal Questions." In *Ethical, Legal and Social Issues in Organ Transplantation,* edited by T. Gutmann, A. S. Daar, R. A. Sells, and W. Land, 49–56. Lengerich, Germany: Pabst Science.

———. 2006. *Für ein neues Transplantationsgesetz. Eine Bestandsaufnahme des Novellierungsbedarfs im Recht der Transplantationsmedizin* [Toward a new (German) transplantation law]. Berlin: Springer.

Gutmann, T., A. S. Daar, R. A. Sells, and W. Land, eds. 2004. *Ethical, Legal and Social Issues in Organ Transplantation.* Lengerich, Germany: Pabst Science.

Gutmann, T., and U. Schroth. 2002. *Organlebendspende in Europa* [Organ living donation in Europe]. Berlin: Springer.

Halpern, S. C., et al. 2010. "Regulated Payments for Living Kidney Donation: An Empirical Assessment of the Ethical Concerns." *Annals of Internal Medicine* 152 (6): 358–65.

Hansmann, H. 1989. "The Economics and Ethics of Markets for Human Organs." *Journal of Health Politics, Policy and Law* 14 (1): 57–85.

Harmon, K. 2009. "For Sale: Human Eggs Become a Research Commodity." *Scientific American,* November.

Harrington, D., and E. Sayre. 2006. "Paying for Bodies, but Not for Organs." *Regulation* 29 (4): 14–19.

Harris, J., and C. A. Erin. 1994. "A Monopsonistic Market: Or How to Buy and Sell Human Organs, Tissues and Cells Ethically." In *The Social Consequences of Life and Death under High Technology Medicine,* edited by I. Robinson, 134–57. Manchester: Manchester University Press.

———. 2002. "An Ethically Defensible Market in Organs: A Single Buyer Like the NHS Is the Answer." *British Medical Journal* 325: 114–15.

Hartmann, T. M. 1979. "Buying and Selling of Human Organs from the Living: Why Not?" *Akron Law Review* 13 (Summer): 152–74.

Hartwell, L. 1999. "Global Organ Donation Policies around the World." *Contemporary Dialysis and Nephrology,* December.

Häyry, P. 2004. "Human Organ Trafficking: Size of the Industry and Means of Regulation." In *Ethical, Legal and Social Issues in Organ Transplantation,* edited by T. Gutmann, A. S. Daar, R. A. Sells, and W. Land, 265–71. Lengerich, Germany: Pabst Science.

Health Council of the Netherlands. 2007. *Living Donor List Exchange: An Addition to the Dutch Living Kidney Exchange Programme?* The Hague: Health Council of the Netherlands.

Health Service Executive. 2009. *Audit of Potential Organ Donors in the Republic of Ireland.* Dublin: Health Service Executive.

Healy, K. 2002a. "Sacred Markets and Secular Ritual in the Organ Transplant Industry." Working Paper, Department of Sociology, University of Arizona, Tucson.

———. 2002b. "The Political Economy of Presumed Consent." Occasional Paper, Department of Sociology, University of California, Los Angeles.

———. 2005. "Do Presumed Consent Laws Raise Organ Procurement Rates?" *DePaul Law Review* 55: 1017–44.

———. 2006. *Last Best Gifts: Altruism and the Market for Human Blood and Organs*. Chicago: University of Chicago Press.

Hee, K. 2008. "Organ Donation Family Refusal Statistics." Department of Public Health, South Australia.

Hilhorst, M. T. 2005. "Directed Altruistic Living Organ Donation: Partial but Not Unfair." *Ethical Theory and Moral Practice* 8: 197–215.

Himmelfarb, J., and A. Kliger. 2007. "End-Stage Renal Disease Measures of Quality." *Annual Review of Medicine* 58 (February): 387–99.

Hippen, B., and S. Satel. 2008. "Crowding Out, Crowding In, and Financial Incentives for Organ Procurement." In *When Altruism Isn't Enough: The Case for Compensating Kidney Donors*, edited by S. Satel, 96–110. Washington, DC: American Enterprise Institute.

Hornberger, J., J. Best, and L. Garrison. 1997. "Cost-Effectiveness of Repeat Medical Procedures: Kidney Transplantation as an Example." *Medical Decision Making* 17 (4): 363–72.

Howard, D. 2007. "Producing Organ Donors." *Journal of Economic Perspectives* 21 (3): 25–36.

Howard, D., and M. Byrne. 2007. "Should We Promote Organ Donor Registries When So Few Registrants Will End Up Being Donors?" *Medical Decision Making* 27 (3): 243–49.

Howard, D., et al. 2007. "Does Quality Improvement Work? Evaluation of the Organ Donation Breakthrough Collaborative." *Health Services Research* 42 (6): 2160–73.

Howard, D. H. 2005. "Quality and Consumer Choice in Healthcare: Evidence from Kidney Transplantation." *Topics in Economic Analysis and Policy* 5 (1), art. 24.

Huang, E., N. Thakur, and D. Meltzer. 2008. "The Cost-Effectiveness of Renal Replacement Therapy." In *When Altruism Isn't Enough: The Case for Compensating Kidney Donors*, edited by S. Satel, 19–33. Washington, DC: American Enterprise Institute.

Hubard, R. G., and A. O'Brian. 2010. *Microeconomics*. 3rd ed. New York: Prentice Hall.

Ibrahim, H., et al. 2009. "Long-Term Consequences of Kidney Donation." *New England Journal of Medicine* 360 (5): 459–69.

Jacob, M.-A. 2006. "Another Look at the Presumed-versus-Informed Consent Dichotomy in Postmortem Organ Procurement." *Bioethics* 20 (6): 293–300.

James, P. T., et al. 2001. "The Worldwide Obesity Epidemic." *Obesity Research* 9: 228–33.

Jansen, N., et al. 2009. "A Plea for Uniform European Definitions for Organ Donor Potential and Family Refusal." *Transplantation International* 22 (11): 1064–72.

Jassal, S., et al. 2003. "Kidney Transplantation in the Elderly: A Decision Analysis." *Journal of the American Society of Nephrology* 14 (1): 187–96.

Jha, V., and K. S. Chugh. 2006. "The Case against a Regulated System of Living Kidney Sales." *Nature Clinical Practice Nephrology* 2: 466–67.

Jingwei, J. A., A. L. Yu-Hung, and L. Ching. 2010. "Living Organ Transplantation Policy Transition in Asia: Towards Adaptive Policy Changes." *Global Health Governance* 3: 1–14.

Johansson, P. O. 2002. "On the Definition and Age-Dependency of the Value of a Statistical Life." *Journal of Risk and Uncertainty* 25 (3): 251–63.

Jonsen, A. R. 1988. "Transplantation of Fetal Tissue." *Clinical Research* 36: 215–19.

Karlberg, I., and G. Nyberg. 1995. "Cost-Effectiveness Studies of Renal Transplantation." *International Journal of Technological Assessment in Health Care* 11: 611–22.

Kaserman, D. 2002. "Markets for Organs: Myths and Misconceptions." *Journal of Contemporary Health Law and Policy* 18: 567–80.

———. 2006. "On the Feasibility of Resolving the Organ Shortage." *Inquiry* 43 (2): 160–66.

———. 2007. "Fifty Years of Organ Transplants: The Successes and the Failures." *Issues in Law and Medicine* 45: 45–61.

Kasiske, B., D. Cohen, M. Lucey et al. 2000. "Payment for Immunosuppression after Organ Transplantation." *Journal of the American Medical Association* 283 (18): 2445–50.

Kass, L. R. 1992. "Organs for Sale? Propriety, Property, and the Price of Progress." *Public Interest* 107: 65–86.

Katz, P., J. Showstack et al. 1999. "Methods to Estimate and Analyze Medical Care Resource Use." *International Journal of Technology Assessment in Healthcare* 15: 366–79.

Keen, J. 2009. "Sperm, Egg Donors Increase during Recession." *USA Today*, July 6.

Kim, D. 2003. "A Study on the Factors Affecting People's Attitudes toward Organ Donation" [in Korean and English]. *KIHASA Policy Review* 23 (2): 23–32.

Kim, J. R., D. Elliot, and C. Hyde. 2004a. "Korean Health Professionals' Attitudes and Knowledge toward Organ Donation and Transplantation." *International Journal of Nursing Studies* 41 (3): 299–307.

———. 2004b. "The Influence of Sociocultural Factors on Organ Donation and Transplantation in Korea: Findings from Key Informant Interviews." *Journal of Transcultural Nursing* 15 (April): 147–54.

Kim, M. S., S. Kim, and Y. S. Kim. 2008. "Current Status of Deceased Donor Organ Recovery and Sharing in Korea." *Journal of the Korean Medical Association* 51 (8): 685–91.

Kimmel, P., and R. Peterson. 2006. "Depression in Patients with End-Stage Renal Disease Treated with Dialysis: Has the Time to Treat Arrived?" *Clinical Journal of the American Society of Nephrology* 1 (2): 349–52.

Kishore, R. R. 2005. "Human Organs, Scarcities, and Sale: Morality Revisited." *Journal of Medical Ethics* 31 (6): 362–65.

Kjellstrand, C. M., and J. B. Dossetor, eds. 1992. *Ethical Problems in Dialysis and Transplantation*. Dordrecht: Kluwer.

Klenow, D. J., and G. Youngs. 1995. "An Empirical Exploration of Selected Policy Options in Organ Donation." *Death Studies* 19: 543–57.

Kliemt, H. 1995. "Wem gehören die Organe?" [Who owns the organs?]. In *Hirntod und Organverpflanzung. Ethische, medizinische, psychologische und rechtliche Aspekte der Transplantationsmedizin* [Brain death and organ transplantation. Ethical, medical, psychological and legal aspects of transplantation medicine], edited by J. S. Ach and M. Quante, 271–87. Stuttgart: Frommann-Holzboog.

———. 2005. "Warum darf ich alles verkaufen, nur meine Organe nicht?" [Why am I allowed to sell everything, except my organs?]. In *Ethik der Lebendorganspende* [Ethics of living organ donation], edited by C. Rittner and N. W. Paul, 167–94. Basel: Schwabe.

Kniesner, T., W. K. Viscusi, and J. Zilink. 2003. "Life-Cycle Consumption and the Age-Adjusted Value of Life." Unpublished paper.

Kreis, H. 2005. "The Question of Organ Procurement: Beyond Charity." *Journal of Nephrology, Dialysis and Transplantation* 20 (7): 1303–6.

———. 2008. "Whose Organs Are They, Anyway?" In *Organ Transplantation: Ethical, Legal and Psychosocial Aspects*, edited by W. Weimar, M. A. Bos, and J. J. Busschbach, 140–43. Lengerich, Germany: Pabst Science.

Kurella, M., et al. 2005. "Suicide in the United States End-Stage Renal Disease Program." *Journal of the American Society of Nephrology* 16 (3): 774–81.

Kwon, Y. M., and E. J. Yeun. 2000. "Subjectivity on Organ Donation and Transplantation." *Journal of the Korean Academy of Nurses* 30: 1437–54.

Land, W., and J. B. Dossetor, eds. 1991. *Organ Replacement Therapy: Ethics, Justice, Commerce*. Berlin: Springer.

Landolt, M. A., et al. 2001. "Living Anonymous Kidney Donation: What Does the Public Think?" *Transplantation* 71 (11): 1690–96.

Landry, D. W. 2006. "Voluntary Reciprocal Altruism: A Novel Strategy to Encourage Deceased Organ Donation." *Kidney International* 69: 957–59.

Larijani, B., F. Zahedi, and E. Taheri. 2004. "Ethical and Legal Aspects of Organ Transplantation in Iran." *Transplant Proceedings* 36: 1241–44.

Lee, L., J. Piliavin, and V. Call. 1999. "Giving Time, Money, and Blood: Similarities and Differences." *Social Psychology Quarterly* 62 (3): 276–90.

Leslie, G. 1995. "The 'Spanish Model'—An Initiative Aimed at Increasing Organ Donation Rates in Australia." *Australian Critical Care* 8 (4): 33–34.

Longworth, L., et al. 2003. "Midterm Cost-Effectiveness of the Liver Transplantation Program of England and Wales for Three Disease Groups." *Liver Transplantation* 9 (12): 1295–307.

Lucan, M., et al. 2003. "Kidney Exchange Program: A Viable Alternative in Countries with Low Rate of Cadaver Harvesting." *Transplantation Proceedings* 35 (3): 933–34.

Luna-Zaragoza, D., and M. Reyes-Frias. 2001. "Donation Transplants and Tissue Banking in Mexico." *Cell and Tissue Banking* 2 (4): 255–59.

Madrigal, G. 1994. "Cost Estimate of Kidney Transplants in Costa Rica: Comparison to Chronic Dialysis." *Transplantation Proceedings* 26 (1): 121.

Mange, K., M. Joffee, and H. Feldman. 2001. "Effect of the Use or Non-Use of Long-Term Dialysis on the Subsequent Survival of Renal Transplants from Living Donors." *New England Journal of Medicine* 344: 726–31.

Manninen, D., and R. Evans. 1985. "Public Attitudes and Behaviour Regarding Organ Donation." *Journal of the American Medical Association* 253 (21): 3111–15.

Matas, A. J. 2004. "The Case for Living Kidney Sales: Rationale, Objections and Concerns." *American Journal of Transplantation* 4 (12): 2007–17.

———. 2007. "A Gift of Life Deserves Compensation—How to Increase Living Kidney Donation with Realistic Incentives." *Policy Analysis* 604: 1–23.

———. 2008a. "Risks of Kidney Transplantation to a Living Donor." In *When Altruism Isn't Enough: The Case for Compensating Kidney Donors*, edited by S. Satel, 10–18. Washington, DC: American Enterprise Institute.

———. 2008b. "In Defense of a Regulated System of Compensation for Kidney Donors." In *Organ Transplantation: Ethical, Legal and Psychosocial Aspects*, edited by W. Weimar, M. A. Bos, and J. J. Busschbach, 55–63. Lengerich, Germany: Pabst Science.

Matas, A. J., B. E. Hippen, and S. Satel. 2008. "In Defense of a Regulated System of Compensation for Living Donation." *Current Opinion in Organ Transplantation* 13 (4): 379–85.

Matas, A. J., and M. Schnitzler. 2003. "Payment for Living Donor (Vendor) Kidneys: A Cost-Effectiveness Analysis." *American Journal of Transplantation* 4 (2): 216–21.

Matas, A. J., and D. Sutherland. 2005. "The Importance of Innovative Efforts to Increase Organ Donation." *Journal of the American Medical Association* 294 (13): 1691–93.

Matesanz, R. 2003. "Factors Influencing the Adoption of the Spanish Model of Organ Donation." *Transplant International* 16 (10): 736–41.

Matesanz, R., and B. Dominguez-Gil. 2007. "Strategies to Optimize Deceased Organ Donation." *Transplantation Reviews* 21: 177–88.

Matesanz, R., and B. Miranda. 2002. "A Decade of Continuous Improvement in Cadaveric Organ Donation: The Spanish Model." *Journal of Nephrology* 15: 22–28.

Matesanz, R., B. Miranda, and C. Felipe. 1994. "Organ Procurement in Spain: The Impact of Transplant Coordination." *Clinical Transplantation* 8: 281–86.

Mathew, T., R. Faull, and P. Snelling. 2005. "The Shortage of Kidneys for Transplantation in Australia." *Medical Journal of Australia* 18 (5): 204–5.

McAlister, V. C., et al. 2003. "Transplantation in Canada: Review of the Last Decade from the Canadian Organ Replacement Register." *Clinical Transplants* 101–8.

McCarrick, P., and M. Darrag. 2003. "Incentives for Providing Organs." *Kennedy Institute of Ethics Journal* 13: 53–64.

McCunn, M., et al. 2003. "Impact of Culture and Policy on Organ Donation: A Comparison between Two Urban Trauma Centers in Developed Nations." *Journal of Trauma—Injury, Infection and Critical Care* 54 (5): 995–99.

Mellström, C., and M. Johannesson. 2008. "Crowding Out in Blood Donation: Was Titmuss Right?" *Journal of the European Economic Association* 6 (4): 845–63.

Mendeloff, J., et al. 2004. "Procuring Organ Donors as a Health Investment: How Much Should We Be Willing to Spend?" *Transplantation* 78 (12): 1704–10.

Merion, R. M., et al. 2008. "Transplants in Foreign Countries among Patients Removed from the US Transplant Waiting List." *American Journal of Transplantation* 8 (4): 988–96.

Metzger, R., F. L. Delmonico, and S. Feng. 2003. "Expanded Criteria Donors for Kidney Transplantation." *American Journal of Transplantation* 3 (Supplement 4): 114–25.

Miranda, B., M. F. Lucas, and R. Matesanz. 1997. "The Potential Organ Donor Pool: International Figures." *Transplantation Proceedings* 29 (2): 1604–6.

Miranda, B., L. Vilardell, and J. Grinyo. 2003. "Optimizing Cadaveric Organ Procurement: The Catalan and Spanish Experience." *American Journal of Transplantation* 3 (10): 1189–96.

Mocan, N. H., and E. Tekin. 2005. "The Determinants of the Willingness to Be an Organ Donor." NBER Working Paper 11316, National Bureau of Economic Research, Cambridge, MA.

Mor, E. 2009. "Kidney Transplantation from unrelated donors." *Current Opinion in Organ Transplantation* 14 (2): 113–15.

Mullins, C. D., et al. 2003. "The Economic Impact of Laparoscopic Living-Donor Nephrectomy on Kidney Transplantation." *Transplantation* 75 (9): 1505–12.

Munson, R. 2004. *Raising the Dead: Organ Transplants, Ethics, and Society.* Oxford: Oxford University Press.

National Center for Transplantation (Israel). kartisadi.org.il/eng/merkaz.html.

National Health Service. 2010. *2009–2010 Annual Report.* www.nhs.uk.

National Health Service Blood and Transplant. http://www.nhsbt.nhs.uk.

Nationaler Ethikrat [German National Ethics Council]. 2007. *Die Zahl der Organspenden erhöhen— Stellungnahme zu einem drängenden Problem der Transplantationsmedizin in Deutschland* [Increasing the number of organ donations—a statement about an urgent problem of transplantations medicine in Germany]. Berlin: Nationaler Ethikrat.

Nyman, J., and D. Bricker. 1989. "Profit Incentives and Technical Efficiency in the Production of Nursing Home Care." *Review of Economics and Statistics* 71 (4): 586–94.

Oberender, P., ed. 1995. *Transplantationsmedizin: ökonomische, ethische, rechtliche und medizinische Aspekte* [Transplantation medicine: economic, ethical, legal and medical aspects]. Baden-Baden: Nomos.

Oniscu, G., and J. L. R. Forsythe. 2009. "An Overview of Transplantation in Culturally Diverse Regions." *Annals of the Academy of Medicine* 38 (4): 365–69.

Organ Procurement and Transplantation Network (OPTN). 2010. *2010 Annual Report.* optn. transplant.hrsa.gov.

———. 2011. *2011 Annual Report.* optn.transplant.hrsa.gov.

Organisation for Economic Co-operation and Development (OECD). 2010. *Health Data.* www.oecd .org.

Ortner, N. J. 2005. *2005 US Organ and Tissue Transplant Cost Estimates and Discussion.* Seattle: Milliman.

Osterkamp, R. 2004. "Health-Care Efficiency in OECD Countries." *Applied Economics Quarterly* 55 (Supplement): 117–42.

———. 2005. "Is There a Hold-Up of Health-Care Reforms in Europe?" In *The Economics of Health Reforms,* edited by J. N. Yfantopoulos, 63–83. Athens: Athens Institute for Education and Research.

———. 2006. "Why a Shortage of Kidneys under an Inconsequently Altruistic System May Feed Itself." Paper presented at the 81st annual meeting of the Western Economic Association, Los Angeles.

Oteifa, N. 2007. "Kuwait to Host 'Organ Transplant' Meeting." *Kuwait Times,* October 23.

Payton, J., et al. 2006. "Cost-Effectiveness of Pediatric Heart Transplantation." *Journal of Heart and Lung Transplantation* 25 (4): 409–15.

Pearson, E. 2004. "Coercion in the Kidney Trade? A Background Study on Trafficking in Human Organs Worldwide." Unpublished paper on behalf of Deutsche Gesellschaft für Technische Zusammenarbeit, Eschborn.

Perez-Pena, R. 2006. "As Diabetes Destroys Kidneys, New York Lags in Dialysis Care." *New York Times,* December 28.

Pilliavin, J. W., and P. Callero. 1991. *Giving Blood: The Development of an Altruistic Identity.* Baltimore: Johns Hopkins University Press.

Pilliavin, J., P. Callero, and D. Evans. 1982. "Addicted to Altruism? Opponent-Process Theory and Habitual Blood Donation." *Journal of Personality and Social Psychology* 43 (6): 1200–1213.

Potts, M., P. A. Byrne, and R. G. Nilges, eds. 2001. *Beyond Brain Death.* New York: Springer.

Radcliffe Richards, J. 1996. "Nephrarious Goings On: Kidney Sales and Moral Arguments." *Journal of Medicine and Philosophy* 21: 375–416.

———. 2004. "The Case for Allowing Kidney Sales." In *Ethical, Legal and Social Issues in Organ Transplantation,* edited by T. Gutmann, A. S. Daar, R. A. Sells, and W. Land, 272–80. Lengerich, Germany: Pabst Science.———. 2008. "Transplants and the Problems of Justice to Groups." In *Organ Transplantation: Ethical, Legal and Psychosocial Aspects,* edited by W. Weimar, M. A. Bos, and J. J. Busschbach, 382–91. Lengerich, Germany: Pabst Science.

Radcliffe Richards, J., et al. 1998. "The Case for Allowing Kidney Sales." *The Lancet* 352: 1950–52.

Radin, M. J. 1987. "Market-Inalienability." *Harvard Law Review* 100 (8): 1849–1937.

Rappaport, F. L., and C. J. Maggs. 2002. "Titmuss and the Gift Relationship: Altruism Revisited." *Journal of Advanced Nursing* 40 (5): 495–503.

Reilly, P., et al. 1997. "The Costs of Altruism: Patient Charges for Organ Donation after Traumatic Injury." *Internet Journal of Thoracic and Cardiovascular Surgery* 1 (2).

Reynolds, R. L., and L. D. Barney. 1988. "Economics of Organ Procurement and Allocation." *Journal of Economic Issues* 22 (2): 571–79.

Rinehart, J. R. 1988. "The Market Approach to Organ Shortages." *Journal of Health Care Marketing* 8 (March): 72–75.

Rittner, C., and N. W. Paul, eds. 2005. *Ethik der Lebendorganspende* [Ethics of living organ donation]. Basel: Schwabe.

Riviera-Lopez, E. 2006. "Organ Sales and Moral Distress." *Journal of Applied Philosophy* 23 (1): 41–52.

Rodrigue, J. R., et al. 2006. "Organ Donation Decisions: Comparison of Donor and Non-Donor Families." *American Journal of Transplantation* 6 (1): 190–98.

Rodriguez-Arias, D., L. Wright, and D. Paredes. 2010. "Success Factors and Ethical Challenges of the Spanish Model of Organ Donation." *The Lancet* 376: 1109–12.

Roels, L., et al. 2003. "Cost-Benefit Analysis in Evaluating Investment into Donor Action: The German Case." *Transplantation International* 16 (5): 321–25.

Rosen, S. 1988. "The Value of Changes in Life Expectancy." *Journal of Risk and Uncertainty* 1 (3): 285–304.

Rosko, M., et al. 1995. "The Effects of Ownership, Operating Environment, and Strategic Choices on Nursing Home Efficiency." *Medical Care* 33 (10): 1001–21.

Ross, L. F., et al. 1997. "Ethics of a Paired-Kidney Exchange Program." *New England Journal of Medicine* 336 (24): 1752–55.

Roth, A. E. 2007. "Repugnance as a Constraint on Markets." *Journal of Economic Perspectives* 21 (3): 37–58.

Roth, A. E., T. Sönmez, and M. U. Ünver. 2004a. "Kidney Exchange." *Quarterly Journal of Economics* 119 (2): 457–88.

———. 2004b. "Pairwise Kidney Exchange." NBER Working Paper 10698, National Bureau of Economic Research, Cambridge, MA.

———. 2005a. "Efficient Kidney Exchange: Coincidence of Wants in a Structured Market." NBER Working Paper 11402, National Bureau of Economic Research, Cambridge, MA.

———. 2005b. "A Kidney Exchange Clearinghouse for New England." *American Economic Review* 95 (2): 376–80.

———. 2007. "Efficient Kidney Exchange: Coincidence of Wants in a Model with Compatibility-Based Preferences." *American Economic Review* 97 (3): 828–51.

Rothman, S. M., and D. J. Rothman. 2003. "The Organ Market." *New York Review of Books* 50 (16): 49–50.

Rottenberg, S. 1971. *The Production and Exchange of Used Body Parts.* In Online Library of Liberty: Toward Liberty: Essays in Honor of Ludwig von Mises, vol. 2, pp. 206–11. Liberty Fund, Inc.

Rudich, S., B. Kaplan et al. 2002. "Renal Transplantations Performed Using Non-Heart-Beating Organ Donors: Going Back to the Future." *Transplantation* 74 (12): 1715–20.

Rufat, P., F. Fourquet et al. 1999. "Costs and Outcomes of Liver Transplantation in Adults." *Transplantation* 68 (1): 78–83.

Sadler, B. L., and A. M. Sadler Jr. 1973. "Providing Cadaver Organs: Three Legal Alternatives." *Hastings Center Studies* 1 (1): 14–26.

Sagmeister, M., B. Mullhaupt et al. 2002. "Cost-Effectiveness of Cadaveric and Living-Donor Liver Transplantation." *Transplantation* 73 (4): 616–22.

Satel, S., ed. 2008. *When Altruism Isn't Enough: The Case for Compensating Kidney Donors.* Washington, DC: American Enterprise Institute.

Savoye, E., et al. 2007. "Survival Benefits of Kidney Transplantation with Expanded Criteria Deceased Donors in Patients Aged 60 Years or Older." *Transplantation* 84 (12): 1618–24.

Savulescu, J. 2003. "Is the Sale of Body Parts Wrong?" *Journal of Medical Ethics* 29 (3): 139–40.

Scandiatransplant Foundation. www.scandiatransplant.org.

Scheper-Hughes, N. 2000. "The Global Traffic in Human Organs." *Current Anthropology* 41 (2): 191–224.

———. 2004. "The Last Commodity: Post-Human Ethics and the Global Traffic in 'Fresh' Organs." In *Global Assemblages: Technology, Politics, and Ethics as Anthropological Problems,* edited by A. Ong and S. Collier, 145–67. London: Blackwell.

———. 2006. "The Tyranny of the Gift: Sacrificial Violence in Living Donor Transplants." *American Journal of Transplantation* 7 (3): 1–5.

Schnitzler, M., et al. 2003. "The Expanded Criteria Donor Dilemma in Cadaveric Renal Transplantation." *Transplantation* 75 (12): 1940–45.

Schnuelle, P., et al. 2009. "Effects of Donor Pretreatment with Dopamine on Graft Function after Kidney Transplantation." *Journal of the American Medical Association* 302 (10): 1067–75.

Schold, J. D., et al. 2008. "The Association of Candidate Mortality Rates with Kidney Transplant Outcomes and Center Performance Valuations." *Transplantation* 85 (1): 1–6.

Schroth, U. 2001. "Das Organhandelsverbot—Legitimität und Inhalt einer paternalistischen Strafrechts-norm" [The prohibition of trading in organs—legitimacy and content of a paternalistic norm in criminal law]. In *Festschrift für Claus Roxin*, edited by B. Schünemann et al., 869–90. Berlin: Springer.

Schwartz, J. 1999. "Blood and Altruism." *Public Interest* 136: 35–52.

Schweitzer, E. J., et al. 1989. "The Shrinking Renal Replacement Therapy 'Break Even' Point." *Transplantation* 66 (12): 1702–8.

———. 1991. "Causes of Renal Allograft Loss: Progress in the 1980's, Challenges for the 1990's." *Annals of Surgery* 214 (6): 679–88.

———. 1997. "Increased Living Donor Volunteer Rates with a Formal Recipient Family Education Program." *American Journal of Kidney Diseases* 29 (5): 739–45.

Schwindt, R., and A. R. Vining. 1986. "Proposal for a Mutual Insurance Pool for Transplant Organs." *Journal of Health Politics, Policy and Law* 11 (3): 483–500.

Seabright, P. B. 2009. "Continuous Preferences and Discontinuous Choices: How Altruists Respond to Incentives." *B.E. Journal of Theoretical Economics* 9 (1), art. 14.

Segev, D., et al. 2010. "Perioperative Mortality and Long-Term Survival Following the Live Kidney Donation." *Journal of the American Medical Association* 303 (10): 959–66.

Sells, R. A. 1979. "Let's Not Opt Out: Kidney Donation and Transplantation." *Journal of Medical Ethics* 5 (4): 165–69.

———. 1993. "Consent for Organ Donation: What Are the Ethical Principles?" *Transplantation Proceedings* 25 (1): 39–41.

Sexton, T., et al. 1989. "The Impact of Prospective Reimbursement on Nursing Home Efficiency." *Medical Care* 27 (2): 154–63.

Shafer, T., et al. 2006. "Organ Donation Breakthrough Collaborative." *Critical Care Nurse* 26: 33–48.

Shapiro, M. H. 2003. "On the Possibility of 'Progress' in Managing Biomedical Technologies: Markets, Lotteries, and Rational Moral Standards in Organ Transplantation." *Capital University Law Review* 31 (13): 13–69.

Sheehy, E., et al. 2003. "Estimating the Number of Potential Organ Donors in the United States." *New England Journal of Medicine* 349 (7): 667–74.

Shiffman, M., et al. 2006. "Liver and Intestine Transplantation in the United States, 1995–2004." *American Journal of Transplantation* 6 (5): 1170–87.

Shimazono, Y. 2007. "The State of the International Organ Trade: A Provisional Picture Based on Integration of Available Information." *Bulletin of the World Health Organization* 85 (12): 955–62.

Siegal, G., and R. J. Bonnie. 2006. "Closing the Organ Gap: A Reciprocity-Based Social Contract Approach." *Journal of Law, Medicine and Ethics* 34: 415–23.

Sievers, K., and G. Neitzke. 2006. "Struktur, Arbeitsweise und Ethik von Lebendspendekommissionen—Ergebnisse einer bundesweiten Befragung" [Structure, methodology and ethics of German commissions on living organ donation—results from a national survey]. *Deutsche Medizinische Wochenschrift* 131: 1283–87.

Singer, P. 1973. *Democracy and Disobedience*. Oxford: Clarendon.

Spital, A. 2005. "Conscription of Cadaveric Organs for Transplantation: A Stimulating Idea Whose Time Has Not Yet Come." *Cambridge Quarterly of Health Care Ethics* 14 (1): 107–12.

Spital, A., and C. A. Erin. 2002. "Conscription of Cadaveric Organs for Transplantation: Let's at Least Talk about It." *American Journal of Kidney Diseases* 39 (3): 611–15.

Stason, E. B. 1968. "The Uniform Anatomical Gift Act." *Business Law* 23: 927.

Steinbuch, R. 2009. "Kidneys, Cash and Kashrut: A Legal, Economic and Religious Analysis of Selling Kidneys." *Houston Law Review* 45: 1529–607.

Stempsey, W. E. 2000. "Organ Markets and Human Dignity: On Selling Your Body and Soul." *Christian Bioethics* 6 (August): 195–204.

Strauss, R. G., et al. 1994. "Concurrent Comparison of the Safety of Paid Cytapheresis and Volunteer Whole Blood Donors." *Transfusion* 34 (2): 116–21.

Sung, R., et al. 2005. "Impact of the Expended Criteria Donor Allocation Systems on the Use of Expended Criteria Donor Kidneys." *Transplantation* 79 (9): 1257–61.

Taylor, J. S. 2005. *Stakes and Kidneys: Why Markets in Human Body Parts Are Morally Imperative*. Aldershot, UK: Ashgate.

———. 2007. "A 'Queen of Hearts' Trial of Organ Markets: Why Scheper-Hughes's Objections to Markets in Human Organs Fail." *Journal of Medical Ethics* 33 (4): 201–4.

Taylor, J. S., and M. C. Simmerling. 2008. "Donor Compensation without Exploitation." In *When Altruism Isn't Enough: The Case for Compensating Kidney Donors*, edited by S. Satel, 50–62. Washington, DC: American Enterprise Institute.

Telser, L. 1964. *Theories of Competition*. Amsterdam: Elsevier Science.

Titmuss, R. 1970. *The Gift Relationship: From Human Blood to Social Policy*. London: Allen and Unwin.

U.K. Transplant Center. 2006. *2006 Annual Report*.

———. 2009. *2009 Annual Report*.

———. 2010. *2010 Annual Report*.

United Network for Organ Sharing (UNOS). www.unos.org.

U.S. Department of Health and Human Services. 2005. *National Survey of Organ and Tissue Donation Attitudes and Behaviors*.

U.S. Renal Data System (USRDS). 2009. *2009 Annual Report*. www.usrds.org.

———. 2010. *2010 Annual Report*. www.usrds.org.

———. 2010. *2010 Annual Report*. www.usrds.org.

———. 2011. *2011 Annual Report*. www.usrds.org.

Van Dijk, G., and M. T. Hilhorst. 2007. *Financial Incentives for Organ Donation—An Investigation of the Ethical Issues*. The Hague: Centre for Ethics and Health.

Vathsala, A. 2004. "Improving Cadaveric Organ Donation Rates in Kidney and Liver Transplantation in Asia." *Transplantation Proceedings* 36 (7): 1873–75.

Veatch, R. M. 2003. "Why Liberals Should Accept Financial Incentives for Organ Procurement." *Kennedy School of Ethics Journal* 13: 19–36.

———. 2004. "Justice, Utility and Organ Allocation." In *Ethical, Legal and Social Issues in Organ Transplantation*, edited by T. Gutmann, A. S. Daar, R. A. Sells, and W. Land, 57–67. Lengerich, Germany: Pabst Science.

Verble, M., and J. Worth. 1996. "The Case against More Public Education to Promote Organ Donation." *Journal of Transplant Coordination* 6 (December): 200–203.

Viscusi, W. K., and J. Aldy. 2003. "The Value of a Statistical Life: A Critical Review of Market Estimates throughout the World." *Journal of Risk and Uncertainty* 27 (1): 5–76.

Volokh, E. 2007. "Medical Self-Defense, Prohibited Experimental Therapies, and Payment for Organs." *Harvard Law Review* 120 (7): 1813–46.

Weimer, D. L. 2010. *Medical Governance: Values, Expertise, and Interest in Organ Transplantation*. Washington, DC: Georgetown University Press.

Wellington, A. J., and J. B. Whitmire. 2007. "Kidney Transplants and the Shortage of Donors: Is a Market the Answer?" *Contemporary Economic Policy* 25 (2): 131–45.

Wendler, D., and N. Dickert. 2001. "The Consent Process for Cadaveric Organ Procurement—How Does It Work? How Can It Be Improved?" *Journal of the American Medical Association* 285 (3): 329–33.

Wertheimer, A. 2001. "Exploitation." *Stanford Encyclopedia of Philosophy*. Stanford, CA: Stanford University Press. http://plato.stanford.edu/entries/exploitation.

Whaples, R. 2009. "The Policy Views of American Economic Association Members: The Results of a New Survey." *Econ Journal Watch* 6 (3): 337–48.

Whiting, J., et al. 2000. "Economic Cost of Expanded Criterion Donors in Cadaveric Renal Transplantation: Analysis of Medicare Payments." *Transplantation* 70 (5): 755–60.

Wilkinson, S. 2003. *Bodies for Sale: Ethics and Exploitation in the Human Body Trade*. London: Routledge.

Wille, S. 2006. "Sozialpflicht zur Organspende?" [Social obligation to donate organs?]. In *Anreize zur Organspende* [Incentives for organ donation], edited by Europäische Akademie, 7–26. Bad Neuenahr-Ahrweiler, Germany: Europäische Akademie.

Williams, C. 1994. "Combating the Problem of Human Rights Abuses and Inadequate Organ Supply through Presumed Donative Consent." *Case Western Reserve Journal of International Law* 26: 315–64.

Wilson, G., and J. Jadlow. 1982. "Competition, Profit Incentives, and Technical Efficiency in the Provision of Nuclear Medicine Services." *Bell Journal of Economics* 13 (2): 472–82.

Winkelmayer, W., et al. 2002. "Health Economic Evaluations: The Special Case of End-Stage Renal Disease Treatment." *Medical Decision Making* 22 (5): 417–32.

Wolfe, R., et al. 1997. "Patient Survival for Wait-Listed Dialysis versus Cadaveric Renal Transplant Patients in the U.S." *Journal of the American Society of Nephrology* 8: 708.

World Health Organization. 2004. *Ethics, Access and Safety in Tissue and Organ Transplantation: Issues of Global Concern.* Geneva: World Health Organization.

Yen, E., et al. 2004. "Cost-Effectiveness of Extending Medicare Coverage of Immunosuppressive Medications to the Life of a Kidney Transplant." *American Journal of Transplantation* 4 (10): 1703–8.

Zajac, E. E. 1995. *The Political Economy of Fairness Games.* Cambridge, MA: MIT Press.

Zaltzman, J. 2006. "Kidney Transplantation in Canada: Unequal Access." *Canadian Medical Association Journal* 175 (5): 489–90.

Zargooshi, J. 2008a. "Commercial Renal Transplantation in Iran: The Recipients' Perspective." In *Organ Transplantation: Ethical, Legal and Psychosocial Aspects*, edited by W. Weimar, M. A. Bos, and J. J. Busschbach, 72–79. Lengerich, Germany: Pabst Science.

———. 2008b. "Commercial Renal Transplantation Program: Results and Complications." In *Organ Transplantation: Ethical, Legal and Psychosocial Aspects*, edited by W. Weimar, M. A. Bos, and J. J. Busschbach, 80–94. Lengerich, Germany: Pabst Science.

Zenios, S. A., G. M. Chertow, and L. M. Wein. 2000. "Dynamic Allocations of Kidneys to Candidates on the Transplant Waiting List." *Operations Research* 48 (4): 549–69.

Zink, S., and S. L. Wertlieb. 2004. "Forced Altruism Is Not Altruism." *American Journal of Bioethics* 4 (4): 29–31.

———. 2006. "A Study of the Presumptive Approach to Consent for Organ Donation: A New Solution." *Critical Care Nurse* 26: 129–36.

Zutlevics, T. L. 2001. "Markets and the Needy: Organ Sales or Aid?" *Journal of Applied Philosophy* 18 (3): 297–302.

Index

Italic page numbers indicate material in tables or figures.